THE FUTURE OF POLICING

The Future of Policing

ROD MORGAN

and

TIM NEWBURN

CLARENDON PRESS · OXFORD
1997

Oxford University Press, Great Clarendon Street, Oxford OX2 6DP

Oxford New York

Athens Auckland Bangkok Bogota Bombay
Buenos Aires Calcutta Cape Town Dar es Salaam
Delhi Florence Hong Kong Istanbul Karachi
Kuala Lumpur Madras Madrid Melbourne
Mexico City Nairobi Paris Singapore
Taipei Tokyo Toronto
and associated companies in
Berlin Ibadan

Oxford is a trade mark of Oxford University Press

Published in the United States
by Oxford University Press Inc., New York

British Library Cataloguing in Publication Data
Data available

Library of Congress Cataloging in Publication Data
Data available
ISBN 0-19-876441-3
ISBN 0-19-876440-5 (Pbk)

Set by Hope Services (Abingdon) Ltd.
Printed in Great Britain
on acid-free paper by
Bookcraft Ltd., Midsomer Norton, Somerset

CONTENTS

LIST OF FIGURES

ACKNOWLEDGEMENTS

This book arose out of our joint participation in the work of the *Independent Inquiry into the Role and Responsibilities of the Police* established by the Police Foundation and the Policy Studies Institute during 1994-6. One of us (Rod Morgan) was a member of the Committee and the other (Tim Newburn) was the Inquiry's Director of Research. The Inquiry produced both an interim and a final report and we were both closely involved in the production of those documents, which we fully supported. However, we thought there was a case for taking the exercise further, an aspiration which our Chairman, Sir John Cassels, encouraged. First, we wished to set out more fully the context of the issues on which the Inquiry concentrated its attentions and, secondly, we wanted to extend some of the arguments developed by the Committee.

We could not have written this book without having taken part in the challenging discussions which the existence of the Committee made possible and we wish to thank all our colleagues in that venture, in particular the Secretary Bill Saulsbury, for the inspiration and knowledge they provided. But in the final analysis the report from any Committee comprising a diverse membership has to carry all of its members with it and we wished to go beyond the recommendations the Committee supported. It follows that though our starting point was the work of the Committee, our colleagues from the Inquiry are in no way responsible for what follows, nor would they necessarily support what we have written. The responsibility is entirely ours.

During the course of our writing several colleagues have assisted us with information and advice. They also are not responsible for the end product. We would like to thank Mike Maguire and PSI's librarian, Sue Johnson, for their help with a number of queries. And we would especially like to thank Mollie Weatheritt for reading an early draft of our manuscript and copiously applying red ink to it. Her comments were invaluable.

August 1996   Rod Morgan
                                                          Tim Newburn

INTRODUCTION

'I believe that we have to seriously consider whether the
time has come to have a totally non-partisan view of what
the police are about, what they should and should not be
doing, and how they should be accountable'.

(Alan Eastwood, Chairman of the Police Federation,
speaking after the release of the Birmingham Six in 1991)

It used to be commonplace for Britons, particularly British politicians, to boast that we have 'the best police in the world'. The
British bobby with his quaint helmet—typified by PC George
Dixon of Dock Green—has been a symbol of political continuity,
cultural homogeneity, and moral consensus: alone, unarmed, he
walked the beat, and the British people really did ask him the
time. Recently, however, we have suffered something of a crisis
of confidence in our police and our policing arrangements.
Crime rates have risen, continually and often sharply. Fear of
crime and a deep sense of insecurity blight many lives. The
police have repeatedly been embattled with inner-city youth,
strikers, travellers, and protesters of various kinds. The long
shield, NATO helmet, and flameproof suit have become almost
as familiar, albeit through television for most of us, as the traditional helmet. The private security industry has greatly
expanded, to some extent providing services that the police are
unable or unwilling to provide. There has also been a spate of
highly publicized miscarriages of justice. Public confidence in
the police, as measured in repeated opinion polls, has declined.
Reflecting this, a cartoon published in the *Gurdian* a few years
ago depicted a man arriving out of breath for a meeting.
Apologizing for being late he said: 'I asked a policeman the time,
and he lied'![1]

The political context of policing has also changed dramatically. 'Law and order' is now the high ground for which the
Labour and Conservative parties are struggling. 'Law and order'
has been party-politicized. The issues matter because voters are
concerned about them. Opinion polls repeatedly show crime to

be a major issue. Difficult as it now is to imagine, until the mid-1970s there existed a large measure of agreement between the two main political parties about the police and policing. However, the increasingly political profile of some serving or recently retired senior police officers and police representatives in the late 1970s, together with a series of public disagreements with Labour Party spokespeople in the early 1980s, undermined the political consensus over law and order policies in general and policing in particular. That consensus has not been regained.

The new Conservative government in 1979 focused the bulk of its law and order attention on the police. A new pay deal was quickly implemented, resulting in very significant rises in police salaries, and money was made available for increases in police complements as well. Mrs Thatcher promised to 'spend more on the police whilst economising elsewhere'.[2] Her expectations, and those of her ministers, were twofold. First, that this would deliver a supportive police service and, secondly, that the increased expenditure would result in reduced crime levels. Neither was to be so easily achieved.

In her speech to the 1985 Conservative Party annual conference Mrs Thatcher was willing to promise that 'the government will continue steadfastly to back the police. If they need more men, more equipment, they shall have them'.[3] Yet in spite of such undertakings and though relationships between the police and the Labour Party continued to deteriorate, it would be wrong to create the impression that a straightforward party political alignment developed during the decade. It was not to be. The public love affair between the police and the Conservative Party was never fully consummated. Government unease about the poor dividends being earned from its very considerable investment in the police began soon to arise and the police were not slow to criticize the measures taken by government in response to its unease. In his memoirs, Kenneth Baker, who had been Home Secretary in 1990, sketches the tension well. He recalls that he:

found that while several of my ministerial colleagues and Tory MPs supported the police in public, they were highly critical of them in private. There was impatience, if not anger, that although we had spent 87 per cent more in real terms since 1979 and had increased police numbers by

27,000, there had still been a substantial rise in crime. 'Where is the value for money?' asked my colleagues' [4]

The reasons for the government unease are readily apparent. Recorded crime continued to rise inexorably despite increasing police resources. Crime clear-up rates fell. And public satisfaction with the police declined. Data from the three British Crime Surveys conducted in the 1980s by the Home Office's own Research Unit showed that the proportion of the public who gave the police the highest possible rating dropped from just over one third in 1982 to under a quarter in 1988.[5] Furthermore, this decline in confidence was observed in most major social groups and communities, including those non-Metropolitan areas traditionally highly supportive of the police.

From approximately 1982 onwards, the government began vigorously to pursue its 'Financial Management Initiative' (FMI), designed to encourage effectiveness, efficiency, and cost savings by applying private sector management methods to the public sector, and imposing market disciplines on them. Both the Association of Chief Police Officers (ACPO) and the Police Federation were generally hostile to the new emphasis on 'value for money'.[6] The police service formed the view that the government's concern was largely to limit expenditure and that the effect this would have on the quality of policing was of secondary importance. Relatively liberal spending policies on policing gave way to a measure of stringency.

The 1980s also saw the emergence of an issue that had begun to threaten other public services: privatization and, in the case of the police, two sub-themes, 'civilianization' and 'voluntarization'. Was it necessary for the police to undertake all the tasks that they performed? Might some tasks not be contracted out? And to the extent that it was desirable that the police retain responsibility for providing current services, did those services have to be delivered exclusively by well-trained, legally-empowered and relatively highly-paid officers? Might they not be done equally well by civilians? Could certain tasks not be performed with the assistance of citizen volunteers?

The impact of both financial constraint and the spectre of privatization was to open up a debate about the future shape of policing in Britain that caused the police representative organizations growing consternation. It was not long before the Labour Party, searching for new foundations for electoral success, began actively to exploit the tensions between the police service and the government in the course of rebuilding its own legitimacy as a party that could deliver 'law and order'. By the end of the 1980s the Labour Party had entered the fray with a range of proposals for policing, many of which were very close to the opinions being expressed by senior officers.[7] The Labour Party repeatedly called for increases in police strength.

Thus whereas the 1980s began with a promise from the newly-elected Conservative Government that it would spend more on 'law and order' while cutting public expenditure elsewhere, the 1990s opened with a series of increasingly searching government inquiries as to whether the police were providing 'value for money'. Anticipating this debate successive commissioners of the Metropolitan Police and several provincial chief constables set in train programmes of reform aimed at making their police forces more responsive to 'consumers'. But these chief officers' programmes of reorganization and their initiatives designed to change the public image of the police failed to satisfy what was becoming an increasingly reformist political administration. The potential scope for radical change was opened up the moment Kenneth Clarke crossed the threshold of the Home Office after the 1992 General Election. Within six months of taking office the new Home Secretary instituted two major reviews of policing.

The first review, which was conducted entirely within the Home Office and had no official terms of reference, eventually gave rise to the 1993 White Paper on *Police Reform*.[8] During the course of the inquiry there were a succession of leaks to the press about reforms that were being considered. These included the possibility of drastically reducing the number of police forces; privatizing a number of current policing functions; funding policing entirely from central government revenue; and replacing the local police authorities with government-appointed boards. In the event the proposals in the White Paper were less radical than the rumours suggested, though they did include far-reaching changes to local police authorities. Though it received less attention at the time, it was arguably what the White Paper had to say about the *role* of the police, however, that was most significant.

The White Paper contains the following simple prescription of the role of the police: 'The main job of the police is to catch criminals.' The very next sentence, however, contains a decription of what the police actually do which would appear to conflict with this prescription: 'In a typical day, however, only 18 per cent of calls to the police are about crime, and only about 40 per cent of police officers' time is spent dealing directly with crime.'[9] There are two possible ways of interpreting this apparent contradiction. The first interpretation, and the one we wish to pursue in this book, is that the role of the police involves, and should involve, much more than simply catching criminals. Catching criminals is certainly an important policing priority. But the fact that the police spend only a proportion of their time dealing directly with crime is not necessarily an indication that they are falling down on the job and that a major restructuring of their responsibilities is warranted.

The second interpretation is that the police are simply spending too much time on activities that are not part of their main job. This is the line the government has taken. As a consequence the keystone of the government's policy in recent years involved finding ways of freeing up police time so as to maximize 'thief-taking' and minimizing distractions from that main task.

While the Government's White Paper was being prepared a further review was under way. Announced to general surprise at the Police Federation conference in May 1992, the terms of reference of the Sheehy Inquiry were: 'To examine the rank structure, remuneration, and conditions of the police service in England and Wales, in Scotland and in Northern Ireland, and to recommend what changes, if any, would be sensible'. The Inquiry was chaired by Sir Patrick Sheehy, the chairman of British American Tobacco, and he was joined by four other members with considerable experience of commerce but little of public service. One member of the Committee was a former civil servant. The Inquiry reported just two days after the publication of the White Paper and put forward 272 recommendations designed, it was suggested, to 'reward good performance and penalise bad'.[10] Sheehy recommended that: new recruits to the police be hired on ten year contracts; the ranks of deputy chief constable, chief superintendent, and chief inspector be abolished; a severance programme be introduced, thereby enabling the termination of up to 5,000 middle-ranking and senior officers' contracts; performance related pay be introduced for chief constables and assistant chief constables; the starting pay of officers be reduced; officers' pay rates be linked to non-manual private sector earnings; and a number of forms of overtime payment be removed and housing allowances frozen for existing staff and abolished for new recruits.

The Sheehy Inquiry Report was predictably not popular with the service and led to the biggest mass rally of police officers held at any point since the introduction of the New Police in 1829. The Police Federation argued that the recommendations would remove the vocational aspect of the work, turning it into a 'job like any other job'. The Superintendents' Association suggested that recruitment, retention, and motivation of staff would all be hit by the proposals.[11] Though many of Sheehy's recommendations were eventually successfully resisted, the very existence of the Inquiry reinforced the police view that, as far as the government was concerned, the police service was increasingly to be run on business lines, that police performance would henceforth be measured, and that the criteria by which the service would in future be judged would largely be laid down by the Home Secretary. However whereas the Home Secretary's view, as set out in the White Paper, was that the primary task for the police was to catch criminals, Sheehy took a broader view. He described the aims of the police as: preventing crime; pursuing and bringing to justice those who break the law; keeping the Queen's peace; and protecting, helping, and reassuring the community. Those observers concerned to discover what the priorities for an increasingly hard-pressed police service were to be, therefore gained little enlightenment and suffered increased uncertainty as a result of the joint publication of the White Paper and the Sheehy Report.

New procedures for the setting of goals and objectives for the police were established as a result of the Police and Magistrates' Courts Act 1994, the legislation that grew out of the White Paper. The original Bill contained far-reaching proposals for the restructuring of local police authorities. Had these proposals been passed they would have reduced democratically elected local councillors to a minority of police authority members and given the Home Secretary unprecedented powers to nominate candidates for such bodies. In the event these proposals were in part successfully resisted in the House of Lords. Nevertheless, the eventual package of reforms was still significant. Under the Act, the newly constituted police authorities are required to: determine objectives for the policing of the authority's area during the forthcoming financial year; issue a plan setting out the proposed arrangements for the policing of the authority's area for the year ('the local policing plan'); and include in the plan a statement of the authority's priorities for the year, of the resources expected to be available and of the intended allocation of those resources. The new authorities are to do all this on the advice of their chief constables who are to prepare a draft of the local policing plan for their authorities' consideration. But local policing plans must also take into account national objectives for policing laid down by the Home Secretary. This and other provisions alarmed the police. Sir John Smith, then President of ACPO, took the view that 'we are witnessing a move, perhaps unintended, for national control of the police by central government'.[12]

Misgivings within the police service about the government's intentions were exacerbated when, in 1994, it was announced that another internal Home Office review of policing was to take place. This exercise, which became known as the Review of Core and Ancillary Tasks, was led by a civil servant and was given terms of reference: 'To examine the services provided by the police, to make recommendations about the most cost-effective way of delivering core police services and to assess the scope for relinquishing ancillary tasks'. The review team's starting point was the observation that demands on the police continue to grow at a rate that outstrips increases in police resources and places a strain on the service. They suggested, therefore, that 'some of the resources needed to improve performance in core areas of work supporting key and national objectives will have to be found by releasing resources currently absorbed by peripheral non-essential tasks or by finding more cost-effective ways of delivering core tasks'. In layperson's language: 'it is no longer possible to meet the bill for the police to perform all the tasks they are called on to perform; therefore we will have to see if some of these tasks can be passed on to someone else'.[13] The Inquiry excited all the police service's worst long-incubated fears. It appeared to signal a major step along the road towards the privatization, or contracting out, of certain police functions. As has so often been the case in recent years however, a major rearguard action of resistance was mounted by the police behind the scenes. Insofar as these things can be judged, the campaign appears to have been successful, at least in the short term. After a protracted delay the review led to relatively innocuous recommendations: contracting out such police tasks as the accompaniment of wide loads on motorways scarcely represents the fundamental reform of the police service.[14] It is doubtful, however, that the impetus that led to the review will go away.

Of all the bodies examining policing in the last ten years the most important has probably been the Audit Commission. Designed to examine economy, efficiency, and effectiveness in public sector services, the Commission is an independent and powerful body which, because at its heart lie questions of finance, has commanded considerable attention in policing circles. The Audit Commission has produced a raft of new performance indicators based on specified standards of service delivery and, more recently, in its studies of police patrol[15] and, particularly, crime investigation,[16] has begun to develop a model for the future of policing that has many supporters within the service. We will consider this model in some detail later in the book but, in brief, it is underpinned by the argument that the police service can make significant inroads into crime levels if the service is properly organized and resourced. More particularly the Audit Commission has argued that policing should: become more 'proactive' and less 'reactive' in what it does; prioritize prevention and investigation; place greater emphasis on information technology and the management of information; and target known repeat offenders who, it is argued, are responsible for so much crime. The Audit Commission espouses an optimistic vision of what the police can do to reduce the level of crime. Though the Commission's view of policing is in many ways much more sophisticated than that which the Government appears to hold, it nonetheless incorporates some of the same characteristics. The Commission holds out the promise of controlling crime by means of policing policy:

By adopting [our] recommendations . . . the police can help to prevent crime and raise clear-up rates significantly, which itself will help to deter would-be criminals. The ultimate prize for the police is the development of a strategy in which the crime rate could be brought under control.[17]

As we shall explain in the chapters that follow we question this viewpoint on two counts. First, though it is right and proper that the police should be encouraged to make the most effective use of the resources available to them, neither they nor the public should be misled about the causes of crime, and thus the solutions to crime. There is little evidence that anything the police do has much more than a very marginal impact on crime levels. Secondly, to the extent that the Audit Commission, like the government, is sugesting that a significant switch in emphasis by the police towards crime-fighting, as opposed to the other functions the police perform, will in the long-term be more effective in preventing crime this is, we think, a dangerous illusion.

This brief introductory sketch of developments in policing in recent decades should be sufficient to indicate that the role and responsibilities of the police are a contested issue. Contrary to the background assumptions informing the establishment of the major inquiries into aspects of policing since 1992, the role and responsibilities of the police are neither well known nor subject to consensus. The reports emanating from the government's inquiries have contradicted each other. That there should be confusion or disagreement among policy-makers about the fundamental role of the police causes concern within the service and provides little comfort to an increasingly insecure public.

It is of fundamental importance, therefore, to establish and reinforce in the public mind what the major functions of the police are. This is vital because it is apparent that in the hands of a reformist government determined to overhaul public services, particularly by applying private sector management strategies and increasing competition through privatization, what has been referred to as 'market-based criminal justice' is beginning to touch policing. It is of course possible that as a result of the changes being instituted the police are becoming a more efficient organization. But there is also a danger of much being lost as a consequence of the changes that are taking place. We risk squandering a policing tradition that, despite the problems experienced in recent years, nevertheless retains at its core much that is valued by the British public and which is still looked to with envy in countries where the democratic tradition and the doctrine of 'policing by consent' are poorly understood and have few firm roots.

It was against this background that an Independent Committee of Inquiry was set up in 1993 by the Police Foundation and the Policy Studies Institute. The Independent Committee arose out of a concern that changes in policing policy might be instituted without adequate reflection on the police role considered in the broadest terms and that, further, such initiatives might endanger the British policing tradition. For despite the controversy that inevitably attends their work, it remains the case that the British police continue to enjoy a high level of public regard and trust. Our police remain largely unarmed, retain the principle of the minimum use of force, continue to patrol on foot, have strong local ties, and encourage community consultation. The Police and Criminal Evidence Act 1984 (PACE) is regarded as a model of operational accountability in much of the rest of the world. The British policing tradition is something of which the country can be proud. Nevertheless, it also clear that we cannot go on as we have been doing. With crime continuing to increase, a more general sense of public insecurity becoming entrenched and the financial cost of policing continually rising, it is vital to establish some consensus about the core role and responsibilities of the police. This prompts a number of questions. We must establish what the fundamental role and functions of the police are to be. But we must also decide: how and by whom these responsibilities and functions are to be defined; how they should best be achieved; what the role of other agencies is to be in delivering broadly defined policing services; and how the boundaries and the division of labour between these agencies and the police are to be drawn and, where appropriate, properly regulated. It is these and related issues that we address in the rest of this book.

1

THE CHANGING SOCIAL CONTEXT
OF BRITISH POLICING

Were we to resuscitate PC George Dixon he would find his sur-
roundings somewhat strange. His uniform would be fairly familiar—though he would notice that even that has subtly been
altered—but the entrance to his police station would be star-
tling. There would no longer be uncontrolled access to members
of the public and he would see that the open counter across
which officers and local residents could in his day talk freely has
been replaced with a glass screen and a voice box. Indeed he
might think that the place had been re-designed with a siege in
mind, an impression reinforced by the large police vans parked
out back with wire-mesh visors to pull down over their wind-
screens. He would be equally struck by the changes in the cell
block, now strangely termed the custody suite. Why, he might
think, this extraordinarily elaborate form-filling, confinement
for several hours, and recording by a sergeant for petty
shoplifters and other minor offenders? Elsewhere there would be
computers and electronic communications wizardry unknown
in his day. But he would probably be most surprised that most of
these aids—aids handling vital and confidential information—
were being operated by civilians. Indeed he might remark that
few of the personnel around the station were now in uniform.
What are they? Detectives? Officers off duty? Clerks?

Policing, like most activities, has been transformed in the last
thirty years. These changes reflect the changing character of the
environment being policed. And the changes that have occurred
in Britain reflect global trends. In this Chapter we shall consider
some of these contextual trends in order to prepare the way for
our discussion, in later chapters, of how and why policing has
developed in the way that it has and what the options are for
policing in the future.

Income, Wealth, and Inequality

In spite of the recessions of the 1980s and the re-emergence of widespread poverty we are, in 1996, a more prosperous nation overall than at any point in our history. The standard measure of economic growth, gross domestic product (GDP), though subject to criticism, remains the most widely accepted indicator. The annual GDP figures show that the output of the British economy has risen by approximately one half since 1970, and has almost doubled since 1960.

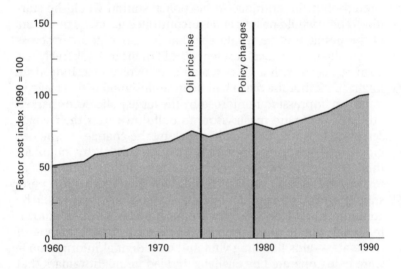

Fig. 1. Gross Domestic Product, 1960–1990
Source: Northcott, J. (1991) *Britain in 2010*, London: PSI

The nation is both more prosperous and better off in a variety of other ways. A few indicators will suffice to illustrate the point. For every 1,000 births in 1940, fifty-six babies died. Today the figure is eight deaths per 1,000 births. In 1951, forty per cent of homes had no bath. Today this is the case for less than one per cent. In 1950, more than two thirds of 15-year- olds were no longer at school compared with fewer than one twentieth today.[1]

But this growth in prosperity has not been equally shared.

From the mid-1940s to the mid-1970s economic equality increased, at least as measured by the distribution of income. Since then the trend has been reversed. Income inequality grew quickly after 1977 and by 1990 had reached a level higher than at any time since the end of the Second World War. What happened? In short, the skilled industrial worker disappeared. He— because such workers were largely male—was replaced by casualized, low-paid, temporary, part-time workers, a growing proportion of them female.

These trends are neatly illustrated by Government statistics on *Households below average incomes*. These show that the incomes of the top and bottom of the population have been diverging. They show that, overall, incomes have continued to increase during the past ten to fifteen years, with the exception of those of the poorest.

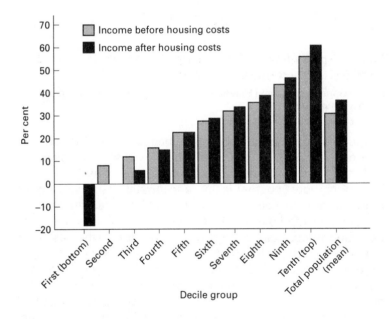

Fig. 2 Percentage changes in real income between 1979 and 1992/3 by decile group

Source: Oppenheim, C. and Harker, L. (1996) *Poverty: The Facts*, London: Child Poverty Action Group

The same pattern emerges from the statistics on pay. Again, inequality remained largely level up until the late 1970s and has since increased.

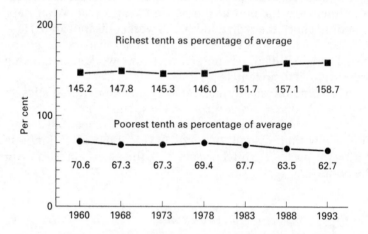

Fig. 3 Dispersion of weekly earnings of manual men 1960–1993 (earnings as a percentage of median)

Source: Oppenheim, C. and Harker, L. (1996) *Poverty: The Facts*, London: Child Poverty Action Group

A local study comparing income inequalities in Oldham and Oxford in the 1980s found that inequalities were widening in line with the national picture. But low-income households were becoming more geographically concentrated, especially on the more disadvantaged housing estates. Stated briefly, the researchers found that since 1981 the better-off households and neighbourhoods had increased in prosperity, whereas those households with the lowest incomes had progressively clustered together. They concluded that what was already a very marked difference in 1981 had grown significantly in the intervening decade. What is true of Oldham and Oxford is largely true nationally.[2] We are becoming a more polarized society, both ecomonically and geographically.

Quite apart from any moral objections we may have to progressive economic polarisation the process involves social consequences which should be of concern. The recent Joseph

Rowntree Income and Wealth Inquiry chaired by Sir Peter Barclay argued that:

there has been a shift towards double-income families, where both parents work but can spend less time with their children, and lone parenthood, with its associated vulnerabilities and stresses which also reflect on the children.[3]

The Committee expressed particular concern about the non-white population of Britain which, it argued, is at much greater risk of poverty than the white population. It suggested that there was a real possibility that poverty would overwhelm the investment that has been made in the people and fabric of some of the poorest council estates in the country. In addition, of course, the welfare state infrastructure is increasingly preoccupied with sustaining the safety net, rather than maintaining and improving the major public services. Indeed so often have we been told in recent years that there is no alternative to this trend, that most people have come to accept that budgets for services like health and education will have to be progressively reined in. The police have been affected by this trend like all the other public services. The police, of course, are also affected by the consequences of increasing inequality, particularly where this means the further marginalization and alienation of sections of the population where crime—both in terms of its commission and its impact—is already concentrated. Central to such trends have been changes in the labour market and to levels of, and the nature of, unemployment.

Employment and Unemployment

Anyone over the age of about forty and living in the UK or countries with similar economies will in his or her adult life have witnessed a series of quite remarkable changes in the pattern of employment and the nature of work. In the UK there have been several economic recessions; manufacturing industry has declined at a staggering rate whilst the service sector has expanded exponentially. Part-time and flexible working have become commonplace. One of the consequences of these changes is that, arguably, an increasing proportion of people in the labour market face growing levels of job insecurity. It is briefly worth considering the evidence behind this feeling of insecurity.

First, there have been major changes in the type of work done, and this has led to the decline of communities founded on long-standing local industries. Employment in agriculture has been in decline for many decades. In 1948, for example, agriculture, forestry, and fishing accounted for almost 8 per cent of employment, whereas by 1994 this had dropped to just over 1 per cent.

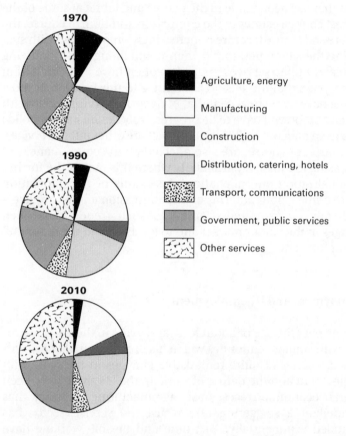

Fig. 4 Distribution of employment by sector, 1970, 1990, 2010

Source: Northcott, J. (1995) *The Future of Britain and Europe*, London: PSI

The decline of employment in the coalmining industry in recent years is perhaps the most graphic of these changes.

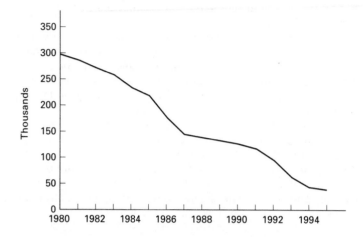

Fig. 5 Employment in coalmining, 1980–1995
Source: Annual Abstract of Statistics

Such trends will not be reversed. These industries will not be resurrected, and the communities that were founded upon them will, where they survive at all, be lastingly affected. Crucially, the most significant change in employment we have mentioned already, namely, the enormous decline of employment in manufacturing. This trend also is unlikely to be reversed.

Changes in the *type* of work done have been more than matched by changes in the *composition* of the work force and the *circumstances* in which people work. There is now a far greater number of women in work than was the case twenty years ago, though almost half of women in employment work part-time, and women's average earnings continue to lag far behind those of men. Furthermore the legal rights of many workers have deteriorated and the conditions of work of the poorly paid have been particularly badly hit. Though it is clearly the unskilled who are most at risk in the labour market, job insecurity is by no means confined to those in manual occupations. As the government's own publication, *Britain 1995: An Official Handbook* puts it:

In the 1950s, '60s and '70s most men—certainly skilled manual workers and white collar workers—believed they had a right to a job for life. They might not expect to stay with the same company from school or university to retirement, but neither did they expect to move around very much.

The classic example was banking. Get a job with a bank, and your problems were over. You might—just possibly—move to another bank, but only if you were terribly ambitious and weren't being promoted quickly enough. You certainly didn't expect to be sacked, not unless you'd run off with the day's takings. The young lad leaving school clutching his School Certificate who was lucky enough to become a junior clerk in his local Barclays or Lloyds could reasonably expect to be an assistant manager or better when the time came for his retirement party 45 years later.

By the mid-1990s that same lad would have much more trouble landing the job in the first place (his local branch might well have been closed down) and if he did, he could expect to have many more retirement parties. From 1990 the big High Street banks had, between them, reduced their workforce by a staggering 100,000. The concept of a job for life had ceased.

Surmounting all these structural changes, which have disrupted many lives and sapped the lifeblood of many communities, is the the most important change—the growth of unemployment. We have grown accustomed to levels and types of unemployment that would have been regarded as totally unacceptable fifty years ago. In the 1950s and 1960s unemployment remained between 1 and 3 per cent, and it was unusual for the number of people out of work to exceed the number of unfilled job vacancies. The spectre of mass unemployment—it had been as high as 15 per cent in the 1930s—was generally considered a thing of the past and a phenomenon that economic policy could and should avoid. In the mid-1990s unemployment levels of 7–8 per cent (percentages comparable to the past are difficult to establish because of the numerous ways in which the definition of unemployment has been changed, thereby disguising its extent) have come to be regarded as almost an inescapable fact of life such that a significant minority of the adult population available for work will be unable to find a job. Whereas forty years ago there was, for men at least, what is now described as full employment, unemployment rose steadily in the 1970s and 1980s and shows little prospect of disappearing. With unemployment forecast to remain at approximately current levels, the major political parties have generally abandoned full employment as a realistically achievable goal. To a greater or lesser extent this is a feature of most developed industrial economies.

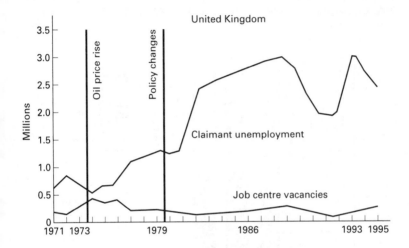

Fig. 6 Unemployment and vacancies, 1971–1995
Source: Northcott, J. (1995) *The Future of Britain and Europe*, London: PSI

Graphs like the one above tell only part of the story, however. A decrease in the unemployment figures does not translate directly into an increase in jobs. Some of those who leave the unemployment register do not do so to take up work: some are merely leaving the labour market. The proportion of men aged 16-64 who were economically inactive increased from approximately 3 per cent in 1979 to over 12 per cent in 1994. Put another way, in the fifteen years from 1979, 9 per cent of potentially economically active men dropped out of the labour market altogether.

Secondly, global unemployment statistics disguise some of the qualitative changes that have been taking place. Not only are more people unemployed than was the case in the past but, crucially, increasing numbers of the jobless are unemployed for longer periods of time: they are long-term unemployed (generally defined as out of work for a year or more). Increasing numbers of potentially economically active adults lack the skills and experience which might make their future employment easy in the ever more demanding labour market. As a consequence they have neither the income nor productive role which has come generally to be regarded as the basis of social standing and the prerequisite for active and dignified citizenship.

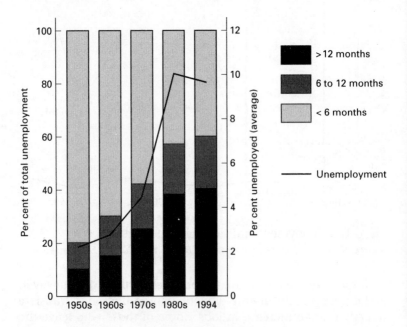

Fig. 7 Length of unemployment, 1950s–1990s

Source: Commission on Social Justice (1994) *Social Justice: Strategies for National Renewal*, London: Vintage

The official statistics tell the story all too clearly. Recent years have seen the chances of unemployed, unskilled men moving into employment drop markedly. Even in periods when the official unemployment rate has declined, as in the financial year 1993–4 for example, long-term unemployment has remained relatively static.

One of the questions raised by the emergence of a body of long-term unemployed people is the extent to which they can be considered to be a social class—an 'underclass' below the working class. There is now a considerable body of evidence to show that there is a distinct social group that faces long-term or multiple bouts of unemployment during their lives and that they encounter other disadvantages—health problems and homelessness or poor housing, and so on—as a result.

There appears at present to be little prospect of this marginal section of the population diminishing in size. The number of unskilled jobs in the labour market will continue to fall, support services for the disadvantaged are not growing in generosity, and the financial and other pressures exerted on the unemployed by political administrations wedded more and more to the application of market incentives seem likely to grow. This pattern may change of course. Future governments may decide it is imperative to invest considerably more money and effort in the training and support of the multiply disadvantaged long-term unemployed than has hitherto been the case. The question at issue is whether they will do so before or after we have faced the socially disorderly consequences—increased protest, crime, riot, and so on—of spawning and then ignoring the aspirations of large and increasingly concentrated disadvantaged communities denied a reasonable share of the growing and flaunted prosperity enjoyed by the majority of the people. As the next section will show, this question has a racial dimension. These are major issues for the future of policing.

Socio-demographic Change

In recent years population increases in the UK have been levelling off, as they have in most European countries. Within this more stable total population, however, a number of structural changes have been taking place which are altering the shape of the population and which are likely to result in further significant changes in the decades ahead. Fertility rates fell sharply in the 1960s, and though they have since increased they remain below replacement level. Moreover, contrary to the impression one might gain from political discussion and media preoccupation, immigration has been roughly matched, in terms of numbers, by migration. Nevertheless the total population continues slowly to grow. A falling death rate is the cause, the result of increasing prosperity and medical advances. The rate of population increase was 1.4 per cent in the five year period to 1990, the total population at that point standing at 57.4 million. It is projected to rise to as much as 62 million by 2020. There are, in simple terms, increasing numbers of people to police.

It follows that the structure of the population is changing. As is the case in most of Western Europe, Britain's population has aged. In 1961 just under 12 per cent of us were aged over 65. By 1995 the figure was 16 per cent. The overall number of those aged 60 or over has risen by one third since 1960 and now stands at approximately twelve million people. By contrast, the juvenile population has fallen. The proportion of the population aged under 16 fell from one quarter in 1961 to 21 per cent in 1994.

This aging of the population will continue. It is projected that the proportion of the population under 16 years will fall to 18.5 per cent by 2021. More striking still is the projected decline in the proportion of young adults. In 1990 it was forecast that the numbers in the 20–34 age group were expected to decrease by almost one fifth by 2010. It is anticipated, therefore, that there will be a marked decline in the number of people of working age, though this will in part be offset by increases in the numbers of people in the older working age groups. The proportion of the population aged over 65 is expected to rise from 16 to over 19 per cent in 2021, and the bulk of this change is expected in the over-80s. There will be many more very old people, though the balance between males and females is not expected to alter greatly: there will continue to be slightly greater numbers of women than men.

Changes have also taken place in the ethnic composition of British society, though the precise nature of these changes is uncertain because reliable data were not collected. The 1991 census was the first in which a question was asked about ethnicity. Prior to 1991, data on country of birth were used as the unsatisfactory basis for deriving estimates of ethnicity. Given that an increasing proportion of the minority ethnic population is second generation—by 1991 well over half of the resident Black Caribbean population in the UK (in terms of origin), for example, were born in the UK—the pitfalls associated with using country of birth as a proxy measure for ethnicity are obvious.

According to the 1991 census 94 per cent of the population of England and Wales is white. The remaining 6 per cent are split as follows:

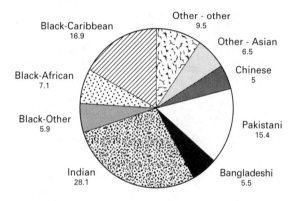

Fig. 8 Ethnic population of England and Wales, 1991
Source: The Census

Although the ethnic minority population is now a substantial and established one, all the evidence is that it has expanded rapidly since 1945. In 1951 there were significantly fewer than 100,000 Black Caribbeans and South Asians in Britain. The ethnic minority population as measured by the 1991 census is now over three million. The rates of growth for different ethnic groups can be seen in Fig. 9.

It is the social and economic characteristics of these populations that are most important for our purposes here. Rates of unemployment, for example, are generally higher for ethnic minority groups. Unemployment rates for Black Caribbeans are approximately double the national average, for Black Africans three times as high, and higher still for Pakistanis and Bangladeshis (see Fig. 10).

Moreover, there is considerable evidence that most ethnic minorities are doubly disadvantaged: not only are their chances of finding employment relatively poor, but those who do find

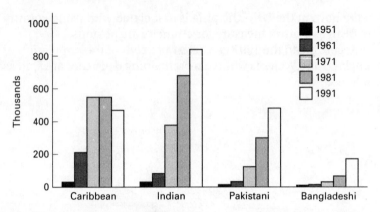

Fig. 9   Estimated size and growth of the main ethnic minority populations, GB, 1951–1991

Source: Peach, C. (1996) *Ethnicity in the 1991 Census*, London: HMSO

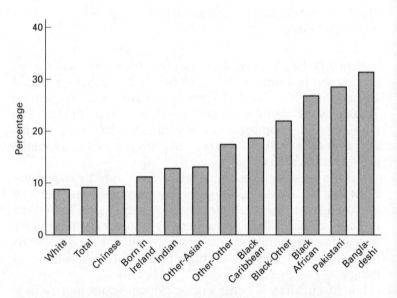

Fig. 10   Percentage unemployment by ethnic group, 1991

Source: Peach, C. (1996) *Ethnicity in the 1991 Census*, London: HMSO

work are less likely to occupy secure, well-paid jobs. In terms of housing tenure, the ethnic minority population is again disadvantaged. Black groups have far lower rates of owner-occupation than most other ethnic groups, particularly Indians and Pakistanis, and the latter are concentrated in inner-city accommodation with relatively high levels of overcrowding. Only approximately 3 per cent of Britain's ethnic minority population live in rural enumeration districts compared with the national average of 24 per cent.

The ethnic minority populations are largely urban. They are also geographically concentrated and residentially segregated. Thus, whereas approximately one quarter of the British population lives in Greater London, Manchester, and the metropolitan counties of the West Midlands and West Yorkshire, the comparative figures for ethnic minority groups are: 83 per cent of Black Africans, 79 per cent of Black Caribbeans; and 75 per cent of Bangladeshis. Moreover, although, the degree of visible 'ghettoization' is not as pronounced as, say, that in the United States, nonetheless approximately half the white population of Britain lives in areas in which ethnic minorities account for less than one half of 1 per cent of the population, and only 6 per cent of the white population lives in areas where ethnic minorities represent more than 5 per cent of the population. Such segregation reflects both class and race divisions. In the most deprived areas of England and Wales there are frequently relatively large concentrations of people from ethnic minorities, and an analysis of both the 1981 and 1991 censuses suggests that it is in the most deprived areas of England that ethnic minority populations are growing. Elsewhere these populations remain relatively stable.[4]

These 'deprived areas' have themselves not been standing still. A century of urban growth has begun to be reversed in recent decades. We are witnessing what is generally referred to as a process of 'urban decline'. As a result of technological change, de-industrialization, and the contraction of domestic manufacturing industry many of the large metropolitan cities have seen their populations shrink, their housing stocks decay, their transport and other infrastructures disintegrate, and poverty and social stresses—including crime—become increasingly concentrated. In Britain, for example:

- lone parent households and ethnic minorities are disproportionately concentrated in the most deprived areas;
- unemployment increased absolutely and relatively in deprived areas between 1981–91; unemployment rates in these areas are highest among young men;
- the stock of low-cost social housing available to poor residents in deprived areas has declined; in most of these areas homelessness has increased;
- the proportion of households in the most deprived areas with dependent children but no economically active adult increased three-fold between 1981–91, compared with the two-fold increase nationwide;
- crime is a feature of the culture of poverty; crime is concentrated in poor areas; people living in the highest crime neighbourhoods (the top decile in Fig. 11) are over ten times as likely to become victims of property crime as those living in the most orderly areas.

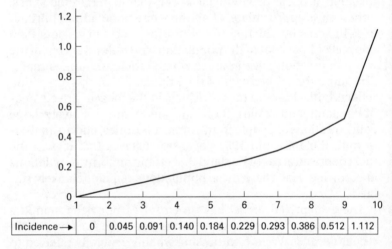

Incidence →	0	0.045	0.091	0.140	0.184	0.229	0.293	0.386	0.512	1.112

Fig. 11 The distribution of property crime

Source: Hope, T. (1996) Communities, crime and inequality in England and Wales, In Bennett, T. (ed) *Preventing Crime and Disorder*, Institute of Criminology, Cambridge

Data from the British Crime Survey demonstrate that ethnic minority respondents are more likely than white respondents to report being victims of crime (see Fig. 12).

England & Wales   Percentages

	Black	Indian	Pakistani/ Bangladeshi	White
Household offences[1]				
Vehicle crime (owners)				
Vandalism	12	9	11	8
All thefts	26	22	25	20
Burglary	13	10	6	6
Home vandalism	4	4	5	4
Other	9	7	11	10
All household offences	36	35	34	33
Personal offences[2]				
Assaults	7	2	4	4
Threats	4	2	4	3
Robbery/theft from person	3	3	4	2
Other personal theft	5	4	2	4
All personal offences[3]	13	9	10	8

[1] Percentage of households in each ethnic group who had been a victim once or more.
[2] Percentage of people aged 16 and over in each ethnic group who had been a victim once or more.
[3] Excludes sexual offences.

Fig. 12 Ethnic minority victims of crime by type of offence, 1993
Source: Office of National Statistics (1996) *Social Focus on Ethnic Minorities*, London: HMSO

In addition to these general demographic and environmental trends, the character of families and households has changed. New patterns of marriage, divorce, and family formation have transformed the social landscape. Thus, for example, the marriage rate (for first marriages) halved between 1971 and 1991 and the divorce rate more than doubled.

There is now quite strong evidence that parental conflict and separation are related to 'delinquency' among young people, as

Fig. 13 Divorce rates, 1950–1992

Source: Utting, D. (1995) *Family and Parenthood*, **York: Joseph Rowntree Foundation**

is harsh or erratic parental discipline. It is among those families experiencing low income and poor housing that there are most likely to be conflict and separation and dysfunctional forms of discipline. These pressures on family units and changes in traditional family forms may be linked to trends in crime. Remarriages, where at least one partner is divorced, now account for over a third of all marriages and the rate of cohabitation has increased over the past twenty-five years from 6 per cent of couples before their wedding day to 60 per cent. Families are now generally smaller, are started later in life, and are increasingly divided between 'work rich' (two incomes) and 'work poor' (no regular income other than benefits). The proportion of families with two incomes was 43 per cent in 1973 and 60 per cent in 1994, whereas the percentage of dependent children living in families with less than half the average household income increased from 10 in 1979 to 32 in 1992. Lone parenthood is increasingly common. Whereas in the early 1960s approximately 6 per cent of births occurred outside marriage, the figure was 31 per cent in 1992. Of these births 45 per cent were registered either by two parents living at different addresses or by mothers alone. The estimated number of one-parent families with dependent children more than doubled in the period 1971–92. The proportion

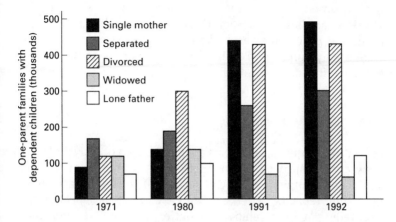

Fig. 14 Numbers of one-parent families, Great Britain, 1971–1992

Source: Utting, D. (1995) *Family and Parenthood*, York: Joseph Rowntree Foundation

of dependent children living in one-parent families has risen from 8 per cent to almost 20 per cent.

The merchants of doom in the tabloid press interpret these trends as indicating the terminal decline of marriage and the family. There are a number of reasons for rejecting such pessimism. First, despite the increasing number of marriages ending in divorce, the rate of remarriage is such that, as one commentator has put it, *hope is, thus far, triumphant over experience*. Secondly, there are clear indications that the upward trends in cohabitation, divorce, and the proportion of births taking place outside marriage are already flattening out. The emergent picture is one in which more fragmented patterns of marriage and family-formation are developing. People are now more likely to experience a variety of relationships during their lifetimes: these may include periods of cohabitation, marriage, separation or divorce, remarriage, parenthood, and step-parenthood. These changes affect both the *experience* of parenthood and, in some respects, the *character* of parenthood.

There is, of course, considerable debate about what the consequences of these changes might be. How, for example, they might be linked to changing patterns of criminal behaviour. For our purposes it is important to note that all these social processes are linked—though there is considerable uncertainty about how exactly they are linked—with those things which are traditionally considered to be the core business of the police: levels of crime and disorder.

Levels and Patterns of Crime

As everybody knows, crime has risen, and risen quickly and relatively consistently, since the 1950s. This is arguably the most significant change in the social context of contemporary policing. Crime rates, however, are not easy to measure accurately, especially not over relatively lengthy historical periods. For example, in relation to those crimes recorded by the police (generally speaking those more serious offences eligible to be tried on indictment, that is, before a jury), there have been a number of far-reaching changes in the law which have either created new offences or redefined old ones. In 1980, moreover, the basis on which national criminal statistics were compiled was changed substantially. It is possible, however, to make adjustments to take account of the most significant of these legal changes and recording conventions. Figure 15 illustrates the increase in the rate of offences recorded by the police in England and Wales between 1950 and 1993—an increase from around one offence per 100 of the population in 1950 to ten offences per 100 of the population in 1993. Increases in relation to some specific offences have been even greater than this. There was, for example, a twenty-eight-fold increase in motor vehicle theft in the same period, and a forty-eight-fold increase in robbery.

Changes in the law and police-recording conventions may be relatively unimportant compared to other factors which influence the manner in which we view crime and how we react to it, thereby affecting the likelihood of its being officially recorded. Using a second source of data—the British Crime Survey (BCS)—it is possible to get a more accurate picture of trends in crime in the more recent period of 1981–93. If we consider those offences where it is possible to make comparisons between the amount of crime officially recorded and the amount of crime which respondents to successive sweeps of the BCS

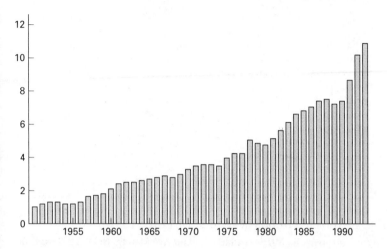

Fig. 15 Recorded crime per 100 population in England and Wales, 1950–1993

Source: Criminal Statistics

report having experienced, Home Office researchers estimate that only just over a quarter of (comparable) crimes noted by the BCS currently end up being recorded by the police. Although there are differences between the two sources of information, the underlying upward trend in the amount of crime is not in dispute. Whereas between 1981 and 1993 police-recorded crimes more than doubled (rising by 111 per cent), the incidence of the crimes recorded in the BCS rose by 77 per cent.

It is significant, however, that both the police statistics and the BCS show that 'acquisitive' crimes—which account for around two-thirds of all recorded crime—more than doubled between 1981 and 1993, with especially large increases in vehicle thefts and burglary.

In the public mind, by contrast, there is perceived to have been a dramatic rise in violent crime and some support for such a view is found in the official statistics. These show recorded crimes of violence to have doubled between 1981 and 1991. Estimates based on the BCS, however, indicate that offences of violence (wounding and robbery) have increased by only approximately one fifth.

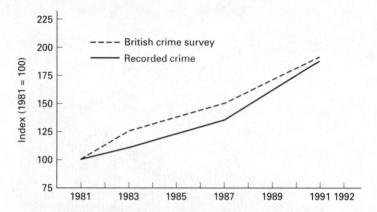

Fig. 16 Indexed trends in acquisitive crime 1981–1991

Source: Mayhew, P., Mirrlees-Black, C., and Aye Maung, N. (1994) *Trends in Crime: Finding from the 1994 British Crime Survey*, Home Office Research Findings No.14, London: Home Office

We have not become a dramatically more violent society. Indeed, to the extent that members of the public are now reporting to the police a greater proportion of the violence suffered, we may have become less tolerant of violence.

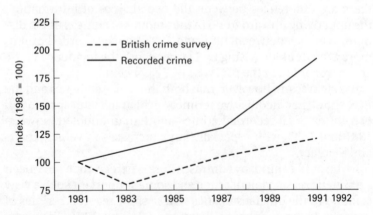

Fig. 17 Indexed trends in violence, 1981–1991

Source: Mayhew, P., Mirrlees-Black, C., And Aye Maung, N. (1994) *Trends in Crime: Finding from the 1994 British Crime Survey*, Home Office Research Findings No.14, London: Home Office

Most countries with advanced economies are recording similar trends in crime as are found in Britain. The notable exception is Japan where recorded crime has remained relatively steady throughout the whole of the post-war period and, to a lesser extent, the United States, where recorded crime has fallen in recent years after previously reaching extremely high levels, particularly for crimes of violence, by the standards of the United Kingdom and all the other member countries of the European Union.

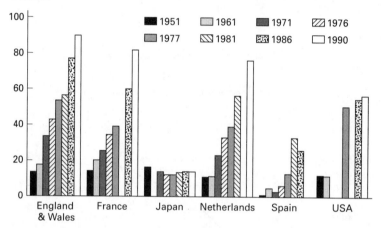

Fig. 18 International comparisons: rates for all offences recorded by police, 1951–1990

Source: Smith, D. (1996) Explaining Crime Trends, In Saulsbury, W. et al (eds) *Themes in Contemporary Policing*, London: PSI

A wide variety of reasons have been advanced to explain the relentless rise in crime since 1945 in most developed societies. Many of these explanations are contested, but there is general agreement that an increase in the opportunities for crime combined with a decline in effective informal social controls has played a significant role. Certainly the fact that motor vehicle crime accounts for upwards of one quarter of all recorded crime points to the increasing importance of the car—and all the expensive and portable equipment that is often contained therein—as a target for criminal activity.

These crime trends demonstrate two things fairly conclusively. First, in advanced economies the pressures on the police

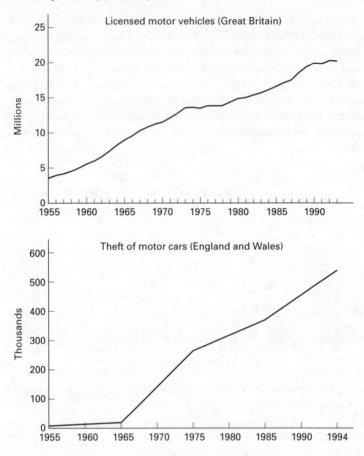

Fig. 19   Number of licensed motor vehicles, Great Britain, 1955–1993/Theft of motor cars in England and Wales, 1955–1994
Source: Annual Transport Statistics/Annual Criminal Statistics

have increased significantly in recent decades. Much more crime is occurring and is being reported to the police, and public expectations that the police will be able to do something about the rate of offending have risen. Secondly, and contradictorily, all the evidence suggests it is a mistake to believe that the police, or indeed the wider criminal justice system, are, or ever could be, the most decisive factor in determining crime levels.

Crime levels have risen steadily in spite of substantial increases in police resources and in spite of constant amendments to the sentencing powers of the courts. In part this is because, as successive British Crime Surveys have shown, something less than one half of all offences committed actually come to the attention of the police. Furthermore, of those crimes that are brought to the attention of the police not all are recorded, let alone cleared up. Because of what is known as the high 'attrition' rate, a very small proportion of all those persons responsible for offending behaviour are brought to book in terms of being sentenced by a court or subjected to a formal caution by the police following their acknowledgement of guilt.

Much contemporary acquisitive crime is committed anonymously in public space. It is estimated that only 30 per cent of all crimes committed are actually *recorded*, and only 7 per cent are *cleared up*, that is, are eventually attributed to specific offenders. Only 3 per cent result in a caution or conviction and 2 per cent in a conviction. If, as the evidence suggests, crime is best prevented by the certainty of detection, conviction, and punishment, then the criminal justice system is implausibly of great deterrent value for those potential or actual offenders who calculate the odds of getting caught.

Most people, most of the time, do not, fortunately, abide by the law because they calculate the likelihood of being caught and punished. They abide by the law because they subscribe to the values inherent in the law and appreciate the social benefits derived from following the rule of law. It follows that any decline in the perceived legitimacy of the law and the law enforcement agencies—because of general feelings of injustice and so on—is almost certainly a much more dangerous social prospect than police ineffectiveness in thief-taking.

Quite apart from the fact that it is only one of the tasks undertaken by the police, 'tackling crime'—in the sense of controlling crime levels—is clearly not a task that the police can realistically be expected to manage alone. The police obviously have a key role to play, but we must not burden them with expectations they cannot possibly fulfil. One of the questions which arises therefore is: how is crime to be controlled, and what is the role of the police (and other policing organizations) in crime control? We return to this question at several points in later chapters.

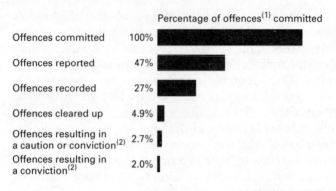

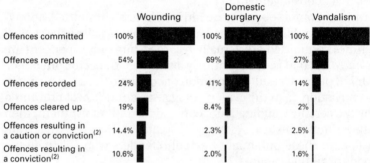

Fig. 20 Attrition within the criminal justice system
Source: Digest of Statistics 2, London: Home Office

It is depressingly evident then that crime has become a relatively pervasive feature of contemporary life. And the evidence
we have about offenders and offending behaviour confirms this
dismal picture. Crime, at least among the young male population, is relatively common. One third of males have a criminal
conviction by their early thirties. Recent research by the Home
Office found that over half of young men and almost one third of
young women admit to having committed a criminal offence in
their lifetime. Although the estimates vary, it is well established
that a small number of these young people commit a disproportionately large number of offences.

There is considerable political and policy interest in this group
of young people and, for fairly obvious reasons, it is often suggested that they should be the specific focus of efforts by the

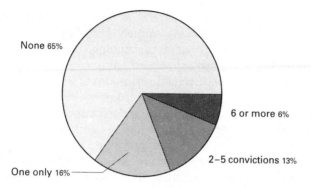

None 65%

6 or more 6%

2–5 convictions 13%

One only 16%

Fig. 21 Males born in 1953 convicted of an offence on the 'standard list' by age 35
Source: Digest of Statistics 2, London: Home Office

criminal justice system. For this reason we shall return to the police response to persistent offenders in a later chapter.

The great majority of young offenders, however, do not persist in a 'criminal career'. Rather than looking always for the causes of crime, therefore, it may be more enlightening to ask why it is that most people do not commit crimes most of the time, given the relatively low chances of detection and conviction. The reasons, it is suggested, lie in the informal sanctions that are brought to bear by families, schools, employers, and the 'communities' in which people live, and the investments in relationships within these settings which they stand to lose if they transgress commonly-held rules. It has convincingly been argued that the nature of change in the late modern world has been characterized by a decline in the effectiveness of these social bonds and informal social controls and that this is central to any explanation of the increase in crime in countries with developed economies since the Second World War.[5] To the extent that this is true it follows that the task of crime prevention involves issues much more far-reaching than police resources, powers, and procedures and that small changes in sentencing practices are likely to be of only marginal significance.

We should note also that crime patterns have changed. In particular, ease of movement made possible by new forms of transport and communication have led to the growth of organized national and international criminal networks involved in activities such as drug trafficking, money laundering, credit card fraud, prostitution, lorry and car ringing, document forgery, counterfeiting, and trading in stolen antiques and works of art.

It is difficult to provide reliable estimates of the extent of these activities. However, information from some of the bodies involved in attempting to prevent or detect and prosecute these forms of crime provides us with some indications. In 1992-3, for example, the Customs and Excise prevented drugs worth an estimated £900 million from entering the country, in the process making over 9,000 drugs seizures and almost 2,700 arrests resulting in 1,700 convictions. Customs and Excise investigations resulted in the breaking up of what the department described as forty-seven major drug smuggling organizations. Or, to take one example of international fraud, in 1990 a messenger in the City of London was robbed of a case containing £292 million of securities. The investigation conducted by the police resulted in the arrest of over eighty people, and involved police operations to recover bonds in the United States, Peru, Cyprus, Germany, Singapore, the Netherlands, Northern Ireland, Scotland, Switzerland, and Brazil.[6]

The development of organized crime structures that cross both local and national police boundaries raises the question of how the police should be organized, and what balance should be struck between local, regional, national, and international policing bodies. We return to this in the following and a later chapter.

Insecurity

As Lord Scarman pointed out almost a decade and a half ago, it is not surprising that the British police face a variety of pressures that go wider and deeper than any which have previously confronted them: 'These pressures reflect changes in society, in social values and attitudes, and in policing itself'.[7] As we have seen, the second half of the twentieth century has brought significant socio-economic structural changes: a massive decline in manufacturing industry; the development of new technologies; the rise of 'consumerism' and the mass ownershop and circulation of relatively anonymous consumer durables; the increasing mobility of capital and of criminal activity; and the growth of long-term unemployment. These changes have altered patterns of social stratification. Social class has been partially replaced by, or overlaid with, other forms of social differentiation. There is now a far greater emphasis on individualism, and this has posed a significant challenge to many traditional forms of social control. There is also a heightened sense of personal insecurity, part of which comprises concern about or fear of crime, and this has added to the demands made on the police.

The fact that the British Crime Survey has now been conducted on four occasions (1984, 1988, 1992, 1994) allows us to get some feel for trends not just about crime but also fear of crime. Some of the findings from the BCS are slightly unexpected, however, and should lead to caution in making general statements about levels of fear and insecurity in contemporary society. Worry about and fear of crime vary a good deal depending on the age and sex of the person concerned and the type of offence involved. Some examples will illustrate the point. Thus, although there was some increase in anxiety about burglary in the period 1984–94, the increase was relatively slight and it was uneven.

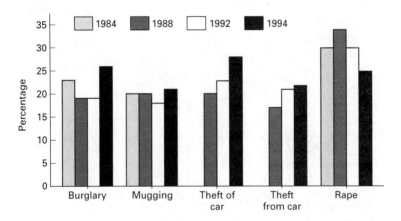

Fig. 22 Trends in worry, percentage feeling 'very worried' about various crimes

Source: Hough, M. (1995) *Anxiety About Crime: Findings From the 1994 British Crime Survey,* Home Office Research Findings No.25, London: Home Office

By contrast, general anxiety about car crime rose steadily during the period, as might have been expected given the significant increase in the risk of being the victim of car crime. Anxiety about mugging was more stable, but the proportion of young women reporting worries about this form of crime rose markedly. By contrast again there was a fall in the proportion of women reportedly 'very worried' about rape, though there was a rise in those 'fairly worried'. One possible explanation for some of these trends is that some of the increases in risk—in relation to burglary, for example—have not been fully appreciated by the public.

Yet according to the BCS concerns about crime top the list of all the 'worries' reported by the public, with anxiety about burglary and rape being more common than other 'life worries' such as possible loss of employment, becoming seriously ill, having a road accident, falling into debt, and so on. Worries, predictably, vary a good deal by age and sex. Women are more fearful of mugging and generally feel less safe than men. Older people are more likely to feel unsafe about going out alone at night.

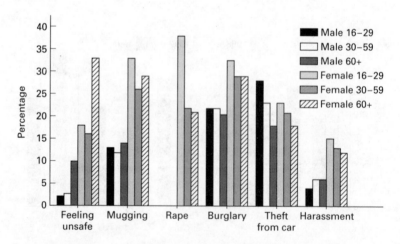

Fig. 23 Variations by age and sex, percentage 'very worried' or 'very unsafe'

Source: Hough, M. (1995) *Anxiety About Crime: Findings From the 1994 British Crime Survey*, Home Office Research Findings No.25, London: Home Office

Most striking, however, is the finding that worries about non-criminal misfortunes are closely linked to anxiety about crime. It is possible, of course, that this may merely reflect the fact that some people are more predisposed to worry (about all sorts of things) than others. This no doubt explains part of the relationship. But we should note that those people who are most at risk of criminal victimization are also those persons most likely to suffer such things as accident and illness. Rather than looking for an explanation in the psychological make-up of these insecure respondents it is likely to be more fruitful to consider their social circumstances. For the BCS data appear to lend support to the proposition that people's fears about crime are largely rational. As Hough, a former senior Home Office researcher, has put it, 'worry about crime is often firmly and intelligently grounded in direct or indirect experience'.[8] A striking illustration of this connection is to be found in the figures on fear of crime for ethnic minority respondents, whose risk of victimization is greatest, compared to white respondents.

In considering our response to crime and fear of crime the message is, therefore, that we should take seriously what people say they are anxious about. It would appear to follow that we

England & Wales		Percentages[1]		
	Black	Indian	Pakistani/ Bangladeshi	White
Burglary	41	49	48	25
Theft from car[2]	39	34	46	21
Theft of car[2]	38	44	51	28
Mugging	33	46	44	20
Racial attacks	28	39	36	7
Street harassment	19	32	31	9

[1] Percentage of people aged 16 and over who were 'very worried' about each type of crime.
[2] Percentage of car owners.

Fig. 24 Fear of crime, type of crime by ethnic group, 1994

Source: Office of National Statistics (1996) *Social Focus on Ethnic Minorities*, London: HMSO

should also be taking seriously what people tell us they would like the police to do. What people want from the police is an issue to which we shall return in the next Chapter. For the moment we should note that in many respects the public continues to view the role of the police as being to stem increases in crime. The police, who have in the past tended to encourage this unrealistic expectation, have inevitably failed in the venture. This has led to an increasing public tendency to turn to organizations other than the police in an attempt to bolster their security.

Concluding Comments

Our world is changing quickly and, so goes the argument, it is the traditional bases of security which are being destroyed. Jobs for life no longer exist. The welfare state safety net has more and more large holes in it through which the unemployed, the poor, the infirm, and the elderly slip in ever-larger numbers. The growth of global markets and consumer individualism has progressively undermined civic society. Local communities and neighbourhoods are increasingly blighted by levels of incivility and crime which leave all but the most hardy fearful for their property and their safety. With increasing prosperity has come increased geographical and social mobility, and a spectacular change in the nature of consumption. There have been transformations in the labour market, perhaps most importantly with the growth of long-term unemployment. As old industries and means of production have declined and been replaced by new technologies and products, so our living environment has been affected. The inner cities have declined and, in some cases, begun the long process of regeneration. What are sometimes referred to as 'sunrise' and 'rustbelt' zones have developed.

This somewhat dystopian view of contemporary society is not experienced equally or generally. It affects certain groups and localities disproportionately while other strata and neighbourhoods enjoy increasing levels of prosperity almost unscathed by the ravages which preoccupy their fellow citizens a few miles away. Crime is part of this differentiated ecological structure. Crime patterns are often highly localized though, paradoxically, they may involve international connections.

These are the changes and features which form the backdrop to current developments in, and the preoccupations of, British policing. In a context where social forces such as these are let loose what can the police be expected to achieve and what should their role be? In the next two chapters we move on to look at recent developments in policing before considering these questions in greater detail.

2

RECENT DEVELOPMENTS IN POLICING

The basis of our contemporary system of policing was laid down in the recommendations of the Royal Commission on the Police in 1962, later formalized by the Police Act 1964. It was the 1964 Act that established what is referred to as the 'tripartite' structure for the governance of the police: the responsibilities of the police authorities, the chief constables, and the Home Office. This structure provides: the local police authorities with the general duty to maintain an 'adequate and efficient' force; chief constables with responsibility for the 'direction and control' of their forces (what has become known as 'operational independence'); and the Home Secretary with powers generally to 'promote the efficiency of the police'. More recently the Police and Magistrates' Courts Act 1994 has restructured local police authorities and instituted some important changes in the powers available to them and to the Home Secretary. The Police Act 1996 has consolidated these changes.

Although there was initial acceptance of the arrangements brought about by the 1964 Act, together with continuing support for the police, this changed significantly, and perhaps irrevocably, during the following two decades. Three developments were important for this change of mood: the move to Unit Beat Policing; the corruption scandals of the 1970s; and the increasing politicisation of policing.

In 1967 the Home Office encouraged police forces proportionately to increase their use of motorized patrols and place less emphasis on foot patrol. The expected advantage was that wider geographical areas could be covered on a twenty-four hour basis and this, allied with the increasing use of personal radios, would enable officers to respond more quickly to calls for service. This, it was thought, would help the police keep the peace, enhance the detection and prevention of crime, and improve police–pub-

lic relations. It is now widely agreed that the reverse was the outcome and that the emphasis on Unit Beat Policing was miscon-
ceived. The initiative reinforced those aspects of police culture
which sought 'action'. The consequence was to highlight the
'crime fighting' aspects of police work and to devalue the service
role. As one commentator put it: 'The "British bobby" was recast
as the tough, dashing, formidable (but still brave and honest)
"crime-buster" '.[1]

Even the image of the honest crime-fighter was about to come
under attack, however. Within a ten-year period there were four
separate public corruption scandals involving Metropolitan
Police officers. They began with allegations that serious crimes
were being covered up and ended with suggestions that some
officers were actively involved in protection rackets and, even,
armed robberies. Moreover, there was evidence that those
officers whose job it was to investigate such allegations were
hampered at every turn, and even the massive *Operation
Countryman* (an inquiry into alleged Metropolitan Police corruption headed by the chief constable of Dorset), set up by Sir
David McNee, petered out in an unseemly exchange of allegations and counter-allegations of malpractice, incompetence,
and corruption.[2]

The smiling face of PC George Dixon seemed a long way off
and it was not long before his impartiality also came to be questioned. Though the emergence of Robert Peel's 'new' police in
the 1820s was the subject of considerable resistance and political
debate, the history of British policing has largely been characterized by an absence of political controversy and a deliberate cultural avoidance of 'politicking' by police representatives.
Beginning with the campaigns for better pay this changed during
what is now seen as the watershed of the 1970s.[3] The Police
Federation became increasingly vocal as a pressure group, and
by 1979 the political territory of 'law and order' had been firmly
captured by the Conservative Party who linked themselves
unashamedly with the interests of the police and were rewarded
with the explicit support of the Police Federation. Soon after the
1979 election, the new Conservative government immediately
honoured its pledge to implement in full the Edmund Davies
Committee's far-reaching recommendations on increasing
police pay, recommendations which the outgoing Labour

administration had been prepared to implement only in stages.

The increasingly party political profile of the major police union and a few senior police officers, together with a series of significant public disagreements with Labour Party spokespersons—over the policing of the Grunwick trade union dispute, rising crime rates in the late 1970s, and the policing of the inner-city riots in the early 1980s—led to the end of any party political consensus over policing. The policing of the Miners' Strike in 1984 brought the relationship between the police and the Labour Party to an all-time low and the calm consensus that had generally characterized relationships between chief constables and police authorities was disturbed by some high-profile conflicts. Since all the major metropolitan police authorities were controlled by Labour county councils these conflicts generally involved senior Labour councillors.

Financing the police

The Conservative Party used the issue of 'law and order' as a central plank in its general election platform in 1979 and, once elected, the Thatcher administration moved quickly to put its promises regarding policing into practice. In addition to the implementation of the Edmund-Davies pay award, police manpower was increased by just over 6 per cent in the period 1979–84 and expenditure on the police was doubled from £1,644 million to £3,358 million (see Fig. 25).

It was not just expenditure on the police that was increased. Against the backcloth of cuts in all the other major public services, spending on the criminal justice system as a whole rose (see Fig. 26).

These investments reaped no obvious 'law and order' dividends, however. Recorded crime continued to increase—the total number of notifiable offences stood at just over 2.5 million in 1979 and rose by 37 per cent to almost 3.5 million by 1984. Moreover the official clear-up rate for notifiable offences declined from 41 per cent in 1979 to 35 per cent in 1984. And these trends continued throughout the 1980s. Notifiable offences rose a further 6 per cent to over 3.7 million by 1987 and clear-ups fell to 33 per cent.[4]

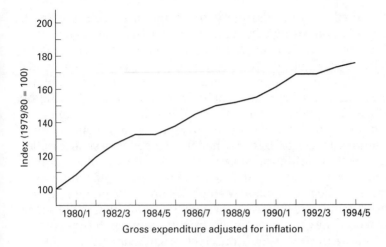

Fig. 25 Expenditure on the police in real terms, 1975–1994
Source: CIPFA Police Statistics adjusted using RPI average earnings index.

It was against this background of major investment and what appeared to be declining indices of police success that the government began, from approximately 1982 onwards, to pursue its 'Financial Management Initiative'. The FMI was generally designed to encourage effectiveness, efficiency, and cost savings in the public sector services by applying private sector management methods and imposing market disciplines on them. Although initially it looked as if the police might be relatively

£million

	1981	1991	% increase	Adj RPI
Police	2,455	6,324	158	23.9%
Prisons	613	1,918	213	31.5%
Legal Aid	160	755	372	55.0%
Probation	102	262	157	23.5%
Law courts	712	3,204	350	52.0%

Fig. 26 Expenditure on the criminal justice system
Source: *Your Police: The Facts*

sheltered from such scrutiny, the publication, largely without consultation with police representative bodies, of Home Office Circular 114/1983 (and later, the even tougher Circular 106/1988), signalled that the financial climate had changed.[5] The 1983 Circular outlined potential new management strategies for the police—now generally referred to as 'Policing by Objectives' (PBO)—many of which had influential supporters within the police. Kenneth Newman, then Metropolitan Police Commissioner, for example, had introduced very similar initiatives within the Metropolitan Police before the Circular was published. Nevertheless, both ACPO and the Police Federation were generally hostile to the new emphasis on 'value for money' and measurement of that value through the application to the police of techniques borrowed largely from the world of business.

One reason why the Conservative government felt able to apply a more stringent financial policy to the police, particularly in its second term of office, was that recorded levels of public satisfaction with the police had been declining for some years. Although public confidence remained relatively favourable compared to other public services, the trend was nevertheless in a downwards direction (see Fig. 27).

Privatization of the police also emerged as an issue. The private security industry was expanding rapidly during the 1980s

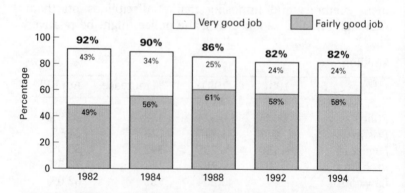

Fig. 27 Trends in public confidence in police, 1982–1994

Source: Bucke, T. (1995) *Policing and the Public: Findings From the 1994 British Crime Survey*, Home Office Research Findings No.28, London: Home Office

and members of the Conservative Party, if not the government at that stage, talked increasingly about the possibility of contracting out discrete policing tasks. Moreover the scope for civilianizing tasks then undertaken wholly or largely by police officers was canvassed more and more vigorously. The use of 'specials' (volunteer unpaid special constables) also assumed prominence in the agenda of Conservative policy-makers during this period. Although the number of specials declined in the late 1970s, it is generally agreed that in part this was a 'paper decline' caused by changes in the rules of service (lowering the retirement age) together with a more stringent application of the hours of service requirements (making the numbers a more accurate reflection of 'active' specials).[6] In the first half of the 1980s the number of specials hovered around the 15,000 mark and reached 20,000 by the early 1990s. In line with their view that 'the community' should be playing its part in policing and crime prevention, and that resources for increases in the mainstream would necessarily be limited, there was official encouragement for increasing the number of specials and Government ministers set targets of 30,000 that they hoped would be achieved in years to come.

As a result of all these developments the accord between the police and the Thatcher government of the early 1980s waned in the second half of the decade. Moreover government moves to exercise greater control over police budgets involved greater centralization of policy making. Policing policy was made more and more by Home Office Circular accompanied by a tighter grip on the financial reins by the Home Office.[7] The Labour-controlled Metropolitan Counties, and their related police authorities, were abolished by the Local Government Act 1985 and replaced by the generally weaker District Council-based Joint Boards for the same areas. Local authority expenditure was capped and the proportion of police budgets met from central government expenditure increased. Central policing agencies, such as the National Criminal Intelligence Service, were created. Local authority control over policing policy, a power that was already vestigial, waned further. The equilateral triangle supposedly represented by the tripartite structure was now isosceles, with ACPO building its corporate strength to take on the increasingly powerful Home Office and the local authorities reduced to what one commentator described as little more than a 'cheer-leader corps', if they were still so minded, for the police.[8]

The Police and Criminal Evidence Act 1984

During the 1980s the Conservative government also introduced what has been described by one commentator as the 'single most significant landmark in the modern development of police powers':[9] the Police and Criminal Evidence Act 1984. The following year the government removed, with the introduction of the Crown Prosecution Service (CPS), the prosecutorial role of the police and in 1986, through the Public Order Act 1986, introduced significant changes to public order law. An important part of the backdrop to these developments was the urban unrest of the early 1980s.

The most infamous of the public disorders in the early 1980s occurred in Brixton in April 1981. During a weekend of rioting, arson and looting, over 7,000 officers were deployed in an attempt to restore order and 400 of them were reported injured. Over 250 people were arrested. The eruption in Brixton ignited serious disorders in Liverpool, and later in Birmingham, Sheffield, Nottingham, Hull, and other cities. Following a police raid on houses in Railton Road, rioting again broke out in Brixton in July 1981, and then, briefly, again in Liverpool.

Lord Scarman was appointed to inquire into the causes of the unrest and to make recommendations.[10] Scarman was highly critical of the policing of Brixton and especially the absence of consultation locally. He described the riots as 'an outburst of anger and resentment by young black people against the police'.[11] Had there been proper police–community consultation the saturation policing exercise that sparked the events in Brixton would in his opinion not have been launched. He concluded that any police force that failed to consult local communities about the policing of their areas would fail to be effective because effective policing required public support. There was, he thought, a danger of the police 'becoming, by virtue of their professionalism, a "corps d'elite" set apart from the rest of the community'.[12]

Lord Scarman made wide-ranging recommendations covering recruitment of ethnic minorities to the police, increasing consultation through the introduction of liaison committees, the lay visiting of police stations, the independent review of complaints against the police, and the tightening of regulations regarding racially prejudiced behaviour by officers. He also reiterated Sir Richard Mayne's 1829 definition of the police function as 'the prevention of crime . . . the protection of life and property, [and] the preservation of public tranquillity' and he argued, controversially, that in the event of a conflict of aims—where law enforcement prejudiced pubic tranquillity—public tranquillity should have priority.[13]

Scarman's was not the only inquiry in the period considering the behaviour and the role of the police. The 'Confait case' in which three young boys were convicted of murder in the early 1970s led, when later it was established that their confessions had been false, to considerable concern about the efficacy of the Judge's Rules which formed the basis of safeguards for suspects detained in custody. The case led indirectly to the establishment of a Royal Commission on Criminal Procedure. The report of the Royal Commission proved controversial.[14] It received a large measure of support from the police but was widely criticized by left-wing and liberal commentators inside and outside Parliament. It gave rise to the Police and Criminal Evidence Bill introduced in 1982 which, after the intervention of a general election and unprecedentedly prolonged debate and amendment, was eventually enacted in 1984.

The Act (PACE) extended police powers in a number of important ways and also introduced far-reaching procedural safeguards (some of which were revised in 1991) to protect suspects against abuse of these powers. Critics argued that the new powers made available to the police represented a serious danger to civil liberties and that most of the alleged safeguards would prove of little worth. By contrast the police maintained that the safeguards were too onerous and meant that they would in future be fighting crime with one hand tied behind their backs. Police powers of arrest, detention and stop and search were enacted and were accompanied by four codes of practice which replaced the Judges' Rules. Research on the impact of PACE has upheld the fears of neither the police nor the critics.[15] There is absolutely no doubt that the legislation has, in a number of vital respects, had a significant impact on the behaviour of the police and on the culture of policing. Moreover, there is little evidence that the effectiveness of the police has been greatly handicapped by the changes. The police have come to accept routine practices—the attendance of legal advisors for suspects in police stations and the tape-recording of all police interviews, for example—which when first mooted were met with considerable hostility and apprehension.

PACE also introduced a statutory requirement on chief constables to make arrangements 'in each area for obtaining the views of people in that area about matters concerning the policing of the area and for obtaining their cooperation with the police for preventing crime in the area'. This has led universally to the establishment of Police Community Consultative Groups (PCCGs—the nomenclature varies but the nature of the groups is largely the same).[16] A considerable body of research on these groups suggests that their operation has not greatly affected police priorities and that they have stimulated few practical crime prevention initiatives.[17] Nevertheless the police have been provided with a mechanism for building improved public understanding of the varied tasks they perform and the dilemmas that they face, and it seems likely that PCCGs, of which there were by the early 1990s approaching 500 with a total membership of 10-15,000 people throughout England and Wales, have helped bring about the modest improvement in public confidence in the police recorded in recent public opinion surveys.

PACE also reformed the police complaints procedure. It replaced the previously existing Police Complaints Board (a part-time lay body) with the Police Complaints Authority (PCA)—a full-time body with the power to supervise the investigation of any serious complaint. Research has come to both positive and negative conclusions about the operation of the new system.[18] It appears to be staffed by committed and able police investigators and those police officers responsible for complaints and discipline are increasingly impressed by its operation. The new 'informal resolution' procedure appears to be promising. On the other hand there continue to be an overwhelming majority of 'dissatisfied customers', be they officers or complainants. The fact that most complaints against officers continue to be investigated exclusively by the police themselves is almost certainly an important factor in explaining why so few complaints are made compared with the proportion of members of the public who report having felt like making a complaint.[19]

Public Perceptions Change

The policing of the Miners' Strike in 1984-5 greatly affected the nature and style of public order policing in Britain and public perceptions about the police generally. During the strike the accoutrements of militaristic policing—visored helmets, flame-proof uniforms, full-length shields, and long-handled batons—were used on a regular basis by thousands of officers transported up and down the country through a system of mutual aid between forces. The costs of the operation were enormous and caused widespread consternation to police authorities whose approval was neither needed or sought by chief constables to whom the government had apparently given a blank cheque. The TV-viewing public watched officers on horseback charging into lines of pickets, followed by sorties of officers with long shields, short shields, and batons, all in a highly organized manner. This drift towards paramilitarism has changed the public image of the police, perhaps for ever: police tactics familiar from filmed images of Northern Ireland or continental France or Germany had come to mainland Britain. The wire-meshed police van could henceforth regularly be seen on the average English high street and, in a related sight linked to another threat, tourists leaving for their overseas package tours got used to seeing police officers equipped with automatic weapons at major airports. As a consequence of these developments the legitimacy of policing policy, and of police tactics and operational decisions, is probably now more closely examined and questioned than it was in the past.

This increased scrutiny of the police which followed the Miners' Strike and the introduction of PACE did not diminish. For within a relatively short time the uncovering of several major miscarriages of justice led to further debate about the accountability and control of the service. The cases of the Guildford Four, the Birmingham Six, the Maguires, and the 'Tottenham Three', together with widespread allegations concerning the methods of the West Midlands Serious Crimes Squad, led to further falls in public confidence in the police. Even the Thatcher administration, which had reportedly set its face against the use of Royal Commissions to review policy, was forced to give way. In 1991 the Royal Commission on Criminal Justice was established.[20]

In fact the Royal Commission was one of several inquiries into policing created in the early 1990s. The arrival of Kenneth Clarke in the Home Office heralded a period of intense activity regarding policing. Within a relatively short space, and without any formal consultation, a White Paper on *Police Reform* was issued,[21] and this began a period of over two years when policing issues were rarely out of the news. Kenneth Clarke's reported initial plans included reform of: police authorities, by reducing their size and the proportion of elected members and appointing independent members; police budgets, by eliminating local funding altogether; police forces, by reducing their number in England and Wales by almost half through a process of amalgamation. In the event the White Paper included a number of proposals for amending the structure and functioning of police authorities, together with powers to amalgamate forces, but the idea of funding local policing entirely by central government was dropped. A compromise proposition reducing the proportion of police budgets derived from local taxation, and cash limiting those budgets, was included in the White Paper instead.

The Government's core reforms for the governance and administration of the police were brought to fruition in the Police and Magistrates' Courts Act 1994. Over three-quarters of policing expenditure is now provided directly by central government (it was previously 51 per cent, though a proportion of the local authority contribution came indirectly from central government). The Act enables the Home Secretary to set national objectives for policing and imposes a statutory duty on police authorities to publish annually a local policing plan. Police authorities are also required to set performance targets for measuring the achievement of objectives. The Act enables the Secretary of State to issue codes of practice relating to the exercise of police authority functions. The majority of police authorities were reduced to seventeen members, nine of whom are now elected to sit with five appointed members and three magistrates. Although Kenneth Clarke's original intention had been to appoint both the independent members and the chairmen of the authorities, amendments to the legislation in the House of Lords meant that independent members are now appointed locally, but only after the Home Office has played a part in the short-listing process. The power to elect or appoint their chairmen remains with the authorities.

These are the most far-reaching changes to the system for local governance of the police for thirty years, though what the changes signify is contested. The Government claims that the Act will strengthen the system of local policing: that the inclusion of appointed members, particularly those with experience of commerce, will invigorate police authorities; and that the police authorities and chief constables now enjoy increased devolved powers to determine local policing policy. Detractors see the Act as representing the very opposite trend: local democratic accountability of the police having been undermined by the appointment of what are likely to be political placemen and women, the police authorities now being part of the government's quangocracy; and the powers now held by the Secretary of State, including powers of the purse, mean that we have a national police in all but name. It should be noted that some seasoned observers of the British policing scene argued that our ostensible system of local policing was largely a constitutional fiction *before* the Police and Magistrates' Courts Act: the manner in which chief constables are groomed and apppointed; the previously existing Home Office powers to control budgets, determine regulations, impose standards of equipment, and arrange central services; and the influence of Her Majesty's Chief Inspector of Constabulary and now the Audit Commission; all signify centralized policy making with police authorities exercising little more than a not particularly influential consultative role.[22]

In May 1992 what became known, after the name of its Chairman, as the Sheehy Committee of Inquiry was announced. Its terms of reference were: 'To examine the rank structure, remuneration, and conditions of the police service in England and Wales, in Scotland and in Northern Ireland, and to recommend what changes, if any, would be sensible'. The Committee reported in mid-1993,[23] within days of the publication of the White Paper. Sheehy recommended: flattening the pyramid of police ranks; reducing the initial salaries of recruits to the police;

instituting fixed-term contracts for new recruits; and a system of performance-related pay for senior ranks. These proposals were met, not surprisingly, with a barrage of criticism from the police service. In particular Sheehy's proposals for performance-related pay, which many commentators saw as reflecting the government's obsession with commercial management methods—though, ironically, many commercial enterprises had decided that performance-related pay was counter-productive for motivation, teamwork, and productivity—was singularly inappropriate for a public service in which desirable 'performance' was notoriously difficult to measure. Sheehy's most radical proposals have so far been shelved. However, the rank structure has been thinned—deputy chief constables (at least in name) and chief superintendents have gone—and fixed-term appointments are now the norm for officers of ACPO rank.

By the end of 1993 a further inquiry—the *Core and Ancillary Tasks Review*—had been set up within the Home Office. Its purpose was: 'To examine the services provided by the police, to make recommendations about the most cost-effective way of delivering core police services and to assess the scope for relinquishing ancillary tasks'. The review, not surprisingly, was interpreted by the police service as potentially the most threatening planning exercise for a programme of privatisation, or contracting out, of certain police functions yet undertaken by a Government highly committed to this approach. The brief given to the civil servants carrying out the review neatly expressed the police service's worst forebodings:

to see whether there are tasks which it is no longer necessary for the police service to carry out [and] to see where there is scope for using money and manpower more effectively to carry out tasks, which everyone agrees are for the police service.[24]

The background to the review was ominously clear. Police costs were growing, as were the demands made on the police. How great was the increase in demand relative to the additional staff provided was graphically illustrated by the Audit Commission (see Fig. 28).

Some indicators of police performance were deteriorating: the clear-up rate for recorded crime had fallen to 26 per cent in 1992 from 41 per cent in 1979, for example. At the same time the

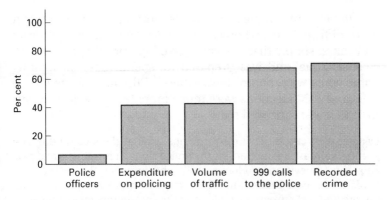

Fig. 28 Changes in police resources and demand for police services, 1981–1992

Source: Audit Commission (1993) *Helping With Enquiries*, London: Audit Commission

Government was trying to exercise firm control over public expenditure. It was no longer possible for the police to do, and the government to pay for, everything the police were currently doing if, as the White Paper had signalled, the police were to perform their 'core tasks' well. And as Michael Howard had indicated in his introduction to the White Paper, the priority for policing was waging an effective *'war against crime'*.[25]

Though the initial aims of the Inquiry were modified as work progressed, possibly as the Government drew back from radical plans in the face of a sustained campaign of resistance from the police representative organizations (ACPO, the Superintendents' Association and the Police Federation), the underlying rationale continued to be the limitation of public expenditure on policing. In the event the report from the review was something of a damp squib, its recommendations being largely confined to relatively peripheral police activities such as the escorting of wide-bodied loads on motorways.[26]

Policing, Crime Prevention, and Proactivity

As crime continued to rise, despite the increase in resources devoted to policing in the early 1980s, the causes of crime were said to be more complex and the responsibility for preventing it more diffuse. Thus, whereas the 1979 Conservative Manifesto had stated simply that the Party gave high priority 'to the fight against crime' and was prepared to 'spend more on fighting crime while we economise elsewhere',[27] the manifestos for the 1983 and 1987 Elections were much more tentative documents. In 1983 it was conceded that:

Dealing with crimes, civil disobedience, violent demonstrations and pornography are not matters for the police alone. It is teachers and parents—plus television producers too—who infuence the moral standards of the next generation. There must be close co-operation and understanding between the police and the community they serve.[28]

In 1987 the Party stood by its law and order guns, but no longer 'underrated the challenge'. The Manifesto pointed out that 'crime has been rising steadily over the years; not just in Britain but in most other countries too. The origins of crime lie deep in society'.[29]

One of the key messages put out by the Government and the police as the decade advanced was that the police could not be expected to carry responsibility for the prevention of crime unaided. Increasing emphasis was placed on the responsibility of the 'community' both in relation to policing generally and, more specifically, to crime prevention.

This message was not new. It was merely emphasized with new, possibly defensive, vigour. As early as 1965 a Home Office report had recommended that sections of the public, particularly the business community, be enlisted to assist the police with the development of local crime prevention initiatives. Local Crime Prevention Panels were established as a consequence.[30] Though Crime Prevention Panels initially tended to emphazise a technological 'locks, bolts and bars' approach to crime prevention—what has since become known as 'target hardening'—by the mid-1980s panels were being persuaded to adopt a more 'situational' approach, along the lines being pursued within the Home Office. Efforts were now made to 'design out' crime. The new emphasis was on reducing the opportunity for crime less through fortification and more by local planning designed to affect the motivations of offenders. These efforts included siting vulnerable facilities—like telephone boxes—in locations where they were subject to better natural surveillance. Situational crime prevention initiatives tended, however, to require the co-operation of local agencies typically unrepresented on Crime Prevention Panels. A wider framework was required.

During the late 1970s John Alderson, until 1982 the Chief Constable for Devon and Cornwall, argued, in a series of books and pamphlets, for what he termed a 'new social contract for police' based on 'community policing principles'. For Alderson this meant the establishment of 'community police councils'— bodies not far removed from the PCCGs established under the Police and Criminal Evidence Act—systems for inter-agency co-operation for crime prevention, and the appointment of 'community constables', officers attached to particular localities with a high level of continuity.[31] Alderson was convinced, as was Lord Scarman after him, that the police had become too distant from the communities they allegedly served: what was required was the establishment of a new partnership between the police and public. The police must in turn emphasize that theirs was less a 'force' and more a 'service', a theme taken up by the police generally after the conflicts of the early 1980s. All police representatives now emphasize that whatever the role of the police is, it is the 'police service' that provides it. Moreover, most constabularies were to claim during the 1980s that they were committed to 'community policing' in one form or another, usually by allocating a proportion of their patrol force to permanent community beats.

The idea of 'inter-agency co-operation' soon became more than the reformist vision of advocates of change like John Alderson. In 1978, for example, a Home Office circular recommended improved co-ordination between criminal justice agencies, combined with community-based initiatives, as a solution to what was perceived at the time to be the piecemeal approach for dealing with juveniles offenders.[32] During the 1980s inter-agency crime prevention became a major strand of policy, initially advocated by means of Home Office circular and later the subject of Home Office grants to specific programmes. Though initially treated as a peripheral specialism of low status and interest when placed alongside crime fighting, the decade saw crime prevention attract increasing publicity if not police commitment. In 1983 the Home Office Crime Prevention Unit was established, and in the following year an interdepartmental circular on crime prevention was issued.[33] In 1986 two seminars on crime prevention were held by the Prime Minister at 10 Downing Street. In the same year the 'Five Towns Initiative' was launched, followed by the Safer Cities Programme in 1988, initiatives focused on locations identified as suffering from high levels of crime and urban deprivation.[34] In 1989 the charity *Crime Concern* was established, pump-primed with government money and thereafter encouraged to seek sponsorship, particularly from the commercial world, to support its crime prevention projects and training programmes for practitioners. The Home Office Standing Conference on Crime Prevention was reconstituted as the National Board for Crime Prevention. In turn ACPO formed a sub-committee on crime prevention.

In 1995 an even more corporate approach was adopted. The government created a Ministerial Group on Crime Prevention, a committee on which twelve departments are represented, the idea being that every government department should be mindful of crime prevention when pursuing other policy objectives. The Group is advised by a new National Crime Prevention Agency on the Board of which the Home Office, ACPO, Crime Concern, local and police authorities, the business community and others are represented. This structure, the government claims, will lead to a 'sharper, more focused approach to the development of crime prevention strategy'.[35]

These inter-agency initiatives moved proactive crime prevention beyond the realms of 'situational' crime prevention towards what is widely referred to as 'social' crime prevention. The focus was no longer on crime targets, or crime events, but the social environments within which crime—offenders and offending—flourishes. Yet though the government stresses the importance of crime prevention activities and, at least at a rhetorical level, argues that the prevention of crime should be considered a central part of the standard policing function, the reality is that crime prevention remains fairly marginal, and is narrowly defined, within most police forces. There is what one expert observer has described as a 'grotesque mismatch' between the alleged primacy of crime prevention and the resources devoted to the task by the police.[36] Police Crime Prevention Officers comprise less than 1 per cent of force strength, are to be found in

either 'community involvement' or 'criminal investigation'
departments depending on what view is taken of the nature of
the activity, and most police crime prevention initiatives have
been poorly served when it has come to evaluative study.[37]
Nearly every official publication regarding policing now includes
brief accounts of inter-agency initiatives that have allegedly produced excellent crime-reducing results.

Merseyside Police and Urban Crime Fund money to install closed-
circuit television cameras at the entrances to sheltered accommodation for the elderly which had been plagued by 'bogus official'
burglaries, where thieves had talked themselves into homes by pre-
tending to be council or utility company officials. In the twelve
months prior to the installation there had been 51 burglaries, all
investigated exhaustively by the police. In the year since the cameras
were installed, only nine burglaries have occurred.

A joint police/local council project in inner city Leicester reduced
burglaries by 62%, through improved domestic security.

The establishment of the Motor Education Project in Bradford has
coincided with a reduction of 75% in the number of new autocrime
offenders coming to police attention during the 18 months up to
June 1993.

The introduction of closed-circuit TV cameras into Airdrie town
centre, with public support, has had dramatic results. In the first
twelve months of operation, recorded crimes dropped from 2,475 to
627, of which 447 (71%) were cleared up. Break-ins to commercial
premises dropped from 263 to 15 and incidents of vandalism from
207 to 36. The reduced workload in incident response has allowed
increased patrol in rural areas. The costs of installation and maintenance are met by the local business community.

Fig. 29 Crime prevention in action

Source: Audit Commission (1996) *Tackling Crime Effectively vol.2*, London:
Audit Commission

However, in 1991 the Standing Conference on Crime
Prevention (in a report that is generally known as the Morgan
Report) found that in many local authority areas the challenge of
'community safety'—this was now the preferred phrase, in order
to emphasize the fact that crime is only part of a more general
pattern of neighbourhood insecurity—had yet to be taken up.

The Morgan Report argued that if concerted community safety effort was to be undertaken then inter-agency working had to be encouraged through a statutory framework with local authorities being given a clear responsibility. The Government rejected this proposal, a topic to which we return in Chapter 6.

There are two further policing developments from the 1980s which are noteworthy and linked to the account that we have given so far. The first is the extension of the idea of community partnership of which members of the public are almost certainly most aware—neighbourhood watch. The second is in a sense the corollary, *within* police forces, of the information that ideally the police should gain from neighbourhood watch—the formation of intelligence-led crime management desks or units.

In the early 1980s the idea and terminology of neighbourhood watch was imported from North America: Cheshire Constabulary claims to have been the first in the field in 1983. The vogue was encouraged by the Home Office, in the form of guidance issued by the Crime Prevention Unit,[38] and the idea took off with astonishing rapidity. Within two years the Inspectorate of Constabulary reported that there were 3,500 neighbourhood watch schemes in operation in more than half the police forces in England and Wales. By 1987 it was estimated that more than 2.5 million people lived in areas covered by neighbourhood watch. According to the British Crime Survey neighbourhood watch continues to increase in popularity with one in five households members of a scheme.[39] The Government's most recent White Paper suggests that there are now some 143,000 schemes covering 6 million households.[40]

The idea of neighbourhood watch is grounded on three propositions. First, that the police are unable to prevent or detect crime on their own. Secondly, that the public are able to prevent and detect a good many forms of crime and, most importantly, that they have a duty to do both. And thirdly, that the crime prevention and detection efforts of individuals are made more effective when those individuals act as members of a group or community. Areas covered by watch schemes are signposted and co-ordinators appointed, principally to liaise with the police. Neighbourhood watch rapidly proliferated into Business Watch, Vehicle Watch, Farm Watch, and so on. Some police forces enthusiastically pioneered the formation of neighbour-

hood watch groups; others were sceptical. Some chief constables, for example, anticipated—accurately as it turned out—that
schemes were most likely to take off in residential areas where
the crime-preventive need was least and there was a danger,
therefore, that scarce police resources would be sucked into the
support of watch schemes, thereby further depriving high crime-
risk areas. In the event public enthusiasm for neighbourhood
watch outstripped all police caution: the evidence shows that
most schemes are initiated not by the police but by local residents.

True to tradition, neighbourhood watch was initially pushed
without there being much evidence that criminals were deterred
by the street signs and window stickers or that the police
benefited greatly from any enhanced flow of information about
crime and criminals from the better organized participating citizenry. When systematic evaluative studies were undertaken the
findings were as usual compromised by shortcomings in the
implementation of schemes—thus raising the usual question of
whether better results might have been achieved had greater
efforts been invested.[41] Generally speaking there is little evidence that watch schemes reduce the incidence of crime or that
the police derive more and better quality criminal intelligence as
a result of their existence. However, there is evidence that neighbourhood watch participation serves to reassure local residents
and make them less fearful of crime. Furthermore, it is argued
that what begins as a neighbourhood watch effort has beneficial
side-effects, enhancing people's sense of community and
encouraging neighbourliness. This is the view now taken by
Crime Concern.

It is very doubtful that the value of neighbourhood watch
should be judged only according to short-term technical crime
preventive criteria. As in the case of changes in police operational methods, there are long-term consequences to be considered. Neighbourhood watch has the potential for forging a
greater sense of partnership between the police and the community and of making the police better aware of what it is that
the public wants and is concerned about. Neighbourhood watch
representatives are prominent, for example, in the membership
of most Police Community Consultative Groups. Equally, however, mass neighbourhood watch participation may stimulate a

public demand for policing services which, if not met by the state police, may lead to the growth of other 'policing' initiatives of a self-help or commercial nature. Some of these outgrowths—local patrols, as in 'street watch' which is said now to be a feature of 15 per cent of all neighbourhood watch schemes,[42] for example—may officially be approved, while others—various forms of vigilantism—may be regarded as profoundly undesirable. One thing is clear. The amazing growth of neighbourhood watch during the 1980s reflected a latent public concern about policing, crime, and community safety which demands urgent analysis.

Whereas crime prevention remains the Cinderella role within the police, the detection of crime has always been seen as the prime activity. Detectives in the Criminal Investigation Departments enjoy high status. Yet, according to the Audit Commission, the work of detectives and the activity of crime detection have historically been subject to remarkably little scrutiny.[43] Further, though the majority of crimes, particularly those that are less serious, are in fact investigated by uniformed officers, the work of detectives has traditionally been very poorly integrated into the work of basic police administrative units. Detectives are constantly in 'fire-fighting' mode, unable usually to see the wood for the trees and bogged down by paperwork. Crime intelligence has typically been gathered in limbo. Local Intelligence Officers (LIOs) comprise, like Crime Prevention Officers, less than 1 per cent of a typical force strength and instead of being high status individuals at the centre of operational management their few posts have been what the Audit Commission has described as the 'refuge of the lame, sick and elderly', often untrained, on the periphery and frequently disregarded.[44]

The Audit Commission, in a report which all the evidence suggests has been highly influential, has recommended a proactive intelligence-led crime management approach to remedy these deficiencies. The approach is based on the proposition that a small proportion of offenders are prolific in their offending and that these individuals can be better targeted if crime pattern analyses and enhanced use of intelligence is brought to the centre of police operations through the establishment of a crime management desk or unit staffed by the most able officers available. According to this model every Basic Command Unit (BCU) should have a Field Intelligence Officer and more personnel resources should be allocated for proactive use on the basis of intelligence. Greater use of surveillance and informants should be used as part of this strategy. In a follow-up report the Audit Commission states that police forces are increasingly pursuing this approach.[45] Two thirds of forces are said to have introduced crime desks or units, and this is said to have inspired focused operations in selected areas against particular types of offences or offenders with greatly improved results for both the incidence and clear-up of those crimes.

These are important developments though, despite the glossy accounts of encouragingly positive results, it is too early to assess what the overall impact of these organizational shifts will be. It is not at all clear, for example, what policing activities are possibly being displaced by the intelligence-led proactive policing that appears now to be so popular with senior officers. At least one chief constable, for a force which sees itself as a front-runner in the pursuit of the new proactive approach, has privately said to us that the concept of the community constable is no longer feasible, if it was ever sensible, and that he could envisage a time when up to three quarters of all calls from the public to his force would no longer result in attendance by an officer. To the extent that this is so, the public may be educated to the view that this shift in prioritizing the allocation of police resources is sensible and acceptable. But there is substantial room for doubt whether the public will be satisfied by any significant diminution in the visible presence of uniformed officers in their neighbourhoods, a question to which we shall return in Chapters 5 and 6.

Regional, National, and International Developments

Some of the most significant organizational developments in policing have involved the formation of regional, national, and even international structures.

These supra-force policing organizations have developed in order to counter the threat posed by the mobility and global networks to which we referred in Chapter 1. The existence of these broader policing structures has implications for the future of local policing and in Chapter 6 we make recommendations in relation to regional, national, and international policing organizations and the mechanisms by which they are made accountable. First, it is worth reviewing briefly the nature and history of these organisations.

There is first the Regional Crime Squads, first established under provisions in the Police Act 1964. There are currently six RCSs in England and Wales, each of which covers an area comprising several police forces. The squads are staffed by officers on secondment from those forces. The main functions of the RCSs are: to identify and arrest persons responsible for serious criminal offences which transcend force and regional boundaries; to co-operate with regional intelligence offices in generating intelligence; and, where appropriate, to assist in the investigation of serious crime.

Since the establishment of the RCSs there has been increasing pressure to create more specialist national units to combat various forms of criminal activity which, it is argued, cannot effectively be countered by existing force or regional units. There has also been pressure for increasing international co-operation as a result of the developing European Union. In 1989 the Home Affairs Committee of the House of Commons, as part of their investigation of drug trafficking and related serious crime, heard evidence from several senior police officers that there was need for greater national co-ordination of certain policing activities. Plans for a National Crime Intelligence Unit (NCIU) got underway in 1990, the intention being to integrate the work of the existing National Football Intelligence Unit, the Art and Antiques Squad, the National Drugs Intelligence Unit, the regional criminal intelligence offices, and a variety of other bodies. The NCIU was established in 1992. The Unit: 'gathers, collates, analyses and disseminates intelligence and information on major criminals', it works closely with the RCSs, with local forces, and with HM Customs.[46]

At the 1995 Conservative Party conference the Home Secretary announced that he intended creating an operational National Crime Squad to deal with serious crimes, a proposition implicitly endorsed by the House of Commons Home Affairs Committee in its 1995 report on organized crime.[47] While the Home Affairs Committee accepted that organized crime in the UK did not exist on the scale found in many other countries, the Committee nevertheless considered the evidence on its extent to be a cause for concern. The Committee thought there was scope to develop the role of both the NCIS and the RCSs. The White Paper *Protecting the Public*, published in March 1996, confirmed the government's intention of forming a National Crime Squad and announced that it would be led by a co-ordinator with 'executive power to direct its resources from a national and international perspective'. The government has said that the National Crime Squad will not be the equivalent of a 'British FBI', and that it will not so develop—'the primary focus for policing in the UK will remain at the local level'—but it nevertheless intends to establish the Squad on a statutory basis.[48] What that statutory arrangement will be, and how the National Crime Squad is to be made accountable for its actions, has yet to be announced. Moves to make the NCIS autonomous of the Home Office and place it on a statutory basis—thereby giving it 'the freedom both to manage its own affairs and to review and improve its effectiveness'—have also to be announced.[49]

In addition to these structures at a regional and national level there have also been developments in international policing arrangements. The oldest and largest of these, Interpol, is a communications network which passes criminal intelligence and other messages and requests between national police authorities. Interpol is international rather than European in its ambit. It has over 150 members. The 'Trevi Group' is the second of the major international policing organizations. It was established in 1975 and was originally intended as a platform for EC Ministers of Justice and Home Affairs to develop counter-terrorist measures. However, its remit has gradually been extended and now covers police training and technology, serious crime and public order and disaster prevention. The 'Schengen Group' comprises a third structure, established after the abolition of border controls between France and Germany in 1984. In 1985 these two nations were joined by the Benelux countries as part of the Schengen Agreement. In 1990 all but three of the EC member nations—the UK, Ireland, and Denmark—were brought into the agreement. In addition to the removal of border checks the agreement provides for increased police co-operation between countries within this new 'border'. Key to this is a common information system—the Schengen Information System—and, potentially, the possibility of the right of 'hot pursuit', entailing the use of police powers by officers outside their own jurisdictions.

Finally, there is Europol. The Maastricht Treaty, signed in 1991 and in force since November 1993, brought policing and criminal justice policy under the umbrella of the European Community. This was the beginnings of what is known as the 'third pillar' of what became the European Union in late 1993. More specifically, under Articles K.1.9 and K.4 the Maastricht Treaty established new structures—to repace Trevi—which were to form the basis of Europol. The intention was to develop an information exchange system which could be used to help prevent and combat terrorism, drug-trafficking, and other serious organized crime. It would also help co-ordinate international investigations and encourage other forms of international co-operation.

Private Security and Municipal Policing

Not only is policing delivered by an increasing array of public bodies organized at a variety of geographical levels, but the private and municipal sectors are themselves becoming more visible in this arena. It is far from clear, however, to what extent the growth of policing services delivered by agencies other than the state police represents the filling of a gap left by the inability or unwillingness of the state police to provide services the public wants. It may represent changes in the nature of modern life and institutions in which the growth of these services lies alongside, is complementary to, the steady growth in expenditure on the state police and other public policing services like Environmental Health Officers or the Post Office Investigation Department. Nor is it clear that there has been the massive growth in non-police 'policing' which is often claimed. Certainly there has been a huge increase in the employment of uniformed private security personnel. But if 'policing' in its broadest sense is interpreted to include those people who, like wardens, caretakers, park-keepers, and gamekeepers, have always been employed to guard, protect, and oversee both public and private property and locations, then much of this growth may simply reflect changes in the *way* the task is done.

What is clear is that, for a variety of reasons, the respective roles of the police and private security organizations now increasingly overlap. The boundaries between them are becoming less well defined. This is the result, in part at least, of a process referred to as the 'decreasing congruence between private property and private space'.[50] The second half of the twentieth century has seen a rapid growth in property which is privately owned but to which the public usually has access. This property includes shopping centres, residential estates, educational institutions, parks, offices, and leisure centres. More and more public life is being conducted on private property. Thus the protection of private property—a central aim of private security—has increasingly come to encompass the maintenance of public order as when, for example, there are demonstrations against new road construction. Private security services have impinged more and more on what used to be considered the exclusive domain of the state police.

The boundaries between public and private policing have further been blurred because of the operations of an increasing number of agencies whose formal status and functional activities are difficult to classify. These have most commonly been referred to as 'hybrid' or 'grey' policing bodies. They include, for example, the surveillance, investigative, and regulatory sections attached to central and local government departments. The position of some of these bodies has been made even more 'grey' by the privatization programme the government has pursued. For example the British Transport Police will continue to police our railway network: they will, for the forseeable future, provide a contract service that the new railway companies have been given no option but to receive.

The private security industry is a large, profitable, and growing part of the UK economy. Various estimates of the annual turnover of the industry are available. A 1979 Home Office Green Paper suggested an annual turnover in 1976 of £135 million and, according to the marketing consultancy Jordan and Sons, total annual sales during the early 1980s were in excess of £400 million. Jordan's 1989 and 1993 reports suggest respectively that the annual turnover of the industry increased from £476.4 million in

1983 to £807.6 million in 1987 and £1,225.6 million in 1990. One recent estimate by one of the regulatory bodies in the private security industry has put the turnover for 1994 at £2,827 million.

Although there are various estimates of the number of organizations trading in the private security sector, and the numbers of people employed, few of them appear to be reliable. The best available figures suggest that, in broad terms, the number of private security employees, including those persons involved in the manufacture and installation of security devices, is at least the equivalent of the total complement of the forty-three constabularies in England and Wales; data from the government's Labour Force Survey suggest that there are almost certainly over 162,000 people working in the private security industry, but the actual total may be at least half as many again.[51]

This rapid growth in private security provides a vivid illustration that policing involves much more than the police and what the police do. The point is made all the more clear if one considers that most symbolic of all police tasks, mobile patrol. It is briefly worth considering two examples where a 'police patrol' presence is provided by personnel other than police constables. First is the Sedgefield Community Force. For many years local councils have employed in-house security operations to protect council property and employees. The Sedgefield Community Force, a local authority police force in County Durham, became operational in January 1994. The force provides a 24-hour patrolling service within the geographical confines of the District—an area of 85 square miles and a population of 90,000 people. The ten patrol officers wear uniforms similar to those worn by police officers. They travel mainly in cars, though they are encouraged to leave them to patrol on foot. They received 1,284 calls from the public in their first year.

Although the Sedgefield Community Force provides a visible patrol it was set up as a non-confrontational force and has a policy of 'observing and reporting' based on a presumption of *not* using officers' citizen's powers of arrest. A small-scale piece of research on the Sedgefield Community Force carried out about six months after it was set up[52] found that just under two-thirds of local residents said without any prompting that they had heard of the Force. This proportion of respondents increased to three-quarters after the force was described to them. There is some indication from the survey that the public feels safer since the Force was introduced, and a significant proportion of those questioned felt that the Community Force would act to deter criminal activity. There was clear evidence that local residents saw the Force as complementing what the local constabulary was doing. In general respondents said they would not be happy to have the members of the Force as the sole deterrers of crime. But when asked who they would be happy to have patrolling their streets: 91 per cent said police specials or a new rank of police patroller; 83 per cent said a council-employed community force; 43 per cent said ordinary citizens; and 33 per cent said private security guards. A further survey[53] of residents who had asked for assistance from the Sedgefield Force discovered that the vast majority of calls concerned vandalism, anti-social behaviour, and nuisance—incivilities about which all the research evidence shows the public is generally concerned— though a sizeable minority, about a fifth, concerned straight-for- ward crime. Moreover those persons calling for assistance were highly appreciative of the service they received. Though direct comparisons cannot easily be made, the residents who call the Sedgefield Community Force are at least as appreciative of the service they receive, perhaps more so, than are people who call the police.[54]

The second example is the Wandsworth Parks Constabulary. Under the Public Health (Amendment) Act 1907, all local author- ities in England and Wales can swear in park employees as spe- cial constables though there are few examples of any doing so. Legislation, bearing upon London only, has however been used by several boroughs in the capital to set up Parks Constabularies. Under the Ministry of Housing and Local Government Provisional Order Confirmation (Greater London Parks and Open Spaces) Act 1967, Wandsworth established its Parks Constabulary in 1985.

There are thirty full-time uniformed officers and twenty-five part-timers (effectively 'specials') in the Wandsworth Parks Constabulary. They patrol the parks and open spaces in the bor- ough—about 850 acres in all—and provide security services in council premises, notably the branch libraries, leisure centres, and youth and recreation facilities. The constables aim to act pri- marily as a deterrent rather than an enforcement body. The problems with which they deal appear to be similar to those dealt with in Sedgefield. They include incivilities associated with drunkenness, the control of dogs, the use of bicycles, and the like. But they also deal with crime. In 1994 and 1995 the Wandsworth Parks Police made 105 and 134 arrests respectively: these included alleged offences of dishonesty (including burglary, theft, and robbery), criminal damage, gross indecency, and drugs offences. They took their arrestees to Metropolitan Police stations where there appears to have been little difficulty in getting the majority of their charges accepted. Indeed the research evidence is that the relationship between the Parks Police and the Metropolitan Police is a positive and close one.[55] In addition the constables monitor the CCTV cameras that are positioned in Wandsworth's parks, act as keyholders in relation to a large number of local authority buildings, provide a cash-in-transit service for some local authority functions, and escort some local authority employees. Similar, though generally less wide-ranging, parks police also operate in Kensington and Chelsea, Barking and Dagenham and in Greenwich.

Conclusion

On two counts it is no longer possible to maintain the idea that the police represent the 'thin blue line' between us and social disorder and collapse. First, as the two examples above have illustrated, policing has become much more complicated in the last twenty years. Policing involves much more than what the police do. There are many more 'boys in blue' around (they are generally male), but the uniforms they wear sport an increasing variety of insignia. Secondly, as both the language and the practice of contemporary crime prevention illustrate, there is a far wider range of organizations involved in 'community safety' than just the police and, indeed, much more to community safety than just policing.

It also appears to be the case that the emphasis during the 1980s on two aspects of policing—crime prevention and crime detection—pulled the police in quite different directions, outwards and inwards. Crime prevention is now seen to require the involvement of the community and other public services in partnership. Moreover, though the police have an essential part to play in inter-agency co-operative crime prevention initiatives, it is by no means clear that it should any longer be the lead part. Yet this diffuse communitarian aspect of policing is being pursued alongside a much more specialized effort within the police on targeting serious repeat offenders. It is noticeable that the Audit Commission is employing military terminology—intelligence and Field Intelligence Officers—which meshes closely with the Home Secretary's enthusiasm for the language of war, against crime. How and whether these two aspects of policing fit comfortably together is something we shall consider in the next chapter on the role of the police.

3

THE ROLE OF THE POLICE

There is, we have argued implicitly, a fundamental tension within contemporary policework. Law enforcement and crime control are juxtaposed against a broad variety of activities which have a more preventive and problem-oriented focus and are often to be found under the umbrella of 'community policing'. This is an important, but by no means the only, tension facing the police. As will be clear from the preceding chapter, policing involves the activities of a far broader range of organizations than simply the police. However, it is the police who are the primary focus of this chapter. We shall consider their role and function, and look at how the general trends identified in Chapters 1 and 2 have been translated into police organizational practice.

Most realistic discussions of police work suggest that at the very least the police role includes: order maintenance; crime control; environmental and traffic functions; assistance in times of emergency; crime prevention; and conciliation and conflict resolution. In most countries the police have also been given various regulatory or administrative functions considered consistent with their general role. The police in Britain are no exception in this regard. In recent years greater emphasis has been placed on the 'service' rather than the 'force' element in the police role—possibly because during the early 1980s the element of force became all too apparent—and though this distinction is of limited usefulness, there now exists a fair measure of agreement, at least amongst ACPO ranks, about the importance of the community-oriented service function of the police. Yet, despite the best efforts of senior officers to change the image of policing, it continues to be associated with crime-fighting. All the evidence suggests that this is the role with which the lower ranks most closely identify. Detectives, the officers generally taken to be the embodiment of crime fighting and thief taking, occupy high status within the police. And, as we highlighted in Chapter 2, the government's 1993 White Paper on *Police Reform* represents an attempt to return the police to an old-fashioned and narrowly circumscribed crime-fighting or law enforcement role,[1] a role that the Audit Commission appears to be encouraging and some chief constables are now grasping with enthusiasm.

Our purpose in this Chapter is to look behind these terms and arguments and focus more closely on what the police do, how they do it, and how what they do is perceived and assessed by the public.

The Role of the Police

The police undertake crime control. They are the principal law enforcement agency. They provide the only real 24-hour general emergency service. But they also constitute an all-purpose social service. All these descriptions make up part of what we understand the police to be. But none on its own describes accurately or fully what the police are. Whilst we may shy away from doing so now, until relatively recently the British police were often described as the 'best in the world'.[2] Such a view was underpinned by a number of considerations. The office and powers of the constable in England and Wales are long-standing. They are rooted in the common law principle, as interpreted by the 1929 Royal Commission on the Police, that a police officer is only 'a person paid to perform, as a matter of duty, acts which if he were so minded he might have done voluntarily'.[3] Whilst the struggle to establish the legitimacy of the new professional police after 1829 was a long and difficult one, by the middle of the twentieth century the police in Britain enjoyed widespread, though by no means universal, support. It is not misleading to talk of the affection, albeit abstract affection, of the British for their police. It was certainly reasonable to talk seriously about our system of 'policing by consent'. This was brought about, in part, by the fact that the police were not armed, claimed to eschew force wherever possible, avoided overt political partisanship, and were seen to provide a variety of services broader than those simply associated with law enforcement.

The Metropolitan Police's first instruction book, for example, indicated that 'every effort of the police' was to be directed at the prevention of crime. It went on:

The security of person and property, the preservation of the public tranquillity, and all other objects of a police establishment will thus be better effected than by the detection and punishment of the offender after he has succeeded in committing the crime. This should constantly be kept in mind by every member of the police force, as the guide for his own conduct. Officers and police constables should endeavour to distinguish themselves by such vigilance and activity as may render it impossible for any one to commit a crime within that portion of the town under their charge.[4]

This short description covers a wide range of responsibilities—the prevention of crime, the maintenance of order, and the detection and punishment of the offender. A wide variety of other 'service' or administrative functions were soon acquired by the police. These included: being inspectors of nuisances, weights and measures, diseases of animals, dairies and shops, contagious diseases, explosives, and bridges; in the case of some borough forces, the running of fire and ambulance services; and the provision of informal services such as 'knocking up' people for work. Though they were never important enough to form the defining characteristic of the police, all these activities, because they were widely seen to be positive functions, were important in securing the legitimacy of the police in the nineteenth century. As local authority responsibilities expanded, however, many of the major service functions held by the police were transferred. Law enforcement and order maintenance came increasingly to be considered by officers and public alike as the core of policing.

By the second half of the twentieth century the police had come to believe, as one scholarly commentator put it, 'that their survival depends upon their capacity to control crime'.[5] Indeed, when attempts were made to capture the breadth and complexity of police work in official documents, and in legislation, *enforcement* rather than *service* was emphasized. Even the 1962 Royal Commission—usually taken to be one of the more considered views of what policing is about—relegated the 'helping' function to eighth and last place in a long list of responsibilities. In so doing, the committee reflected not just public perceptions of policing functions and priorities, but the general view of policing put forward by senior officers. This was certainly the preferred image of policing among the rank and file of police officers.

While the service element of the police role never entirely disappeared from popular view, it appears to have been the decline in public confidence in the police in the 1970s and 1980s that prompted chief constables to place increasing emphasis on those elements of the job that would not generally come under the rubric of law-enforcement or order maintenance. Changing views of the nature of policing at the top of the organization is not necessarily translated into changed views and practices at the 'sharp end', however.[6]

In the aftermath of the riots in the early 1980s, and the Scarman Report which followed, significant changes occurred in the public presentation of the nature and limitations of policing. The process was initiated by Sir Kenneth Newman, then Commissioner of the Metropolitan Police, though he drew on many ideas vigorously pressed by John Alderson, Chief Constable of Devon and Cornwall, in the late 1970s. Newman stressed that crime could not be controlled by the police alone and that significant levels of public co-operation were needed if inroads were to be made. His successor as Commissioner, Sir Peter Imbert, continued the process of reorientation with his 'Plus Programme' in London. This programme, together with the subsequent publication by the staff associations of a corporate mission statement, heralded a view of policing that increasingly emphasized public service and responsiveness to the 'community'. The Statement of Common Purposes and Values read:

The purpose of the police service is to uphold the law fairly and firmly; to prevent crime; to pursue and bring to justice those who break the law; to keep the Queen's peace; to protect, help and reassure the community; and to be seen to do this with integrity, common sense and sound judgement.

We must be compassionate, courteous and patient, acting without fear or favour or prejudice to the rights of others. We need to be professional, calm and restrained in the face of violence and apply only that force which is necessary to accomplish our lawful duty. We must strive to reduce the fears of the public and, so far as we can, to reflect their priorities in the action we take. We must respond to well founded criticism with a willingness to change.

We do not think that this mission statement has subsequently been improved on. Nor is it easy to see how one might improve on it. The statement is easily understood, concise, balanced, and comprehensive.

Ever since the Statement was agreed ACPO has maintained a 'Quality of Service Sub-Committee' which has identified five 'key service areas' which have become the framework for the work of the Home Office, ACPO, the Audit Commission, and HMIC on key indicators of police performance. The five areas are: the handling of calls from the public; crime management (including crime reduction, victim support, and crime investigation); traffic management; public reassurance and order maintenance; and community policing. The espousal of this service-based, consumer-oriented style of policing is now common ground, officially at least, among chief constables.[7] To the extent that the police could realistically ever have been described as primarily a 'law-enforcement' or crime-control agency, the 1980s and early 1990s witnessed, in the changing 'public face' of policing, a significant movement away from this role. Whether the public noticed this shift during a period when public events exhibited the more militaristic public order aspect of contemporary policing is questionable however. Moreover, whether the new police 'image' is a more realistic presentation of what the police *actually do* is open to debate. And to what extent such a public face is sustainable in a political climate which emphasises 'the war against crime' is even more problematic.

What Do the Police Do?

We turn now to the empirical evidence about policing. The question: *what do the police do?* actually raises two related questions. First, following on from the discussion above: what are the police for? Is their basic function catching criminals, preventing crime, keeping the peace or something else? Secondly, how are police resources used? What proportion of police staff and police time is devoted to patrol, criminal investigation, traffic, administration, management, and so on, and how are the major time and resource-consuming activities organised? We begin by looking at the basic function of the police.

The Police Function

The police frequently are the only 24-hour service agency available to respond to those in need. The result is that the police handle everything from unexpected childbirths, skid row alcoholics, drug addicts, emergency psychiatric cases, family fights, landlord–tenant disputes, and traffic violations, to occasional incidents of crime. The latter wording is deliberate, for Canadian and American studies agree that relatively little police time is spent on actual criminal cases.[8]

John Hagan, a Canadian academic, might well have added England and Wales to his list, for successive studies have suggested that the same pattern holds here. A variety of methods have been employed to analyse what it is that the police actually do. These methods include analysis of police activity, public calls for police assistance and message pads, observational studies of police work, and crime surveys. Home Office research undertaken in 1985 in one police division, for example, studied incidents attended by uniform patrols and categorized them using a fourfold general classification of crime, social service, public orders and accidents.[9] That study, and a second piece of research known as the Urban Workloads study, both concluded that 'criminal incidents' constituted approximately only a third of the incidents attended and of this third 'a number turned out to be false alarms of some sort'.[10]

Analysis of calls by the public to the police confirms this general pattern. Thus another Home Office study conducted in the early 1980s found that 'only a small proportion of calls for police assistance are related to crime matters'.[11] Of the total number of calls received from the public over a period of six days in one sub-divisional control room only 18 per cent required the preparation of a fresh crime report. By contrast, calls relating to 'plight' (persons locked out of their car or home, lost property, person missing from home), administrative matters (sudden death, various licence renewals, or the revision of alarm keyholder records), disputes (commercial and domestic), disturbances, and nuisance (rowdy children or noisy neighbours, for example) made up by far the most significant proportion of demand.

These findings find support in the data collected in the third sweep of the British Crime Survey (BCS) in 1988 which examined contacts between the police and the public. The survey found that only about 18 per cent of contacts with the police involved specific crime incidents and a further 12 per cent involved disturbances of one kind or another. Only 2 per cent of all reported police–public contacts during 1987 involved 999 calls concerning specific criminal incidents. According to the BCS far more contacts between the police and the public involve an exchange of information, apparently of a non-crime and largely non-emergency nature (traffic accidents, obstructions, and so on, or requesting information about property or directions). Information-sharing of one form or another accounted for almost 40 per cent of police–public contacts.[12]

This view of policework has not gone unchallenged, however. The authors of local crime surveys have argued that these national figures tend to underestimate the proportion of police–public contacts that are 'crime-related'. A survey conducted in Islington, for example, found that 51 per cent of police–public contacts concerned crime.[13] This apparent discrepancy may partly be accounted for by the areas covered by the respective surveys: the BCS itself records a higher proportion of crime-related contacts in inner-city areas. Nevertheless, the author of the 1988 BCS concludes that the evidence from the BCS is that:

most public-initiated encounters reflected the integration of the police into the routines of everyday life. They were called upon to preserve tranquillity, ease the flow of traffic, serve as a clearing house for reports of a variety of community problems, assist in civil emergencies, and help people find their way. In this way the police represent the 'visible face of the law'.[14]

This view is reinforced by the data from the BCS on all contacts between police and public. The 1988 survey found that approximately three-fifths of the adult population of England and Wales had some sort of contact with the police during the course of a year. Fifty six per cent of the population initiated contact with the police and 15 per cent were involved in police-initiated contacts. Data from the first BCS showed that 97 per cent of public-initiated contacts could be classed as 'consumer contacts', whereas 86 per cent of police-initiated contacts were classified as 'adversarial contacts'. Whilst such a finding might at first sight not sit easily with the suggestion that more police time is spent on service-type work than crime-related activities, the survey shows that although half the population have some contact with the police during the course of a year, a mere 6 per cent encounter the police only as adversaries, whereas 31 per cent encounter them as 'consumers' only, and 10 per cent experience both types of contact. This, of course, has quite significant implications for public satisfaction.

It is clear, therefore, that police work cannot accurately be encompassed by terms such as 'law enforcement' or 'crime-control'. A considerable proportion of police time is devoted to dealing with tasks other than crime. This view should not be overstated, however. The debate about 'force' versus 'service' has often hindered creative thinking about the role of the police. Though the emerging academic consensus is that the bulk of police time is not spent engaged on tasks that are 'crime-related', how the work being done should be classified is far from straightforward. For some commentators, the conclusion to be drawn is that police officers 'frequently have to act as untrained and temporary social workers' and that the profession is in fact a 'secret social service'.[15] However, several studies have shown that this 'service' work is widely regarded by the mainstream police occupational culture as 'bullshit' and very much the poor relation of 'real' police work—generally viewed as 'law-enforcement' or 'crime-fighting'.[16] It is vital to note, moreover, that the application of labels like 'crime', 'service', 'public order', and so on, generally speaking takes place *post hoc*. The police have typically had to respond—under traditional call systems—to calls from the public on the basis of patchy and often inadequate information. In these circumstances they are seldom in a position to know in advance exactly what calls are about or might lead to. Calls from the public have traditionally involved little more than the recording of the barest of details—the location of the 'incident', the name of the caller, and some feel for how urgent the message is. For much of the time, therefore, the police are working and responding almost as an all-purpose emergency service. Whether or not a call inovolves a 'crime' depends not just on whether an offence has taken place, whether an offender is present, and so on, but also on whether the attending officer(s) decides—in negotiation with others—that he is going to record the incident as a crime.

In categorizing police time, therefore, it is probably more accurate to think of much of the work as 'potential crime'—incidents that *might* involve or lead to a crime being committed, as well as incidents where the caller asserts that a crime has taken place or is in progress. Research employing this approach has found that 'personal services' account for under 10 per cent of calls, whereas 'potential crime' accounts for over half, and 'social disorder' a fifth.

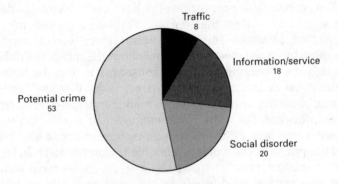

Fig. 30 Messages received by the police
Source: Shapland, J. and Vagg, J. (1990) *Policing by the Public*, **London: Routledge**

Research around the world has shown that peace-keeping is the primary policing function, even in societies where the police are routinely armed, such as the United States, or where the community is seriously divided, as in Northern Ireland. It is a commonplace among sociologists of the police that the scope for discretion is inversely related to status in the police organization: the most junior officers—generally the uniformed patrol strength—have ample opportunity—because of the frequently diffuse nature of the situations they encounter, because they must typically deal with these situations without back-up and because they are subject to little direct supervision—to use the discretion which, in the English system, is every constable's common law power. Thus the law is not invoked because a crime has been committed. The law is invoked because police officers *are satisfied* that a crime has probably been committed and because they deem it *appropriate* to apply the law to the situation. Such decisions are often guided by peace-keeping considerations. As Lord Scarman recognised there are inevitably situations in which the enforcement of the law is not compatible with the maintenance of the public peace. In which event it is the latter, he suggested, which should be the priority. Nothing has happened since his famous report was published which makes us think differently about this issue. Keeping the peace is both what the police do—or attempt to do—and what we think they should do.

This is not to suggest that this question is straightforward. Far from it. It is fraught with problems. Difficult ethical and legal issues of relative power, justice, and equity are raised by the extensive police use of discretion and their emphasis on peace keeping. But it is doubtful whether anyone would consider justice well-served by our police acting like legal automatons. And in any case they could not. Policing situations are often complex and ambiguous. The law is largely silent on *how* the police should proceed in these situations. And the police do not have the resources to arrest and proceed against everyone they encounter breaching the law. Even were they to attempt such a strategy all police resources would be quickly swallowed up— every arrest has now to be followed by a procedure back at the station that typically takes several hours to complete—and we should not thank them for what would undoubtedly be regarded as bureacratic officiousness. We expect our police to use the law with judgement—to keep the peace.

Nevertheless, one is still left with the problem of attempting to distinguish what it is that the *police* do from the activities undertaken by other *policing* organizations. One helpful approach to this question is to be found in a seminal article by the American political scientist, Egon Bittner. He argued that both public descriptions of, and police justifications for, the activities of the police are unrealistic. His view, and one that is now widely accepted, is that the 'potential' duties of police officers are so broad that 'it compels the stronger inference that no human problem exists, or is imaginable, about which it could be said with finality that this certainly could not become the proper business of the police'.[17] Thus, in Bittner's view, it is the very assumption that the police *will* be available to deal with all manner of emergencies that sets them apart. In his famous phrase, people tend to call the police in circumstances that involve their assessment that: 'something-that-ought-not-to-be-happening-and-about-which-someone-had-better-do-something-now!' This is, however, only part of the story. For Bittner it is the capacity that the police bring with them to deal with such eventualities which makes them distinctive. In his words:

'The policeman, and the policeman alone is equipped, entitled and required to deal with every exigency in which force may have to be used, to meet it'.

It is this potential to use legitimate force which is important, for it is rare for incidents to be resolved by the police through recourse to force.

We conclude, therefore, that it is the combination of having access to the legitimate use of force, together with the fact that the police are, in theory, available to anyone, anywhere, at any time of day, that results in such varied and unpredictable demands being made upon them. It is also these factors which separate the police from other policing organizations. However, as we saw in Chapter 2 it is clear that with crime rising, calls from the public increasing steadily, and public expenditure kept under close control, the police are increasingly being forced to prioritize their activities. There are demands for extra resources in all the major areas of policing—patrol, investigation and traffic—there are pressures to reorganise policing within these areas and, at a time when great store is set by consumer opinion, there is growing pressure on the police to pay closer attention to what the public wants from them. Before we look at the evidence on what precisely it is that the public wants, we need first to consider how police resources are divided and how police activities are organized.

The Division of Labour within the Police

In the not so distant past the role of the main grade police officer—the police constable—would probably have been summarized by most members of the public as patrolling a beat on foot. And despite all the changes that have taken place in policing in recent decades patrol remains the staple activity of the majority of police personnel, a good deal of it still on foot. A recent Audit Commission study found that well over half of police effort is absorbed by patrol:[18]

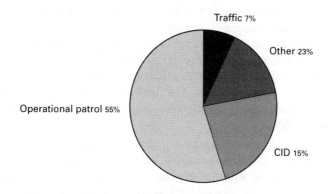

Fig. 31 Police resources
Source: Audit Commission (1996) *Streetwise*, London: Audit Commission

It is not just in Britain that patrol of one sort or another, albeit most of it now in cars, remains the dominant police activity. According to David Bayley, the leading American commentator on comparative policing, a similar pattern is to be found in the United States (where 65 per cent of police officers are assigned to patrol), Canada (64 per cent), and in Australia (54 per cent).[19]

How do police officers spend their time? One study conducted in London in the early 1980s found that on average 55 per cent of all uniformed officers' time was spent outside police premises and 45 per cent on police premises.[20] The bulk of the time spent in police stations was devoted to administration and paperwork. Of total police time, 10 per cent was spent patrolling on foot and 18 per cent patrolling in a vehicle. The rest of the time used up outside the station involved being engaged either on special activities (special events, raids, searches, surveillance, and so on) or in court, contacting or interviewing informants or witnesses, and in 'waiting and taking refreshments' (the latter was found to account for about 5 per cent of time but this, it was suggested, was probably a substantial underestimate). Within the office, 10 per cent was taken up with running the front office and communications system, and 19 per cent on clerical and administrative activities. Only 2 per cent of time was spent interviewing suspects and witnesses.

Given the content of most police television drama, one could be forgiven for thinking that routine police work involved high-speed chases, frequent arrests, and, after a game of cat and mouse in the interview room, the successful charging of guilty parties (we know parties are guilty because in the fictional version they will have 'coughed'). This really is fiction, particularly with regard to patrol work. The best recent description of what much routine police work actually involves has been provided by David Bayley:

The police 'sort out' situations by listening patiently to endless stories about fancied slights, old grievances, new insults, mismatched expectations, indifference, infidelity, dishonesty and abuse. They hear about all the petty, mundane, tedious, hapless, sordid details of individual lives. None of it is earthshaking, or worthy of a line in a newspaper—not the stuff that government policy can address, not even especially spicy; just the begrimed reality of the lives of people who have no one else to take their problems to. Patient listening and gentle counselling are undoubtedly what patrol officers do most of their time.[21]

What Bayley and other police researchers go on to point out is that when they are not 'listening' or 'counselling', patrol officers' work is dominated by responding to calls from the public. The government's White Paper on *Police Reform* highlighted this:

For the police, the 55 per cent of officers assigned to general patrol represents their main response capacity for dealing with all manner of calls, incidents and emergencies. These officers stay on preventive patrol, whether on foot or in a vehicle, only until they deal with and follow through an incident (often back at the station) or are called to more urgent business. Preventive patrol is therefore a temporary condition, and given the press of other business, a scarce resource.[22]

Of course the police, including patrol officers, also engage in proactive activities—the gathering of intelligence, surveillance, and so on. But these activities are not the norm, particularly for those uniformed officers, the majority, engaged in what is called 'relief' policing.

A great deal of police work, then, is instigated by the public.

Indeed, in the recent past, the practice of deploying mobile patrols in response to the vast majority of telephone calls made to the police meant that the public directly and overwhelmingly determined how police resources were used. And, as we have already mentioned, surveys of calls to the police indicate that though reporting crime is the single most common cause of contact, it nevertheless accounts for a minority of calls. Of course, given the burden of work it never was possible for the police to respond immediately to all calls for service. Thus calls have long since been graded, at least in theory, according to their importance and urgency. How does this work in practice?

Calls are received by the police mostly in one of two ways: via the 999 system (less than 30 per cent of calls[23]) or through the general telephone network. Surprisingly, there is very mixed evidence as to whether the former are generally more urgent than the latter. Research on call-grading shows some other interesting patterns. Waddington found that approximately 90 per cent of 'alarm calls' (activated silent alarms or automatic contact via the 999 system) received an instant response as did two-thirds of requests for help (covering everything from traffic accidents to minor domestic problems).[24]

Approximately half of calls reporting crimes or suspicious incidents receive an immediate response, though the proportion is higher if 'crimes in progress' are separated from other reports. Moreover, research has demonstrated consistently that despite the theory of graded response, the vast majority of incidents reported to the police lead to the dispatch of a patrol within a relatively short period of time. Yet the most likely outcome of the response is no police action.

False alarms, no trace of the incident or person, arriving after the incident has been resolved, all use up considerable quantities of police time and result in little or no action being taken. Indeed though a significant amount of patrol work is thought by officers to be 'boring', reacting to calls and looking for excitement (and 'real' police work) have tended to be the dominant *modus operandi* among uniform reliefs. Thus, though a substantial proportion of a patrol officer's time is taken up by 'uncommitted patrolling', any directed activity tends to be grasped in the form of a fire-brigade-type response to a perceived emergency. Officers in patrol cars like switching on their sirens and

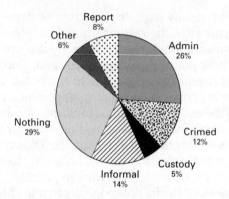

Fig. 32 Outcome of police action
Source: Waddington, P. (1993) *Calling the Police*, Aldershot: Avebury

flashing blue lights: indeed new recruits may be as much influenced by television imagery of police work as members of the public appear to be.[25]

The next major segment of police work is criminal investigation. Dedicated detectives account for approximately 15 per cent of police resources in England and Wales. The first specialist investigation department was set up in London in the 1860s. By the 1960s such departments were to be found in all police forces and had primary responsibility for investigating most crime. Although levels of crime have risen markedly—including serious crimes—the proportionate strength of criminal investigation departments (CID) has remained relatively static. As a consequence CID no longer have a relative monopoly over criminal investigation: most crime, the Audit Commission estimates over three quarters, is now handled by uniformed officers.[26] Which crimes are investigated by CID and which by uniformed officers varies to some extent from force to force, though more serious offences are handled by CID and the vast majority of minor offences by uniformed officers.

Just as patrol activity is largely reactive, so is criminal investigation. There are a variety of reasons for this. First, the workload of the average detective rose by two-thirds between 1982 and 1992 and, faced with this heavier burden, officers have found it difficult, it is argued, to do more than cope with the new files presented to them. Secondly, criminal investigation departments have often resembled little more than collections of individuals working side by side but separately—team working and formal supervision have generally been absent.[27] Thirdly, the time available to detectives has been squeezed by the administrative burden they face: much of their work has involved preparing paperwork for the prosecution file. Fourthly, but most importantly, relatively little emphasis has traditionally been placed by the police on the systematic use of intelligence. As we outlined in Chapter 2, a number of developments have recently taken place—the formation of Administrative Support Units and Crime Management Desks—in an attempt to remedy this failure to work in a more proactive investigative manner.

Leaving aside administration and related activities, the final major segment of police work is traffic, which accounts for 7 per cent of police strength. We showed in graphic form in Chapter 1 (see Fig. 19) the rate of increase of motor vehicles on the roads in recent years. As the volume of traffic has increased so pressure on the traffic police has grown. The rate and scale of the increase have been immense. There are now some 5,000 deaths and 350,000 injuries a year on the roads. Maintaining order, enforcing traffic laws and regulations, and responding to and dealing with accidents alongside the other emergency services, are major tasks for the police. However, the primary goal of traffic policing is generally agreed to be accident prevention and road safety though, as in the other branches of police work, in practice responsive rather than preventive traffic policing accounts for a high proportion of officers' time.[28] The total annual cost of traffic policing in England and Wales is in the region of £350 million (see Fig. 33).

Because it is perceived to be a relatively discrete type of police work, traffic policing has been focused on by those observers who favour contracting out some police functions. Accident reduction, the main objective of traffic policing, includes a number of activities which, arguably, could be carried out by other organizations. These include: enforcing the traffic laws, educating drivers, and helping to maintain the free flow of traffic. It is also suggested that these tasks could be separated from other police activities without major implications for remaining police activities and functions. A good many traffic-related operations

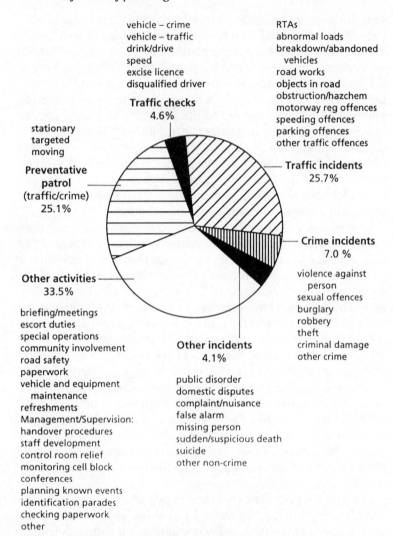

vehicle – crime
vehicle – traffic
drink/drive
speed
excise licence
disqualified driver

Traffic checks
4.6%

stationary
targeted
moving

**Preventative
patrol**
(traffic/crime)
25.1%

Other activities
33.5%

briefing/meetings
escort duties
special operations
community involvement
road safety
paperwork
vehicle and equipment
   maintenance
refreshments
Management/Supervision:
handover procedures
staff development
control room relief
monitoring cell block
conferences
planning known events
identification parades
checking paperwork
other

Other incidents
4.1%

public disorder
domestic disputes
complaint/nuisance
false alarm
missing person
sudden/suspicious death
suicide
other non-crime

RTAs
abnormal loads
breakdown/abandoned
   vehicles
road works
objects in road
obstruction/hazchem
motorway reg offences
speeding offences
parking offences
other traffic offences

Traffic incidents
25.7%

Crime incidents
7.0 %

violence against
   person
sexual offences
burglary
robbery
theft
criminal damage
other crime

Fig. 33 Distribution of police traffic officer resources

Source: Ogilvie-Smith, A., Downey, A. and Ransom, E. (1994) Traffic Policing: Activity and Organisation, Police Research Series Paper 12, London: Home Office Police Research Unit.

could also be carried out by personnel lacking the powers of con-stables: most forces have for many years employed traffic war-dens to enforce parking laws and carry out some other traffic duties. A separate traffic police for London has, for example, been considered by Home Office ministers. There are organiza-tions willing and, probably, able effectively to carry out these tasks. In 1994, for example, the Automobile Association ran an advertising campaign selling itself as the 'fourth emergency ser-vice'. This was interpreted in some quarters as a bid by the AA to establish itself as a possible alternative provider of traffic polic-ing services.[29]

Police resistance to the contracting out or privatization of their functions is, however, strong, and a review of traffic policing undertaken as part of the Inquiry into Core and Ancillary Tasks went no further than suggesting that there might be some scope for privatizing or civilianizing all or part of the responsibility for escorting abnormal loads, dealing with broken-down and aban-doned vehicles, roadworks, and obstructions, and carrying out accident and vehicle and tachograph investigations. In total these activities represent less than 6 per cent of the overall traffic policing function.[30]

Public Views and Assessments of Policing

In Chapter 2 we suggested that, partly as a result of various devel-opments in the 1980s, the activities of the police are now almost certainly subject to greater public and media scrutiny than has ever been the case in the past. This trend was spurred by the fashion, encouraged by the government, of consumerism—the idea that public services generally should be made more respon-sive to 'customer' demands in a more market-oriented climate. The police emphasis on *service* reflected this trend. The Citizen's Charter set out the general parameters of what the public could and should expect from public services, including the police. In 1990 the Victims' Charter outlined what victims of crime should expect from the police. This service ethic has led to much greater emphasis being placed on 'public opinion'. To some extent this is a trend which some forces have encouraged in order to resist what they consider to be the potentially misleading or distorting

'hard' measures of effectiveness being pressed by the government. Thus although the Audit Commission's police performance indicators include no measures of public satisfaction,
those developed by ACPO do, and surveys of public views of
policing have become *de rigueur* in many forces. What expectations do 'the public' have of the police and how does it regard the
services it receives?

Before looking at some of the available data it is important to
note some of the factors that affect the responses people make to
surveys regarding the police. People vary greatly in their knowledge about and experience of the police. A minority of the population has a great deal of contact with them, and this contact is
often adversarial. A minority of people are repeatedly victimized,
may often have to seek assistance from the police, and are well
qualified to judge whether help and information are forthcoming. By contrast a sizeable proportion of the public, between two
fifths and one half, report having had no contact with the police
of any sort during the course of the past year. It follows that many
respondents' views are based less on first-hand experience than
on second-hand accounts or media images, which may, as we
have seen, accord poorly with the reality of policing. Expressions
of public satisfaction with the police are a function, therefore, of
a variety of intervening factors and may be based on experience
of only part of what the police do. Finally, it is worth noting that
even well designed public opinion surveys are not particularly
sophisticated instruments. They require respondents to answer
discrete questions which are seldom able to explore the dynam-
ics of choice. It is one thing to want a particular service. It is quite
another to express a preference if there is some appreciation of
the trade-off between services.

All the survey evidence points to there being significant differences in attitudes to the police between different ethnic groups.
The 1994 BCS found, for example, that of those who had con-
tacted the police, 21 per cent of whites, 39 per cent of Afro-
Caribbeans, and 40 per cent of Asians gave them low marks.[31]
The differences are large. Similarly, a series of surveys on public
attitudes to the police conducted at three-monthly intervals in
the early 1990s found that three quarters of whites thought the
police did a 'very' or 'fairly good' job, whereas only six out of ten
Asians and five out of ten Afro-Caribbeans held this view.

Furthermore, large proportions of the ethnic minority groups—one in six overall, and nearly one in four Afro-Caribbeans—were unwilling or unable to express an opinion on this question.[32]

The surveys also show that the ethnic minorities are less likely to initiate contact with the police—the type of contact which, not surprisingly, is more likely to result in satisfaction—and when they do initiate contact they are less often satisfied and more often dissatisfied with the result. This is particularly so for Asians.

There is a large body of research from both the US and UK which has shown that black people are substantially more likely to be involved in adversarial contact with the police. This phenomenon has a long history. Sherman has argued that the history of police–black relationships in the USA was characterized from an early stage by harassment by both legal and extra-legal means.[33] Unjustified use of force, illegal searches and interrogation, trumped up charges and fabrication of evidence, and general 'over policing' were common features in the black experience of policing. Robert Reiner, the foremost academic commentator on policing in Britain, has noted that whilst racial prejudice is a prominent feature of street-level police culture, and that these rank-and-file views predate any evidence about over-representation in crime involvement on the part of black people, there is evidence of continuing racial prejudice in police ranks.[34] The Scarman Report located the problem of racial prejudice as firmly one of rank and file culture, and explicitly dissociated command-level officers from such views though Reiner, in his study of chief constables, found that many chief constables in the non-Metropolitan areas (i.e. not those areas where the majority of ethnic minority people live) tend to see black people as a source of crime, tension, and disorder.[35]

One of the assumptions often made about police–public relations is that they vary considerably by age or, more specifically, that young people are more likely to hold negative views of the police than older people. The most recent British Crime Survey casts some doubt on this assumption. Almost nine-tenths of 12–15- year-olds (88 per cent) agreed with the statement 'We need a police force in this country to keep law and order', and over three fifths (63 per cent) thought that the police did a very (10 per cent) or fairly (53 per cent) good job in their area. Less than one tenth said they felt the police did a very poor job. The least favourable views of the police were held by young Afro-Caribbeans, mirroring the views held by black adults. Indeed, the views expressed by young people generally were found to correspond closely with the views expressed by the adults in the household who were also interviewed. Unfortunately, the study was not able to explore these links in detail, but it is more likely that young people are affected by their parents' views of the police than vice versa. The author of the survey report concludes, therefore, that one of the lessons for policing is 'that how the police treat both young people *and* adults may well influence the attitudes the other group holds'.[36]

As we have suggested, the data from crime surveys suggest that people in contact with the police because of crime problems are less satisfied with the outcome of the contact than those contacting the police for other reasons or, as the authors of the Islington Crime Survey put it: 'the less urgent the matter the more satisfied the public'.[37]

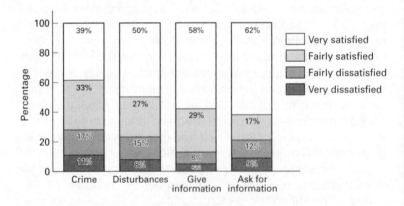

Fig. 34 Satisfaction with public-initiated contacts with the police

Source: Bucke, T. (1995) *Policing and the Public: Findings From the 1994 British Crime Survey*, Home Office Research Findings No.28, London: Home Office

It is clear, then, that dissatisfaction tends to be most common in those cases where contact is made to report crime or disturbances (that is, what we earlier described as 'potential crime')

whereas rather higher levels of satisfaction were reported in relation to the police handling of contacts about more 'service-oriented' issues. Dissatisfaction is most likely to result, therefore, from event-driven contacts, that is, as the author of the BCS report phrased it, the, 'activities which lie at the heart of the traditional police function'.[38]

The most recent large survey of public views, conducted by MORI on behalf of the Audit Commission, illustrates one further key element in public views of policing.

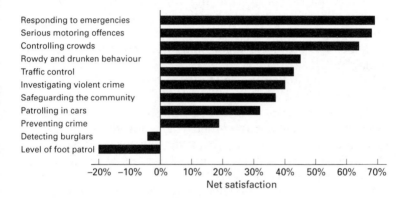

Fig. 35 Public satisfaction with policing
Source: Audit Commission (1996) *Streetwise*, London: Audit Commission

The graph shows that when the police act as an emergency service—and this includes controlling large crowds and dealing with car crashes—a high proportion of the population perceives them to be doing a good job. In relation to serious crime and some forms of prevention they score moderately well. However, in relation to that most symbolic of police tasks, foot patrol, there is net public dissatisfaction.

There are also the related issues of *how* the police respond following a call from a member of the public and how they handle contacts they initiate themselves. A significant proportion of calls from the public results from involvement in or the witnessing of some form of conflict or disturbance. Such calls result from disturbance to 'normal' social order. Such disturbances

often involve nothing criminal, but the public generally understands that it is to the police that one turns on such occasions. In
most cases callers are fairly realistic about what the police can
achieve. Catching the criminal—when a crime has been committed—or solving the 'problem'—when a dispute or other disturbance has occurred—will always be the hope. However the
survey evidence suggests that it is whether the police are perceived to take the 'problem' seriously that is crucial to determining levels of public satisfaction with the response. As Home
Office researchers Ekblom and Heal found in the early 1980s the
level of public satisfaction did 'not originate in the achievement
by the police of tangible and constructive outcomes . . . [but] . . .
seemed to stem from the provision of reassurance and the fact
that the police officers' behaviour matched callers' expectations'.[39]

By the same token the 1994 BCS found that the majority of
members of the public were not angered or irritated by being
stopped in their cars or on foot by police officers. Satisfaction
levels of 85 per cent were recorded where officers were perceived
to be interested in what the person who had been stopped had to
say, whereas they dropped to only 31 per cent where they were
perceived not to be interested.[40]

It is, then, the willingness of police officers to take *responsibility* for dealing as best they can with the problem at hand that is
the most frequent source of public satisfaction or dissatisfaction.
Perceived lack of interest or failure by the police to take a complaint seriously is generally more crucial than the ability to
'solve' the case in some way, and is perhaps the key to under-
mining public confidence in the police. Despite the fact that the
vast majority of police–public encounters apparently concern
issues of a minor nature, there is a good deal of evidence to suggest that the police should not underestimate the importance of
such incidents to those reporting them—especially when the
callers are 'witnesses' or 'victims'. And, regrettably, the evidence
suggests that the proportion of victims who are dissatisfied with
police performance in this regard is certainly not diminishing
and may be increasing.[41]

What do the public want the police to do? The answer does of
course depend on the questions they are asked, but it would
appear that one of the most consistent expectations held by

those calling the police is that the call will result in an officer being sent to the 'scene'. Home Office research in the early 1980s found that in only 6 per cent of cases did respondents admit to not wanting, expecting, or seeing the need for the police to come in response to their call. Given the finite police resources available this factor may in itself create some potentially dissatisfied customers, that is, unless the police are able, through general education or the manner in which they handle the caller on the telephone, to change public expectations.[42]

In terms of policing priorities the public sets great store by foot patrols. So consistently do many sections of the public complain that they hardly ever see a police officer that it is hard to take seriously the fact that once upon a time, in the nineteenth century, they complained about the 'plague of blue locusts' visited on them.[43] On occasion 'more bobbies on the beat' has been ranked more highly by the public than the police responding quickly to emergency calls or investigating and detecting crime.[44] In the Operational Policing Review undertaken jointly by the police representative bodies in 1990 respondents were offered a long list of policing tasks and priorities and asked to rank them in order of importance.[45] The results are presented in Figure 36.

There are some fairly predictable results here. Responding to emergencies (though these are not defined) is clearly identified as being a core police task, followed by investigating crime and arresting offenders. Foot patrol produced a mean score of 60 per cent—very high compared with 24 per cent for patrolling in a car. Just as interesting, however, is to compare public priorities with public perceptions of what takes place (see Fig. 37).

The public believes the police to be responding to emergencies and investigating crime at about the predicted levels. However the police are perceived to be spending less time (or being less successful) at detecting and arresting offenders and doing comparatively little patrolling on foot. This, in part, explains the popularity of patrol as recorded in public surveys. It is not simply that the public perceives patrolling to be a positive activity, it is also that it thinks insufficient police resources are being devoted to this activity. As we will later argue there are no doubt many misconceptions built into this public affection for patrol. Nevertheless, the appeal of foot patrol is a lasting and widespread one, and is something that cannot lightly be dis-

Base All = 1085	Mean score (12 = high, 1 = low)	All ranking among top five
Police Tasks		%
Respond immediately to emergencies	10.42	87
Detect and arrest offenders	8.63	70
Investigate crime	8.54	68
Patrol the area on foot	8.01	60
Set up squads for serious crime	6.96	46
Provide help and support to victims of crimes	5.89	33
Get to know local people	5.77	30
Give advice to the public on how to prevent crime	5.76	27
Patrol the area in cars	5.34	24
Work closely with local schools	5.30	22
Work with local council departments such as housing to plan crime prevention	3.94	12
Control and supervise road traffic	3.56	9

Fig. 36 Police tasks and priorities
Source: Operational Policing Review (1990)

missed. There is a conundrum however. As the American criminologist Wes Skogan has put it:

Foot patrol may be the issue that most clearly highlights the potential clash between popular and administrative concerns. It certainly presents a hard set of choices for police forces pressed on one side to reduce costs and control the growth of personnel, and on the other to respond to the expectations of very large sections of the public who want a visible police service.[46]

Finally, the public likes a particular *style* of foot patrol. Respondents to the Operational Policing Review were asked to express a preference between two different types of neighbourhood police patrol. Two police officers were described to them: PC Smith who spent most of his time arresting and detecting offenders, who concentrated on major incidents, and believed

Base : All = 1085	Extent to which police do this			Top Five most important
	Great deal/ Fair amount %	Not very much/ not at all %	Don't know %	%
Police Tasks				
Respond immediately to emergencies	74	13	12	87
Investigate crime	68	18	14	68
Patrol the area in cars	67	32	1	24
Detect and arrest offenders	54	25	21	70
Work closely with local schools	50	22	28	22
Give advice to the public on how to prevent crime	39	49	12	26
Set up squads for serious crime	26	31	44	46
Get to know local people	23	67	10	30
Work with local council department to plan crime prevention	21	35	45	12
Provide help and support to victims of crime	20	36	44	33
Patrol the area on foot	20	78	2	60

Fig. 37 Police tasks: what police actually do and top five important tasks

Source: Operational Policing Review (1990)

that officers should be firm and should be given more powers; and PC Jones who spent most of his time working with local people to solve crime problems, believed prevention to be the best way of dealing with crime, and dealt with both major and minor matters. Approximately one quarter of the respondents favoured PC Smith and three-quarters PC Jones. By contrast, though they were not asked the same question, respondents in the survey of police officers placed much less emphasis on community liaison and related activities than they did on a desire to see 'strong, positive policing' and stricter laws and fines. It appears that there are differences between what officers want to do and what the public want them to do.

This point has been re-emphasized in a 1996 *Which* report on police–public relations.[47] Presented with a list of ten options the members of the public surveyed considered 'increase foot patrols by full-time officers' the most effective crime preventive option, whereas the police respondents placed 'set up special squads to target specific crimes' first and saw further foot patrol as less effective than 'work with local agencies such as councils and housing associations' and 'increased local authority use of CCTV in public areas'. Survey results like these are not easy to interpret. It can reasonably be argued that they simply reflect public ignorance and police sophistication as to 'what really works'. But the Consumers' Association has persuasively argued that more is at stake. When asked what offences should get policing priority members of the public and police officers do not wholly agree. Both members of the public and police officers agree that burglary should get the highest priority, but thereafter their opinions differ. The public put 'vandalism and deliberate criminal damage' second and 'dangerous driving, including drink driving' third, both offences accorded lower priority by the police who attach greater priority to 'dealing in or using hard drugs' and 'car-related crime'. It may be, as the Consumers' Association argues, that the public attachment to foot patrol is in part a reflection of the fact that they want the police to do more about neighbourhood offences like criminal damage about which they think, probably correctly, the police are less concerned. This possible connection may be crucial for some minority sections of the public. Ethnic minority respondents to the Consumers' Assciation survey, for example, placed 'racial attacks and abuse' as their second offence priority, an offence which the police respondents placed low down in their priorities. We shall return to these issues in Chapter 6.

Concluding Comments

The work of the police incorporates a diversity of activities and functions. For a considerable part of their history the police stressed the importance of their role as law enforcers over and above other aspects of their work. However, as evidence of police limitations in controlling crime increased, so a broader service mandate has come increasingly to the forefront. As we saw in Chapter 2, however, for a variety of reasons there is now pressure to move crime control back towards the centre of police work.

To what extent are such debates merely presentational? What do the police actually spend their time doing? The empirical evidence confirms the general impression that crime-related matters are not overwhelmingly what the police are called upon to deal with, though they do perhaps represent a greater part of police work that has sometimes been suggested. Patrol continues to be the major police activity with 60 per cent of police resources devoted to it. For some time now, however, the car has predominated over the Doctor Marten, and the evidence suggests that most patrol work, especially that in cars, is of the reactive, fire-brigade variety. Furthermore, it is apparent that most police work—be it general patrol work, criminal investigation, or traffic policing—is overwhelmingly reactive rather than proactive in nature and organization. Hence the Audit Commission's recommendations in relation to intelligence-led policing.

So reactive has much policing traditionally been that its overall shape has been largely determined, or mediated, by public demand. What, then, does the public want and think? Not only does it want, unsurprisingly, more than it is ever likely to get, but it makes demands that in some ways reflect the tensions facing the police that we outlined in the last chapter. We must take a step back here, however, for the use of the word *they* disguises one of the important truths about policing. That is that there are many publics. 'Community'—that warm, comforting, and consensual term—has been much used in relation to policing as it has been used in relation to many public services. But the available evidence shows clearly that there are divergent views of the police among different sections of the populus. What people want from the police depends on their circumstances, both in the long and short-term. Whilst these divisions are not always predictable—the young often have more traditional views than might be expected—it is generally the case that it is the most 'disaffected' communities which have the most problematic relationships with the police.[48] If for no other reason, this should make us especially concerned about some of the demographic and social trends highlighted in Chapter 1.

In very general terms, however, the 'public' wants the police to respond promptly. In particular, it wants emergencies dealt with quickly. It wants officers to behave responsibly and politely. It would like crime investigated seriously. Overwhelmingly, however, it would also like a more visible foot patrol presence on the streets. Moreover, presented with a choice, it would choose problem-solving over crime-fighting as the approach the police should adopt in such work.

Unfortunately, patrol work has low status within the police. It is generally undertaken by the least experienced officers, often by those who are still on probation. Moreover, what we described in Chapter 2 as the more communitarian aspects of contemporary policing tend to be least popular with officers. Indeed, one recent study of community policing contained several illustrations of the difficulties of filling community constable vacancies. Most telling in relation to the values dominant in the police service was the report that at one of the research sites, in order to overcome officers' general reluctance to participate, it had been signalled that doing time in community policing was a route into the 'prestigious crime squad'.[49]

We conclude, therefore, that there are a series of additional tensions facing the police:

- *Demand for their service outstrips their ability to supply.* In part, this is simply because public expectations are unrealistic. In part, it is because neither politicians nor the police have been totally honest about what the police can and do achieve. The police service, moreover, has never settled on a consistent explanation of what it is.

- The public continues largely to believe that the police are the most important institution in 'tackling crime' and, yet, when asked, their preference is generally for a community-based problem-solving approach to police work, rather than a 'tough crime-fighting' approach. This may reflect differences between the public and the police about what sorts of offences should get the highest priority for prevention.
- The public values those aspects of police work that the police like least, and are least happy with their contacts with the police in relation to those bits of policing that officers say they value highest.

4

QUESTIONS POSED

One of the concomitants of the consumerist approach to public services generally made fashionable during the 1980s was the growth of the opinion survey. This affected policing as all else. Surveys had been conducted before, but not to the same extent. Now the public was periodically asked—by newspapers, the police, by local authorities, and by academics—what it thought about the police, whether it felt safe in its neighbourhood, what it wanted from the police, and so on. These surveys—some of them crude and others sophisticated—revealed, as we have seen, if not a crisis of confidence then certainly a cause for concern. The evidence showed unequivocally that people were increasingly preoccupied by crime, were more fearful, and had less confidence in the police than they or their forbears used to have. 'Law and order' assumed a progressively prominent position on the public agenda. Whilst the behaviour of young people has always been considered retrograde by older generations, never previously this century had crime generally been considered so great a problem.

The consequence was that increasingly politicians gave undertakings about 'law and order' policy and rhetorically sought to reassure the public that they represented the party which, if elected, would by implication make the streets of Britain safer. They would support the police and provide more of them. They would introduce better technology, enabling offenders to be targeted more effectively. They would introduce measures so that particular groups of offenders could be cracked down on. They would give the police and the courts increased powers. They would restore the balance within the criminal justice system in favour of the victim and away from the offender. The evidence from surveys of voters' behaviour suggests that these undertakings and this rhetoric were often persuasive.[1] They were sometimes critical to electoral success. This trend continues. As a result aspiring politicians are now advised that they cannot risk even the *appearance* of being soft on crime. They must sound tough.

This phenomenon is not unique to Britain. It seems to be general to many advanced industrial nations. Throughout Western Europe and North America and the expanding economies of the Pacific region similar processes appear to be at work. Policing, criminal justice, and penal policy are now at least as prominent on the political agenda as those economic and welfare issues— employment, housing, education, health, and so on—which used almost exclusively to dominate electoral hustings. In the United States, for example, a country which is often said almost disturbingly to point to our own future, it was Richard Nixon who in 1968 first took a 'get tough' stance on crime issues in a presidential campaign, a posture adopted in Britain shortly thereafter, most notably in the Conservative electoral campaign of 1979. In the USA support for the death penalty is now taken to be a virtual requirement for a credible candidate for high political office. More and more well-to-do citizens opt for housing arrangements within physical compounds, barricaded against the outside world and privately policed.[2] In recent years most states have adopted tougher measures—more restrictive bail policies, longer mandatory sentences, less liberal parole provisions—resulting in the prison and gaol population tripling to a staggering one and a half million since 1980, a figure which at 555 prisoners per 100,000 population represents the highest incarceration rate found in any industrial democracy. In 1989, the state of Michigan opened a new prison every nine weeks.[3] California, with a population half that of the UK has a prison population almost three times as high. The same state now spends as much on prisons as on higher education. Nationally, between 1980 and 1993 total federal spending on employment and training programmes was almost halved whilst spending on 'correctional activities' increased by over 500 per cent. And, of course, the impact of these changes is not felt equally. Some of the most chilling statistics concern the experience of America's contemporary urban young black populations. It has been calculated that one in three black men aged 20–29 are now either in prison, on probation, or parole in the US and that in a city like Baltimore, which has a majority black population, *a majority* of the city's young men are under the control of the criminal justice system. As the leading American criminologist Elliott Currie put it: 'it's not much of an exaggeration to describe the city of Baltimore as itself a sort of minimum security penal colony'.[4]

The American situation is as yet nowhere matched in Europe. In England and Wales, for example, which has one of the highest incarceration rates in Western Europe, there are approximately 108 prisoners per 100,000, about one fifth of the number in the United States. But the European trends, including those in England, are in the same direction, not least because of the increasing supra-national co-ordination of an increasing number of policies through agencies like the European Union and the Council of Europe. In the Netherlands, the country traditionally lauded by penal reformers as the most progressive in Western Europe and with the lowest incarceration rate, government plans have been laid for a prison building programme which, if realized and then filled, will result in the number of people in prison per head of population matching that in neighbouring countries, including Britain, by the late 1990s: the incarceration rate will have been quadrupled within twenty-five years.

During the last decade successive administrations have introduced major criminal justice legislation almost annually.[5] Every passing exigency or media-generated folk-devil, from dangerous dogs to ravers to squeegee merchants, is seen by politicians to demand a statutory initiative, thereby demonstrating those politicians' political virility. We have more police officers, more courts, more prisons, and more prisoners in them. Yet still the 'get tough' political rhetoric does not abate and public confidence is not restored. If the most recent Government White Paper is any guide it would seem that the Home Secretary is not forewarned by developments in the United States but takes its recent initiatives as positive examples which we should emulate. Despite the almost universal opposition of the senior judiciary it appears that we are to have a British version of the American penchant for 'three strikes, you're out', with minimum sentences for burglars and drug dealers and automatic life sentences for serious violent and sex offenders, and also our version of 'honesty in sentencing' with the abolition of automatic early release and parole. These changes, it is estimated, will greatly increase our already large prison population.

What are British voters to make of these trends? Is the government really being tough on crime? Should we be as anxious about crime as many of us apparently are? What would best prevent crime? Do we get the policing we need and deserve? And how are ordinary citizens to judge whether their local police are doing a good job? These are the questions that citizens do and should ask. However, they are more easily posed than answered. There are no simple solutions to the law and order difficulties we face. But then that is the first important lesson to be learned. There *are* no simple solutions. There are no quick fixes, and any politician who gives the impression that there are—who suggests that we shall all sleep safer in our beds if we vote for some tough-sounding immediate measure—is almost certainly selling the public short. Therein lies public irresponsibility and social danger; the whittling away of civil liberties dearly fought for over many years; the granting of powers to state bureaucracies that in the long run may serve to oppress rather than safeguard the citizen; the growth of public expenditure which serves little purpose other than the vested interest of those minorities who derive income from it; the scapegoating of minorities whose commitment to the rule of law and the democratic process is undermined; the division of communities into the have-nots who are vulnerable to crime and the haves who, either because they live in low-crime areas or because they are better equipped to protect themselves, are largely immune to its ravages.

The real dangers are these: that social conflicts may be stimulated as much by our response to crime as by the condition of crime itself; that the law and the processes of law enforcement may have criminogenic consequences; that the law and its enforcement may serve not as a source of security and order but of anarchy and fear; that by focusing our efforts at crime reduction on reforming the police and the wider criminal justice system we will fail to identify and address the more fundamental social and economic changes which lie at the heart of the problems we face.

Why are some of these things happening? Is our preoccupation with crime getting out of proportion? It is as well to remember that crime is big business. When saying this we are not referring to the commission of crime, though that business is big enough, particularly in the sphere of corporate and white collar crime, the monetary value of which all analysts agree far out-weighs the street crime of which citizens are most fearful and on which the police largely concentrate their attention. The point is that there are other groups which benefit from crime and the fear it engenders. So-called crime *control*—so-called because it is questionable whether crime *is* controlled by much 'crime-control' activity—is a major industry, a business that is growing faster than most. Many analysts refer now to the 'prisons-industrial complex', a complex into which, with the end of the Cold War, the major corporations that made up the 'military-industrial complex' have moved or are moving. It should be termed the crime-industrial complex, not least because policing and private security is the major part of it. In addition to the £9,400 million spent annually by central government on law and order services, there is the rapidly expanding private security industry to which we referred in Chapter 2 and the ever-growing expenditure by central government, local authorities, firms, and households on the protection of property and the safety and sur-veillance of personnel. It is estimated, for example, that the Home Office alone spends over £40 million *per annum* on pri-vate security.[6] There is now a massive and expanding market in everything from traditional locks, bolts, and bars, vehicle secur-ity systems and burglar alarms, to surveillance and communica-tions technology, weapons, and protective clothing for the police and individual citizens, and the provision of contracted-out 'law and order' services for government. Twenty years ago who would have believed that by the mid-1990s private corporations would be locking up Her Majesty's guests for profit and that army depots and provincial police headquarters buildings would be guarded, not by their own personnel, but by commercial secur-ity guards? Or that the quaint and much loved nineteenth-cen-tury bobby's helmet would regularly be replaced by visored crash helmets surmounting flame-proof NATO suits, plastic shields, and long batons and that officers might routinely carry CS gas? Or that some chief constables would suggest that the general patrol of their areas was no longer feasible or productive and that community groups would begin making their own pri-vate arrangements?

But that is not the end of it. Crime is our major source of enter-tainment. The film industry is sustained by crime stories, apparently the more violent the better. A major part of our newspaper, radio, and television news coverage is devoted to accounts of crime. A high proportion of television drama, not least in serial form, is taken up with crime and the police response to it. And, perhaps most insidiously, some of the TV programmes with the highest viewer ratings comprise 'true crime' reconstructions allegedly better to enable those crimes to be solved. In North America and on the British video market these crime preventive or crime-solving masquerades are falling away. 'Real crime', recorded 'live' on CCTV, or dramatically reconstructed according to police accounts, is now being purveyed as unalloyed entertainment, as are real-life trials like that of O. J. Simpson. It will no doubt not be long before the equivalent of 'America's Most Wanted' TV programme finds a place in British television schedules. There are many more murders, flashing blue lights, and wailing sirens seen and heard vicariously in our living rooms than are witnessed in reality on our streets. All of which is to say that our experience of crime is largely second-hand, through the media. That experience has profoundly affected our perceptions of crime and our attitudes towards and our expectations of the police.

Crime sells not just newspapers and television advertising. At one remove it also sells mace canisters, police batons, CCTV systems, and, given the trend toward privatization, prisons. 'Security' has itself become a commodity. Moreover, the more citizens are arrested and locked up the larger are the profits to which many of the major corporations are now looking. There are a lot of jobs, large salaries, and company dividends being earned from crime, and a large number of vested interests are now tied up in presentation of crime, and the manner in which we should publicly respond to it, in tough, interventionist, high-tech, and expensive ways. Most people now recognize why there is need to place a health warning beside the advertised pleasure of tobacco. But voters and politicians have yet to apply the same caution to the demand for more resources, greater powers, and repressive measures from members of the crime-industrial complex, be they employed by the state or the private sector.

We need perhaps to be more sceptical. To ask more searching questions about the realities of crime and policing. Only by so doing will we be able to identify the general direction in which we need to travel. We may not be able to identify precisely what policies will work, but we ought to be able to eliminate those policies that on the basis of our very considerable experience we know will *not* work. It is time to give the law and order rhetoric a rest and have a proper public debate, one that is grounded on fact. In the rest of this Chapter we shall consider some of the questions crucial to policing.

Who Commits Crime?

We saw in Chapter 1 that the evidence suggests that the incidence of crime has undoubtedly risen in recent decades, though not as steeply as criminal statistics suggest. The rise is hardly surprising. Despite the recession in the economy during the 1980s and the anxieties that accompany the higher levels of unemployment which are increasingly taken to be normal and acceptable, the bulk of the population is overwhelmingly more prosperous than it was twenty, let alone forty or sixty, years ago. Foreign holidays and car ownership are now normal. The high streets are awash with, and most people are surrounded by, consumer goods that have nothing to do with the satisfaction of basic needs of food, clothing, and shelter but have everything to do with what John Galbraith famously termed the management of demand for style, fashion, and status goods,[7] from trainers to hi-fis, designer clothes to automatic cameras, microwave ovens and videos to rollerblades. Never previously has there been so much property so desperately wanted, so anonymously disposable, so little needed, so casually displayed and replaced, so easily damaged or stolen. It would be surprising were property crime *not* to have risen alongside this explosion in personal consumption. This is all the more the case given that in Britain, unlike Japan where street crime (though not official corruption) has remained within modest bounds, individualism as well as consumerism has been so much stressed (remember Margaret Thatcher's: 'There is no society, only individuals'), where the gap between the employed and unemployed is now so great, and where income and wealth inequality has since 1980 been allowed to grow so significantly (see Chapter 1).

But unemployment and poverty were surely worse in the

1930s, some would object? The relationship today between crime and relative poverty, or between crime and unemployment, is not plausibly similar to that which existed in any previous period. The world has changed. There is now significant long-term unemployment. Lifestyles and expectations have changed, as have people's prospects and values. Moreover, our routine use of the law has changed.

Who commits crime nowadays? The evidence suggests that most of us do from time to time. Self-report studies (in which samples of citizens, generally young people, are asked in confidence what offences they have committed) indicate that the commission of one or two crimes falls within the repertoire of normal behaviour, at least for young males. We persuade ourselves that the crimes we commit cause no great harm, particularly to those who are near and dear to us. Our opportunities to commit offences are great and the chances of getting caught small: tax evasion, small thefts from work and shops, the fiddling of expenses, fare dodging or licence evasion, and all the crimes related to the status icon of the age—the car. Yet though the chances of getting caught are small, many of us are caught, in increasing numbers. Perhaps the most astonishing statistic regularly produced by the Home Office is the proportion of the population which gathers a criminal conviction for a 'standard list' offence. Not a motoring offence of the sort that most people, rightly or wrongly, typically discount. But a listed offence, an offence sufficiently serious for it to be tried on indictment before a jury. Thirty-four per cent of males now have such a conviction by the age of 40, 8 per cent of women do so.

Most households are touched by crime not only as victims: most families also contain proven perpetrators. Indeed all the evidence shows that those citizens with criminal convictions are also those most likely to be victims of crime. But, it will be argued, most people do not commit the serious offences about which the public are really concerned and against which they seeks police protection. What of serious offenders, particularly repeat serious offenders? Leaving aside the fact that, as we have seen, the public seek police assistance about many incidents that do not involve crime at all, let alone those pervasive relatively minor property offences about which we have been speaking, what of the suggestion, often made by some senior police officers, that if they could ensure that all the male members of a relatively small number of families in a given area were locked up, then they could cut the number of crimes by a substantial proportion? This suggestion, as we saw in Chapter 2, is implicitly being encouraged by the Audit Commission.

It is of course true that a minority of offenders are responsible for a disproportionate amount of crime. This is not surprising, given that most things are unevenly distributed: professional burglars and fraudsters, some sexual offenders—those who molest children outside their own families for example—who have a compulsive disposition such that they may be responsible for literally hundreds of offences. Thus when we analyse the numbers of offences which persons convicted by the courts are known to have committed, it is certainly the case that a minority of offenders are responsible for a high proportion of offences. The Home Office estimates that 21 percent of convicted male offenders, that is seven per cent of all males, have four or more convictions and are responsible for 59 per cent of all court appearances.

All the evidence suggests that a relatively small proportion of young males are responsible for a large proportion of crime and that their prolific offending occurs during a relatively short period of their lives: that they grow out of crime.[8] Nevertheless, it is a far cry from this assertion—an assertion often sensationally personalised by popular press stories about particular young offenders said literally to be responsible for 'crime waves', or the suggestion that were the courts to lock up known 'bail bandits' then the police would have remarkably little left to do—to the proposition that *the overwhelming majority* of crimes are attributable to *a few* habitually predatory offenders. Were that the case then the problem of crime would be relatively easy to deal with. The police could simply target this very small minority and the courts could take them out of circulation for long periods, as their sentencing powers enable them to do.

But it is not so simple. Those offenders who are convicted and punished are responsible for a very small proportion of the crime from which we suffer. As we saw in Chapter 2 the proportion of crimes reported to the police is less than half, though the proportion varies from crime to crime and the bulk, though not all, of the crime that goes unreported is relatively petty. Of the

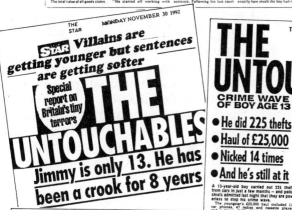

Fig. 38 Press reporting of persistent offenders

crimes that are reported not all are recorded and only a minority—currently 26 per cent—are cleared up. It is estimated that
only about 3 per cent of the sorts of offences uncovered in the
British Crime Surveys (and we should remember that those surveys exclude or understate many categories of crime, some of
them serious) result in a caution or a conviction and only 2 per
cent in a conviction. In relation to some high volume anonymous property offences, such as theft from vehicles, the figures
are even lower. It follows that one simply cannot extrapolate
from the characteristics of offenders convicted to the proportionate responsibility of all the crime that surrounds us. Only a
small proportion of offences committed is attributed by the
criminal justice system to known offenders—7 per cent is the
prevailing estimate. We simply do not know much about the
persons responsible for the vast majority of crime, though the
self-report studies suggest that involvement in frequent criminal acts is relatively rare demographically. Nevertheless the
evidence indicates that responsibility for crime is widely dispersed.[9]

Despite all this, the idea that focusing on the supposedly small
number of high volume offenders continues to be attractive to
politicians, policy-makers, and professionals. Let us look at the
figures a little more carefully. We will start with the baseline used
by the Home Office in their analysis of the Offenders Index: those
males convicted of six or more offences. These men, it is suggested, account for 65 per cent of all convictions. Consequently,
they appear on the face of it to represent a likely target group for
a proactive police service focusing on the repeat offender and
not the crime. How many such individuals are there?

The Home Office states that 7 per cent of males aged under 35
have six or more convictions. To estimate the number of individuals in the population at any one time meeting this criterion is
difficult, however, and involves a degree of educated guesswork.
We will focus on 10–30-year-olds. Let us assume that 7 per cent
of 30-year-olds have six or more convictions (they will have had
twenty years to accumulate them) and that there are no 10-year-
olds with six convictions. We can then devise a sliding scale
between these two points to allow us to estimate the proportion
of 29-years-olds, 28-year-olds, 27-year-olds and so on with six or
more convictions. Then using population totals (we know

roughly how many people there are of any particular age in the population at any time) we can produce a rough estimate of our target population. This rather conservative approach leads us to conclude that at any one time there are well over 300,000 men and women aged 10–30 with six or more convictions for a standard list offence.

There are a few points to add to this revealing statistic. First, it is important to recognize that these are convictions for standard list offences—i.e. relatively serious offences. Lowering the threshold to include those offences which are formally treated less seriously, but which nevertheless cause the public concern and distress, would further increase the number of target repeat offenders. Secondly, as a point of comparison with our rough estimate of 300,000 plus repeat offenders, the forty-three police forces of England and Wales employ approximately 127,000 officers and 51,000 civilians. Any focus on repeat offenders is going to have to be very selective. For example, using the Audit Commission's estimate of the size of population and territory covered by every patrolling officer, there are at least 100 repeat offenders for every officer on the street (see page 126).

Moreover, even though the population is at an all-time high, and expanding more rapidly than most people believed possible, there are currently 'only' 55,000 people in prison. It is a sobering truth, unpalatable or reassuring depending on one's viewpoint, that even if we were to imprison huge numbers of offenders for very long periods indeed, then, as the United States has found to its enormous financial and social cost, there are even larger numbers of offenders left in circulation, or many more potential offenders, willing and able to fill the gap.

None of this should be interpreted as suggesting that serious habitual offenders should not be targeted by the police or punished severely by the courts. That is an obvious crime preventive strategy that should arguably be pursued more vigorously. But it is a 'war on crime' myth that some 'others', some alien outcast group, some morally degenerate minority, can easily be identified, convicted, and neutralized. It really is not the case that all our ills are attributable to some enemy physically and morally distant from the rest of us. The language of war is not appropriate in relation to crime. Crime is not the product of some 'other'. There is no distinctive enemy 'within'. The commission of crime is a fundamental problem integral to the structure and culture of Western industrial society. Crime is pervasive. It is in our neighbourhoods, in our workplaces, in our schools, in our families, in us. For that reason crime prevention is overwhelmingly a problem for us as citizens in all the settings in which we live and play and work. In the same way that doctors can do very little about our health if we smoke and drink and eat to excess, so the police can do very little to prevent the crime about which we complain unless, collectively, we change our economic, social, and political choices. Crime is the deep-seated concomitant of our lifestyles, our culture, and our social and economic relations.

How do the Police Know about Crime and How do They Clear Crime Up?

The television and fictional image of the sophisticated and assiduous detective painstakingly discovering the commission of some heinous crime and then, through some brilliant process of deductive reasoning, fathoming who is responsible, is no doubt appealing, but it has precious little to do with the reality of policing. The police depend crucially on the public to know, first, that crimes have been committed and, secondly, who has committed them. Without public trust in and co-operation with the police, the police are bereft of that stream of information which is the primary source of their effectiveness. That is why—and it is a point to which we shall return—Lord Scarman asserted, following his review of the events leading up to the riots in Brixton in April 1981, that a 'police force which does not consult locally will fail to be efficient'.[10] The police need to know from the public what priorities they should pursue, because only if they deal with the problems about which the public is concerned, and use the methods of which the public approves, will the public tell them what they need to know to get the job done. This is critical because, as we have noted, those members of the community most likely to be the victims of crime are also those citizens most likely to have adversarial contacts with the police.

Most crimes come to public light because members of the public, be they victims or witnesses, *choose* to tell the police about it. Nowadays they do so mostly by telephone, using either the normal telephone system or the 999 emergency procedure. These two methods account for about 95 per cent of all calls to the police though, as we saw in Chapter 3, only about a third of these calls are unequivocally about crime. Other calls *may* concern crime, though this is often uncertain. The latter include reports of suspicious events (people thought to be behaving strangely, persons missing, and so on) reports of trouble (disorders and disturbances) which may be accompanied by a request for assistance (domestic assaults, for example), calls providing information that callers think the police should have (mostly about parked or abandoned vehicles), and the ubiquitously triggered burglar alarms reported automatically or by relay. The latter *may* involve a crime in progress: in fact in 97 per cent of cases they are false alarms.[11]

Not all reported crimes are crimes (items suspected stolen turn out to be mislaid and are recovered) and even if the member of the public continues to think they are, the police may not agree. A proportion of reported crimes are not recorded as crimes. A recent survey of recorded calls to the police found that only 12 per cent resulted in a crime report and even calls to report crimes led to the police generating crime reports in only 39 per cent of cases.[12]

The police discover remarkably little crime for themselves—probably 5–10 per cent of all recorded indictable crime,[13] though it should be remembered that this figure excludes non-indictable offences such as minor criminal damage and common traffic offences such as speeding which are not recorded. Thus, although there is a good deal of talk, not least in the sociology of the police literature, about proactive policing—the police taking their own initiatives to find and deal with the so-called crimes without victims like drug-taking and those surrounding prostitution, for example—in fact these efforts generate a very small proportion of the crimes that are recorded. Furthermore, a good deal of police proactive effort stems from complaints from the public that something be done about a general situation that concerns it—speeding along a particular road, soliciting in a particular neighbourhood, the use of certain public lavatories for 'cottaging' by homosexuals, or more or less open drug-dealing in a particular pub, club or street corner.

Generally speaking, if members of the public choose not to tell the police that a crime has occurred the police will not know about it and it will never get into the official statistics.

This dependence on the public extends to clearing up crime. The research evidence indicates that of those offences that are detected directly—that is, excluding offences that offenders are already admitting, or, having been convicted of one offence, may then be persuaded to confess to by having others 'taken into consideration'—about three fifths are cleared up as a consequence of information given to the police.[14] This is either because the offender is handed to the police on a plate by the reporting agent (as is invariably the case with shoplifting where store detectives report offences by announcing that they have detained a shoplifter) or because the victim or witness is able to provide information to the police leading directly to the identification of the offender. The police methods about which so much is made by the mass media—fingerprinting, DNA samples, forensic tests, house-to-house inquiries, offender profiling, and so on—*may* be very important for clearing up particularly serious crimes about which information is not forthcoming—but they play remarkably little part in the clearance of the majority of recorded crimes. Such methods may be involved in as few as 5 per cent of detections. [15]

It is also worth noting that the indirect methods on which the police largely rely to clear up crime when information from the public is not forthcoming are notoriously subject to abuse. In recent years there have been several scandals involving police officers 'persuading' offenders already in prison or admitting another offence to admit to offences that may either never have been committed, or for which they were probably not responsible.[16] Moreover, the use of informants—a method of which increased use is currently being pressed by the Audit Commission—is a technique both invaluable and dangerous. Several of the police corruption scandals that came to light in the 1970s involved the use of 'supergrasses' and the abuse stemming from the use of informants in Northern Ireland should give further pause for thought.[17] The Audit Commission assertions about the value of informants are worth looking at in a little more detail. The heart of their argument is based on a somewhat naïve cost-benefit analysis of the use of informants in which payments made to informants are balanced against the number of persons arrested or the value of property recovered.[18] This simplistic method fails to take on board a host of other 'costs' involved in the use of informants: the time and organizational resources involved in recruiting and cultivating informants; the operational costs in following up information received; the supervisory and administrative costs involved in registering and handling informants; and, the costs of 'maintaining' informants.[19] Most important, however, are the non-economic costs of using informants. There is the question of legitimacy and trust. If corrupt relationships are wittingly or unwittingly entered into, or if it becomes known that offenders have been able to strike deals or manipulate the system, the potential impact on public views of the legitimacy of the police in particular, and the criminal justice system in general, will be devastating.

This is not to belittle the importance of the police developing improved forensic methods and gathering intelligence about crime patterns, offenders' *modus operandi* and activities, and the routes taken by stolen goods. On the contrary. This expertise and intelligence are vital at the margin and need, as we shall argue, to be cultivated further. They enable the police to make *better use* of the information they receive from the public. Furthermore the degree to which the public is willing to assist depends in part on the perceived professionalism of the police. Eliciting information sensitively, speedily, and accurately from the public is itself a police skill that needs to be cultivated. Nevertheless our central message is that *the police are dependant on the public* for their effectiveness. Were the public to choose, for whatever reason, to report an increased proportion of all the numerous anonymous property offences that we know occur and which currently are not reported, then the aggregate police clear-up rate would inevitably fall, as it has done in recent years. The fall would be no reflection of police effectiveness. By the same token if the public is currently reporting a smaller proportion of anonymous property offences than used to be the case— as the Home Office suggests may now begin to be the case, because of the increased size and application of the waivers and no-claims bonuses now attached to personal property insurance policies[20]—then the police clear-up rate may stabilize or possibly rise. But this will not reflect improved police effectiveness either. All of which must lead us to the conclusion, particularly when we also take into account the capacity of the police to manipulate clear-up rates through use of what we have called 'indirect methods', that aggregate clear-up rates are a poor measure of police effectiveness.

It is precisely because the information that the public holds is so critical to police performance that the police now lay stress on prioritizing their response to calls from the public. If the victim is simply reporting an offence committed by a perpetrator of which he or she knows nothing—a burglary several hours old discovered on return home from work, or a car parked on the street broken into during the night—then there is generally nothing to be gained from the police attending immediately and possibly little to be gained by attending at all, except to collect details of what is missing and to provide an appearance of care. Such commonplace anonymous offences are seldom cleared up unless there are witnesses or the property stolen is found. The best chances of a clearance arise when victims or witnesses are able immediately to provide information to the police, when they are able to identify perpetrators—as is often the case in crimes of violence—or when reporting coincides with apprehension, as it invariably does in the case of shop-theft. Police clear-up rates for different offences by and large reflect the degree to which members of the public are able and willing to tell the police 'whodunnit'. Thus wounding offences, which are rather likely to be reported to the police and where the victim typically knows his or her aggressor and can tell the police—can in a high proportion of cases be attributed to individuals by the criminal justice system, whereas vandalism, where neither of these factors applies, typically cannot (see fig. 20).

There is one further observation that arises out of this pattern of police dependence on the public. It is arguably an excellent thing that the police are so dependent and we should be chary about giving the police investigative powers that might make it less so. Police dependence is a vital safeguard for our liberties and provides the basis of democratic policing. It follows that we should in every way possible seek to enhance police–community collaboration in the interests of what we may term *democratically-informed police effectiveness*. This argument needs a little elaboration.

Some sociologists of the police define police-recorded crimes as crimes-about-which-the-public-think-the-police-should-do-something. The implication is that those crimes not reported are crimes-about-which-the-public-do-not-think-the-police-should-do-something. The basis of this viewpoint is readily apparent from the foregoing account about how crimes predominantly enter the criminal statistics and how they are typically cleared up. Recorded crime is not the crime that occurs—incidents of behaviour that the law proscribes—but the crime that occurs, that someone knows something about, and chooses to tell the police about. It is going too far to say, however, that recorded crime is the crime that the pubic thinks *should be* treated as crime and the offender prosecuted—an arguably attractive communitarian view of law and law enforcement.

There are many reasons why the public may not report crime which involve no such normative judgements. Some victims, for example, may be intimidated into not reporting the offences against them—literally too frightened of the retaliatory consequences of so doing at the hands of some individual or group. Many women repeatedly assaulted by their domestic partners, for example, have found themselves in this position and it is a problem for many young people living in areas where gang or bullying activity is rife. Some victims may not be prepared to report offences because they do not trust the police or because they dislike them—a considerable problem in some countries where police corruption is rife. Or because they doubt, possibly on the basis of past experience, that they will get a sympathetic hearing from the police: this used to be, and possibly remains, a major explanation for the under-reporting of rape.[21] Further, there are some offences that no one, except the perpetrator, knows anything about. Many frauds are of this nature and some people who are missing, but with whom no one had particularly close relations before they went missing, may have been the victims of foul play—a disturbing possibility of which we have been reminded by some recent cases of serial murder.

Finally, large numbers of reporting decisions are made not on the basis of a moral judgement as to whether the police *should* know about it, but because of a bureaucratic requirement—namely that the victim's insurance policy stipulates that a report to the police is the pre-condition for a claim. And the corollary of this consideration is whether, in the absence of a personal bureaucratic requirement, victims and witnesses find it worthwhile or convenient to report crimes; whether they find police bureaucratic procedures too much trouble or doubt that the police will do anything with the information they might give them. Where members of the public are widely put off by such considerations they may even be tempted to take the law into their own hands.[22]

In Britain, fortunately, we do not have to speculate too much about these issues because the British Crime Surveys have explored them closely, at least in relation to that range of street offences which the Surveys cover well.

Fear or dislike of the police, and fear of reprisals, appear not to

	1984	1988	1992
Reasons for not reporting:	%	%	%
Too trivial/no loss	58	50	55
Police could no nothing	17	24	25
Police would not be interested	7	10	13
We dealt with matter ourselves/ inappropriate for police	11	11	12
Reported to other authorities	4	6	6
Inconvenient to report	2	2	3
Fear reprisals	1	1	2
Fear/dislike police	1	1	1
Other	7	13	4
All 'police-related' reasons[1]	24	32	35
Unweighted N	2705	2803	2905

Notes:
1. 'Police-related' reasons comprise any of the following reasons: police could do nothing, police would not be interested, fear/dislike police. Multiple responses were allowed, so these three categories may sum to more than the combined category.
2. Based on all incidents not reported to the police. 'Vague/not stated' responses are excluded from the base.

Fig. 39   Reasons for not reporting crime: 1984, 1988 and 1992 British Crime Surveys

Source: Mayhew, P. et al, (1993) *The 1992 British Crime Survey,* London: HMSO

be a major problem in Britain, though it is worth remembering that young people under 16 years of age are not included in the Surveys, and it is conceded that sexual offences and domestic assaults are not well covered. What is worrying are the considerations that 'the police could do nothing' or 'would not be interested', both of them major and growing reasons for non-reporting. As the Home Office has stated in its commentary on the data, the statistics 'do not suggest any improvement in attitudes among victims as to the ability, or commitment, of the police to deal with the relatively less serious incidents which typically go unreported'.[23]

It follows that we cannot complacently treat the crimes that the public do report as a complete guide to what the public think the police should do something about. What the public reports to the police in part reflects public perceptions of police procedures, attitudes, and performance and there are a good many crimes on which the police ought to be acting proactively as well as making their own procedures more user-friendly. Nevertheless all the evidence suggests that the crimes that the public is able and willing to report *broadly reflect* its view as to what is serious and on which the police should concentrate their attentions. Further, we should regard it as fortunate that our law and criminal justice system are such that for the most part the police cannot clear up crime without our aid: that prosecutions will invariably fail unless complainants are prepared to give evidence; that the police cannot stop and search people and premises without reasonable cause; that suspects cannot indefinitely be detained and oppressively treated until they confess to something; and so on. Long may it remain the case that, despite the increasing array of technological aids available to the police, they are still overwhelmingly dependent on the personal face-to-face co-operation of ordinary citizens to detect crimes and offenders. We shall have things to say in Chapters 6 about formal police accountability, but ultimately the best guarantor of accountability is day-to-day police operational dependency on the public.

One final remark under this head. It is of course a management problem that the public places so many demands on the police, some of them possibly unreasonable. This management problem, and the costs associated with it, is in large measure the reason the present debate about the police is arising. But we should be grateful for the problem we face on two counts. First, the fact that the public takes its problems to the police reflects a relatively high degree of public trust in the police. Secondly, it is not altogether a bad thing that the police have precious little time to do other than react to calls from the public. We should not want them to have time on their hands, able to pursue offences and offenders that, whatever the law might say, the public might think better left alone. It is one thing to encourage the police to be proactive about crimes about which the public at large is *demonstrably* concerned. It is quite another to encourage proactive policing where *the police are unaided in determining the priorities*. The former arguably represents a strand of polic-ing by consent and is to be encouraged. The latter can become the characteristic of a police state.

Does What the Police Do Affect the Incidence of Crime?

In much of what follows the impression may be given that noth-ing the police do is very effective. It is as well, therefore, to set out clearly a cautionary note. We should not place excessive reliance on the various evaluations that have been made of the effective-ness of different police methods in the same way that we should probably be cautious about all short-term social science evalua-tions of social policy options. Such evaluations tend to suggest that nothing much works much better than anything else, or that little difference is made by taking up new options or providing more resources. But seldom are these evaluations ideally con-ducted. The implementation of whatever initiative is being taken is often flawed and both the experiments and their assessment are typically limited to a few months or years. We know that changes in police methods and styles *have* in the long term been associated with changes in public perceptions and that the way the police are regarded by the citizenry in different countries and communities is very different. It is implausible to suggest, there-fore, that what the police do and how many of them do it in no way affects either the incidence of crime or our willingness to co-operate with the police in either preventing crime or clearing it up. The difficulty from an evaluational standpoint is that what the police do is only one part of a criminal justice system, the overall shape of which undoubtedly affects public attitudes and expectations. And, secondly, that the incidence of crime is largely driven by fundamental socio-economic and cultural factors that have little or nothing to do with any aspect of criminal justice policy, let alone policing policy.

We need to be careful, however, about pursuing this argument too far. By stressing that crime is a product of social structural features not easily changed by government policies, at least in the short term, there is a danger that collectively we become fatalistic about crime, imagining either that there is nothing we can do about it or resorting to purely individualistic responses— arranging better personal protection, adopting less outgoing habits, or giving less support to communal arrangements— which ignore and are to the detriment of the public good. Equally damaging is the morale-sapping influence of a 'nothing works' or a 'nothing-works-much-better-than-anything-else' syndrome for the police and other criminal justice practitioners. For in the final analysis, *belief* that effort is worthwhile, that an initiative is capable of changing some aspect of the world, is a *prerequisite* for the success of any effort. Programmes only work if they are invested with personal commitment and enthusiasm. They have to be made to work by the individuals who operate them.

There is no evidence that there is a significant relationship between the number of police officers employed and the incidence of crime, at least within the limits that it is possible to test this proposition on the basis of natural areal variations.[24] Nor, to extend the argument, is there evidence that the provision of more police officers would greatly affect the incidence of crime. Nor does it seem likely, for the reasons that we have implicitly discussed above, that providing the police with more powers or resources would serve to control crime. This conclusion, which the Home Office's own researchers have drawn,[25] does of course fit with the government's generally sceptical attitude towards increased public expenditure and the quality of public services generally. But it also runs counter to the government's generally supportive attitude towards the police whose usual claim is that they need more personnel and resources to do the job required of them. This is where the rub is as far as the reality and politics of policing are concerned.

Doubts about the crime control benefits of providing more police officers apply also to particular methods of policing. On the basis of studies carried out in both this country and the United States, for example, large question marks hang over the crime preventive value of police patrols. Experimental increases in car patrols, though not foot patrols (see below), have generally led to no significant differences in reported crime, rates of victimization, levels of citizen fear or satisfaction with the police. Indeed it seems that local residents seldom notice that any increase in patrols has occurred.[26]

However, it is doubtful that anyone should be surprised by these short-term results. As a recent Audit Commission study of police patrol work demonstrated, once non-patrol personnel (headquarters and management staff, detectives, and specialist officers) have been siphoned off, and allowance made for leave, sickness, training, a shift system, and court appearances, the proportion of officers available for patrol work is typically only about 10 per cent of police strength. Moreover since patrol officers spend nearly half their time in police stations (briefings, meal breaks, and interviewing and completing paperwork for anyone arrested) the number of officers actually on patrol at any one time is only about 5 per cent of strength.

Furthermore, on the basis of current police strengths the Audit Commission has calculated that each officer on patrol—and this assumes that officers are patrolling singly and not in pairs—will be covering a territory in which there are:

- 18,000 inhabitants
- 7,500 houses
- 23 pubs
- 9 schools
- 140 miles of pavement
- 85 acres of parks or open spaces
- 77 miles of road.[27]

And, of course, over 100 prolific offenders, as we calculated earlier.

It does not take much imagination to see that there would have to be very substantial increases in the patrol strength, indeed much larger increases than any police force is ever going to be able to make, for it to be plausible that many local residents

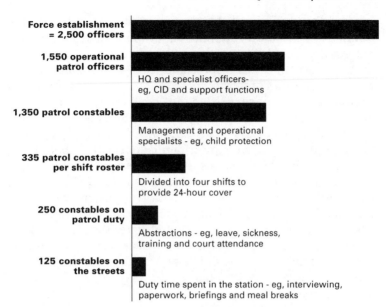

Fig. 40 Officer deployment in a typical force
Source: Audit Commission (1996) *Streetwise*, London: Audit Commission

would notice a significant difference. Unless, that is—and this is a topic to which we return—special efforts are made to make those patrols more visible. Nor, given the relative rarity of visible street crimes—criminals typically do not advertise their activities—is it likely that police patrols, whatever their strength, will often come across crimes in progress, thereby either preventing those offences or catching the offenders red-handed. Such encounters are likely to happen to police officers only occasionally in their careers.[28]

Nor, to take another aspect of police performance, does improving the police response time to calls from the public lead to any great improvement in the crime clear-up rate. Again the reason is not surprising. Most calls from the public do not involve incidents that turn out to involve crime, and when members of the public do call to report an offence, it is usually long after the offenders have left the scene. When they call about an ongoing disturbance—a fight in a pub or a domestic dispute, for example—even if the disturbance has evaporated by the time the police arrive, the likelihood is that whoever called will be able to tell the police who was responsible whether the police arrive within five minutes or thirty.[29]

We should not conclude from this, however, that patrol work and reasonably rapid responses to emergencies do not matter. They do. The public wants both, and since the form of patrol the public particularly favours in Britain is foot patrol, there is an obvious conflict between the two. Officers on foot are not equipped to respond speedily to most calls for assistance. Yet while there is no evidence that foot patrols are any more effective than mobile patrols as far as the incidence of crime is concerned, experimental evidence from the United States suggests that foot patrols have positive benefits in terms of fear of crime, feelings of neighbourhood safety, and public satisfaction with the police.[30] These are important benefits which may be of long-term significance for general police effectiveness. We shall return to the question of police patrols in Chapter 6.

The core of what needs to be said about the effectiveness of detectives and detective methods follows largely from what we have already noted about how the police know about most crime and how they clear it up. A relatively small proportion—about 5 per cent—of crimes are cleared up as a result of deploying the classical detective methods beloved of fiction writers (though these methods may be of enormous importance in some serious cases) and detectives spend a high proportion of their time doing necessary paperwork in order that prosecutions be brought.[31] It is for this reason that the Home Office has calculated that greatly increasing the detective strength would not significantly increase the clear up rate[32] and, self-evidently, such a policy would almost certainly mean further depleting the number of officers available for patrol.

These conclusions have recently been called into question, however. Detectives are now being freed from much paperwork by the establishment of Operational or Administrative Support Units staffed largely by civilians. Moreover, what is required, according to the Audit Commission, is for police work generally to be made more intelligence driven so that the scope for proactive policing can greatly be increased. Crime can be 'managed' into submission. The basic idea is that if a high proportion of offences cannot be solved because they are anonymous, that is, victims do not know who their predators are, then perhaps the police should focus less on offences and more on known 'villains'. By gathering and sharing intelligence more rationally, by setting priorities, planning, and developing teamwork between uniformed officers and detectives more effectively, the argument is that prolific offenders can be targeted and, with the use of informants and surveillance, caught in possession or in the act and, subsequently, many unsolved crimes will be cleared up. Just as importantly, so the argument goes, many further offences can be prevented by taking these prolific offenders out of circulation.[33]

In addition to the myriad practical problems associated with this concept (uniformed and detective branches tend to have separate cultures and styles of working) there are three further major impediments on which we have touched previously in this Chapter and elsewhere. First, there are rather a lot of repeat offenders—they are not rarities. Secondly, most proactive policing techniques are hugely resource-intensive: one cannot put 'the usual suspects' under surveillance for very long, for example, without greatly depleting the delivery of other police services which, as we have seen, the public expects and wants. Informants, moreover, have to be cultivated: that takes a lot of time. Thirdly, proactive policing techniques pose major ethical and civil liberties issues about which the Audit Commission has to date had little to say and other studies have only hinted at.[34] The potential costs arising from these ethical problems may be far greater than any that can be calculated financially. Proactive policing techniques often involve a process which one of America's most scholarly observers of the policing scene has dubbed 'systematic harassment'.[35] It involves, either directly or indirectly through informants, 'getting close to villains'.[36] And it runs the risk of not just corruption for self advantage but of officers justifying to themselves the 'fitting up' of the 'usual suspects' they *know* to be guilty—so-called *noble cause corruption*. This is precisely the set of problems which, the evidence suggests, contributed to a decline in public confidence in the police in the 1970s and 1980s. We should be very wary about treading this path once again.

Crime Prevention by Design: What Works?

In recent years one of the most fruitful aproaches to primary crime prevention has been to assume that many offences, particularly those that are more instrumental, involve a rational choice which can be affected by rearranging factors which curtail the opportunity to commit selected offences and enhance the likelihood, real or perceived, of getting caught. Targets could sucessfully be hardened, as occurred with the compulsory fitting of steering locks on all new cars in the 1970s, or surveillance could be increased, either by re-siting targets—placing telephone boxes in more easily visible locations, for example—or by making use of technological aids—the introduction of CCTV systems in selected London tube stations, for example.

Over the last twenty years a great deal of expertise has been developed in this field based on the publication of a large number of studies. All efforts at primary crime prevention by design are reliant on certain core ingredients. Good data on crimes reported and unreported are required so that a detailed crime pattern analysis can be conducted: Are certain locations repeatedly used to commit particular kinds of offences? Are some victims repeatedly victimized? Are certain types of property, with particular characteristics, more vulnerable to burglary than others? Are some makes and models of cars more likely to be broken into or stolen? In which areas are crimes of all types most commonly committed and how do those areas relate to the areas of residence of known offenders? Through careful analysis of crime pattern data well informed decisions can better be taken about where it might be most fruitful to mount a CCTV system, where police officers might usefully be deployed and at what time of day, which types of property and person might be better protected, where street lighting might be improved, and so on.

Crime prevention by design is of course neither a complete, simple, nor static solution and every initiative has to be tailored to local and changing circumstances. To the extent that offending is instrumental behaviour, and offenders are engaged in a process of calculating the odds of gaining advantage and not suffering consequences, it follows that offenders engage in what is in effect an interactive learning process with those who would prevent their depradations. Every technological advance on the defence side is likely, eventually, to be countered with some new technique for breaching that defence. Much crime comprises a sort of low-key circumstantial arms race. However, unlike the international arms race of the Cold War, the number of players and targets is almost limitless. Thus if one target becomes too difficult, or a particular location too uncomfortable, then there are generally plenty of others to choose from. Crimes prevented in one location may be displaced to another target, place, or time of day. And if a certain type of crime becomes untenable then it may eventually be replaced by a completely new form, a form that may not yet even be designated a crime. Every change in our way of life, every new type of transaction, tool, or technologocal aid, brings with it the possibiity of using that development to take advantage of, rather than to assist, fellow human beings.

However, it is doubtful that one type of crime is mechanically displaced or deflected to another, or that some other site will attract all the criminal activity that used to be conducted elsewhere. Particular locations attract and encourage offending behaviour which is likely to be reduced if the encouragement to such behaviour is absent. There is now a copious amount of evidence as to what is likely to work, where, and under which particular circumstances. This varies from the very general—large-scale architectural redesign for example[37]—to the particular—changing cheque guarantee cards in order to tackle cheque fraud;[38] from the redesign of shops to prevent theft,[39] to the use of publicity to to tackle crime on the underground,[40] and so on. The most popular current strategy which is alleged to prevent crime is the introduction of closed-circuit television (CCTV). Unfortunately, like so many innovations in this area, this is another which has been inadequately researched. Work undertaken by the Home Office and the Scottish Office suggests that the introduction of CCTV is often accompanied by significant drops in crime, but it also casts some doubt on whether such a drop can be sustained.[41]

What is clear is that primary crime prevention involving design and surveillance initiatives can be pursued in almost any setting by a host of agencies providing services to which the public has access or with responsibility for public settings. Highway authorities, housing estates and associations, education departments, town centre trading assocations, major public institutions—all these groupings suffer crime to some degree and would benefit from closer analysis of what form that crime takes. All would benefit from working more closely with the police to explore methods by which that crime might better be prevented.

Conclusion

There are no policing panaceas. We should be wary about the desperate legal and policing measures to which politicians increasingly resort to substantiate their commitment to 'law and order' at a time of general public concern about crime. We should equally be wary of the policing fashions occasionally espoused by new chief constables who, having taken command, feel the need to demonstrate their management virility by juggling with the organization of their forces or by pursuing new initiatives with the methods their forces use. Though the police are a fundamentally conservative body when it comes to basic structural issues, it is a commonplace in the literature on policing that there has been far too much superficial and ill-thought-out change for the sake of change in recent years and, despite the claims often made initially, few of the policy initiatives that have been pursued have been carefully and independently evaluated or have demonstrated significant long-term benefits recognizable to the public.[42]

To the extent that we find there to be major incompatibilities between our current policing arrangements and public demands, concerns, and expectations—the subject of the next chapter—this suggests three important lessons. First, we should be sceptical about claims made by senior police officers and police unions that we need not think about the basic structure of our policing arrangements on the grounds that police management and organizational changes currently underway will lead to significant crime preventive benefits. On the basis of recent experience this outcome is unlikely. Secondly, we should question the credibility of politicians who shy away from pressing forward a searching inquiry into our fundamental policing arrangements, particularly if their first instinct appears to have been to raise such questions. There is a distinct possibility that they have balked at grasping nettles because of police vested interests which, in the current political climate, they wish to have firmly on-side. Thirdly, to the extent that we find it necessary to consider making fundamental changes to our policing arrangements, such changes should be undertaken only in carefully measured steps comprising democratic public consultation, local experimentation, independent evaluation over several years, and yet further consultation.

The British policing tradition is a precious one which has been all too gravely hazarded in recent years as a result of the politicization of 'law and order' policy in general and policing policy in particular. Our debate on this issue needs to be grounded in the realities of crime and the community's multi-faceted responsibility for its control. It was once said of penal policy that changing the sentencing powers of the courts in the hope that criminal activity would thereby be quelled was the equivalent of putting up an umbrella and expecting the rain to stop. Much the same could be said about fashions in policing methods.

5

DILEMMAS STATED

The trends we have described lead us inescapably to the conclusion that senior police officers, and the politicians at local and national level to whom they are accountable, face difficult policy decisions. We think these difficulties revolve principally around four dilemmas to which the remainder of this text is largely devoted. We describe below what we believe these dilemmas to be before setting out the options we believe to be most attractive for responding to these dilemmas.

Dilemma One—**How is the almost insatiable demand from the public that it be provided locally with a visible uniformed police presence to be faced, given that the police increasingly doubt the operational effectiveness of generalized patrol-work, and governments are unlikely to provide resources so as to make such provision possible?**

The public, as we saw in Chapter 3, generally likes the idea of uniformed police patrols within its immediate neighbourhood. It wants more patrols. Every expression of public opinion that has been gathered has underscored this demand. The public particularly likes foot patrols and, as we saw in Chapter 4, when foot patrols are provided the public feels safer even if, statistically, it is no safer in terms of any likelihood, in the short-term at least, of its being a victim of crime. The public also likes the idea, no matter how romantic the notion, or how rose-tinted the implicit recollection that at some time in the recent past it was provided, that there will be continuity of allocation of constables to neighbourhoods such that local officers will be recognizable to residents, and officers in turn will recognize residents.

Chief constables know all of this very well, and many would like to provide more foot patrols, even if privately most of them question whether the public really understands the issues, not least the conflict between the routinely intoned demand for foot patrol and the equally loud demand that the police respond quickly to calls for assistance and deploy greater effort on clearing up those serious crimes about which the public is particularly concerned. Many chief constables have in recent years announced in their annual reports that they *are* devoting a greater proportion of their manpower to community patrols, though whether those undertakings have actually been translated into day-to-day reality on the ground is for various reasons open to doubt. Certainly the evidence has not been forthcoming and the public appears either not to believe it or to feel that it is not benefiting from it.

Some chief constables, however, privately express doubt about the whole notion of so-called permanent beat bobbies. They argue that the institution never really existed, at least in most areas. Further, they contend that the idea that most members of the community could ever know a local beat officer is implausible practically, not least because of the size those beats would have to be, the increased mobility of such a high proportion of the general population, and the fact that police officers, who are now among the best paid of public servants, no longer live or would be willing to live in the less prosperous neighbourhoods from which the majority of calls to the police come and where patrols are arguably most needed. Moreover, even were it practical to provide foot patrols specific to particular neighbourhoods an increasing number of chief constables do not think the policy would represent an efficient use of manpower. The police have too much to do, and no government would be willing to provide resources on the scale which, given the other demands made on police time, would make it possible. The police must prioritize more clearly, responding to calls only where there is a well-founded hope of an immediate crime-preventive dividend or where, when it appears a crime is involved, there is a reasonable prospect of that crime being cleared up. Those officers available for patrol work should be targeted on known offenders or offending 'hot spots'. Of course most chief constables do not find it politic to say much of this bluntly and openly, but an increasing number no longer believe that the public can or should be provided with the neighbourhood patrol officers they say they want. There are more effective uses to which police officers can be put.

Meanwhile the public, whether or not it has really noticed any diminution in the visible local uniformed police patrol presence, has in increasing numbers been giving its support to alternative forms of 'policing' presence. This has so far been largely in the form of advertising its own vigilance through neighbourhood watch schemes and all the other variants of 'watch' initiatives, schemes which, though initially pioneered and advocated by the police (though not in all areas and not by all chief constables), took off in the 1980s to such a popular extent that in many areas the police had to hang on to the tail of the dog they had unleashed in order to try and keep a semblance of control over it. In many areas, as some officers opposed to the concept predicted would happen, the dog has escaped the state police leash. The trend is so far modest, but as we argued in Chapter 2 an increasing number of residential communities have followed the example of commercial companies, groups of traders, and major site-based institutions and begun to employ the patrolling services of private security companies. Moreover, 'street watch' —neighbourhood watch groups patroling their neighbourhoods—an idea that Home Office ministers have encouraged against the advice of the police—is said to be taking off on a large scale. There is also some evidence of community groups engaging in fully-fledged vigilante activity, that is, effectively taking the law into their own hands: patrolling their areas, using force when they consider it necessary, and even meting out punishment to 'offenders' when they consider it justified.[1]

It is going too far to say that the latter developments are the straightforward *consequence* of a decline in state police patrolling activity or that these trends would be reversed were the government to fund and the police to deliver a greater number of permanent beat patrols. There is not the evidence to support so mechanical a relationship. But it is equally implausible to imagine that there is *no* relationship between these developments or that, were the state police largely to abandon general patrol work, as some senior officers now advocate, in order to devote more resources to targeted 'crime fighting', these trends would not sharply increase.

It goes without saying that our first dilemma is only a dilemma if one believes that a problem arises out of the state police not delivering a service the public is adamant it wants. We think this *does* represent a problem for the reasons we set out in Chapter 4. Police effectiveness, be it crime fighting or the maintenance of public tranquillity, depends on public trust, the pursuit of a common purpose, police use of publicly approved methods, personal contact and accessibility, and the flow of information from the public to the police. All the evidence shows—and the pattern is very different in other countries as many British tourists will today be well aware—that most people in Britain meet the police through casual street encounters.[2] Despite the witty use of alliteration by one leading police commentator, the politicization of policing during the last thirty years has *not* led, except for a minority of the populace, to the police being transformed from 'plods to pigs'.[3] Police officers are still asked the way and the time and most citizens want them visibly around so that that can continue. We believe it would be a grave loss, not least for the long-term effective control of crime, were that relationship between police and people to disappear.

Dilemma Two—**How is the growth of self-help and private policing provision to be responded to: should these burgeoning sectors be encouraged and brought into the fold, or should they be resisted on the ground that they represent sectional interests whose activity will undermine the integrity of the state?**

Our second dilemma is inextricably tied to our first, for like the first the growth of self-help and private policing is for some commentators not a problem. Some free market advocates, for example, see the case for subjecting aspects of policing to market competition in precisely the same terms as they have successfully argued the case for privatizing major public utilities like the supply of water or gas or running the railways.[4] The state police, they maintain, have become expensive, inefficient, and unresponsive to public demands by virtue of their monopoly of key services. There is no reason, they assert, why—subject to the accountability inherent in contractual obligations to local residents or government—the private security companies should not compete with the state police for the provision of local patrols or even the investigation of crime in exactly the same way that the government has now accepted that private security companies can manage prisons and autonomous agencies or commercial companies can provide forensic science services for which charges are made to police forces. By such measures will greater innovation and flexibility be achieved, improved responsiveness to customers delivered, and overall costs driven down. There is no essential issue of principle involved: whatever services are provided by whomsoever they will continue to be accountable to the law and to the government. And if it is thought necessary to devise new devices—registration, licensing, or even some form of inspectorate—to regulate this burgeoning market, then they have no problem with that. 'Responsible' security companies would welcome regulation so that the activities of a few rogue outfits do not spoil the pitch and the reputation of the industry generally.

Critics, by contrast, see a great many problems and maintain that there are vital principles at stake. If there is any role for the state then it is irreducibly that of providing for the external defence of the nation and the security of citizens at home. These services must be provided impartially, without fear or favour, respecting principles of justice and treating all citizens as equal. This is quintessentially the role of the state acting on behalf of all. The idea of a market in personal security, or of private corporations making a profit from decisions to invoke the criminal justice system, can only turn policing and punishment into processes that serve sectional interests, particularly those with the means to pay for them at the expense of the less well off. The privatization of these services must in the long-term generate vested interests seeking to promote policing and criminal justice interventions, not because they are in the public interest but because they will generate profits.

Critics also lodge practical and pragmatic objections to the privatization of policing and criminal justice. It is questionable whether any financial savings will be achieved from the commercial supply of services. The entry of commercial suppliers will necessitate regulatory mechanisms currently not necessary, which effectively means introducing a new layer of bureaucracy. Moreover, though commercial tactics may initially reduce the cost of services, once state services have been whittled away to the point of state dependency on commercial suppliers, and the major corporations have squeezed out the smaller companies to create an oligopoly, then prices will rise and rigidity set in such that no operational and fiscal advantage will have been achieved. Quite the contrary. By this stage, however, the state will have become dependent on commercial suppliers of services.

Market advocates answer that these objections make little sense. No one is suggesting that decisions to invoke criminal justice or allocate punishment should be made by persons other than crown servants, nor that commercially employed personnel should be given the power to deploy force. The state will remain totally responsible for the size and quality of the system.

Somewhere between these two often abstract positions lies the reality of what is happening on the ground. The bulk of the work currently undertaken by those corporations which have moved into the security field is not in the mainstream of policing or criminal justice. It involves the by now traditional activities of guarding cash in transit and providing surveillance of private premises, mostly commercial premises and the grounds and buildings of major institutions. However, the latter activity is expanding rapidly because of the growth of public services provided on private property—hospitals, shopping malls, higher education institutions, and now, similarly, railways and so on. These areas of private property almost entirely privately policed are assuming greater importance because the services provided on them are vital to the public generally. It follows that the manner in which they are policed—whether particular groups are excluded or harassed, for example—has a general bearing on social equity and justice. And though the activity is as yet relatively little developed, the same issues arise out of, for example, local authorities employing private security personnel to police council estates and other properties. Moreover, though in Britain private security personnel have no greater powers than the ordinary citizen, the evidence indicates that they are deferred to as figures of authority, and the fact that they may be trained to use force and are dressed in uniforms or protective clothing means that they are better prepared to deploy force when they consider it necessary and justified.[5] It follows that, *de facto*, many private security personnel now occupy important positions of trust and authority.

The question therefore arises whether private security

companies and their personnel are worthy of the trust invested in them. The state police—who, it has to be said, have both a public responsibility and a vested interest with regard to this question—have suggested that some private security personnel are not worthy of trust and that this is socially dangerous.

This issue has assumed particular significance because of the current government's apparent openness to propositions that mainstream criminal justice services might be contracted out to commercial or other providers. In 1987, Douglas Hurd, then Home Secretary, announced in response to a suggestion from the House of Commons Home Affairs Committee, that it was unthinkable that prisons be managed commercially. But today, nine years later, five prisons are so managed and the guards within those prisons are not members of Her Majesty's Prison Service but employees of Group 4, UK Detention Services, and so on. These privately employed custody officers, as they are called by the legislation introduced to cover their duties, have coercive powers, though the officers concerned are vetted and their performance is overseen by a crown servant statutorily appointed for the purpose. This development at the core of the penal system has opened up the suggestion that some policing tasks might equally be contracted out, and certainly the police interpreted the setting up of the Home Office Inquiry into Police Core and Ancillary Tasks in 1994 as an exercise which might lead to just such proposals. In the event the scrutiny resulted in no major challenges to the current organization of policing. However, given that such proposals *are* now being made in other common law jurisdictions how long will it be before they are made here?[6]

To conclude, therefore, a 'market' in policing, is developing whether we like it or not. As a result the boundary between state, commercial, and voluntary police services is becoming increasingly complex and blurred. If present trends continue there is a very real danger that we may end up with the worst of all possible worlds: an increasingly centralized state police system in which officers are given ever-growing powers and become increasingly specialized, alongside an anarchic plethora of more or less local unregulated self-help and private police/security services in the hands of sectional interests which can afford to pay for them or are able to mobilize them.

Dilemma Three—Given all the evidence that the incidence of crime is only to a very limited extent related to anything that the police do, where should the locus of responsibility for crime prevention and community safety lie: should it remain with the police who currently have the task and wish to keep it, or should it be given to others whose involvement would be appropriate but who show no great enthusiasm for taking it on?

All the actions taken by the police and criminal justice agencies should ideally be directed at and achieve crime prevention, whether those actions involve the identification, detention, and change of those persons responsible for crime or the example those exercises have for onlooking actual or potential offenders. There is a division of labour regarding these decisions within the criminal justice and penal systems and a reasonably settled set of understandings as to who is and should be responsible for what. There is less agreement, however, about who is or should be responsible for what we have termed *primary crime prevention* policy—that is the reduction of crime opportunities and motivations without reference to criminals and potential criminals, apart from the self-evident caveat that all theories of crime and thus crime prevention must be grounded on an analysis of crime patterns and offending behaviour.[7]

Since arguably everything the police do should have crime preventive consequences—the very presence of a visible patrolling police officer is generally assumed to constitute a form of crime prevention, which explains the popularity of the device—it has traditionally been assumed that crime prevention is *the* paramount police role (the 1829 Act which established the Metropolitan Police stated that it was their primary goal) and the police have *naturally* assumed responsibility for dispensing basic crime prevention advice. All police forces have long since had specialist 'crime prevention officers', part of either their criminal investigation or community relations departments. The fact that 'crime prevention' has been designated a specialism, but the lack of agreement as to where that specialism should be located organizationally, reflects the uncertainty surrounding the activity within the police. All the evidence demonstrates its marginality, low status, and low priority. Crime prevention specialists are poorly regarded by their police colleagues (not 'real' police work), few of them are employed (less than 1 per cent of all personnel is the usual estimate), they have low status and are allocated minimal resources both locally and nationally (the usual joke is to refer to the Portakabin behind the headquarters of the Staffordshire Police where until recently at least four officers had responsibility for training most of the nation's crime prevention officers).[8] Thus despite much rhetoric within the police and Home Office about crime prevention being the central thread running through all policing activity, with all officers having a duty to contribute to the task, the organizational reality has historically comprised a peripheral specialist preoccupation with security measures, the derided 'locks, bolts and bars', and liaison with community 'crime prevention panels', groups often dominated by shopkeepers.

This narrow police record has to be set alongside the observation, stressed throughout this book, that the incidence of crime is only marginally related to policing policy. This has for some time been recognized in Whitehall where, theoretically at least, crime prevention is now seen as something about which all government departments should be concerned. To begin with this global approach concentrated on 'situational' prevention, reducing the physical opportunities for crime by means of 'target hardening', enhancing natural surveillance of crime-prone sites and objects, and so on. However, with the publication in 1991 of the deliberations of the Home Office Standing Conference on Crime Prevention (the Morgan Report), attention shifted to the various factors which may predispose potential offenders to take the multifold opportunities to commit crime and, at the other end of the continuum, might assist victims to overcome crime and potential victims to resist it.

It had by this stage become commonplace to talk of 'partnerships' between various agencies, including the police, and the community to prevent crime or promote 'community safety', the latter now being the preferred term, given the narrow security and police connotations of crime prevention. Various multi-agency crime preventive initiatives were promoted by the Government via the Home Office—most notably the 'Safer Cities' programme—and ministers began promulgating the concept of 'active citizenship'. From now on, it appeared, crime prevention was to be the responsibility of everyone.

Tackling the causes of crime
- Family support initiatives
- Youth programmes
- Community developments programmes and neighbourhood initiatives
- Pre-school programmes
- Alcohol and drug misuse prevention schemes
- Education and school based programmes
- Work with offenders and their families
- Employment and training programmes
- Debt counselling

Reducing the opportunities for crime to be committed
- Improved security in homes, public buildings and business premises
- Improved lighting in streets and public areas
- Improved security and design of residential areas, city centres, and car parks
- Security considerations in planning and managing public transport
- Safety considerations in the management of licensed premises
- Good management and delivery of local services
- Adequate levels of preventive patrolling

Tackling specific crime problems
- Domestic burglary
- Domestic violence
- Auto crime
- Racially motivated crime
- Crimes against children
- Crimes against the elderly

Helping victims of crime and reducing the fear of crime
- Victim support schemes
- Self-protection initiatives
- Securing positive publicly for successful initiatives

Fig. 41 A portfolio of community safety activities: some examples

Source: Morgan Report (1991)

Such developments logically prompted certain fundamental questions: should there be a lead agency for crime prevention or community safety? Should that lead agency be the police and, if not the police, then who?

As far as the police are concerned the answers to these questions are fairly straightforward. Everything they do is ultimately related to crime prevention, they have assumed responsibility for the activity and they are the custodians of all the principal data on which any crime preventive policy must surely be grounded. It makes no sense, therefore, for them not to continue taking the lead and co-ordinating role. Against this, however, is the view that primary crime prevention, particularly that broad view of primary crime prevention which now goes by the name of community safety, is never likely to enjoy high priority in police circles: the concept is too diffuse and the activity involves none of the specific measures of performance and pay-off to which police commitments are increasingly geared. Community safety is ideally the task for those authorities with the widest remit for the provision of public facilities and the delivery of local services. The difficulty, however, is that in recent times local government has both been reorganized and stripped of many of its traditional responsibilities. In the present climate it is unlikely that central government will provide adequate resources to underpin any new allocation of responsibility for community safety. Therein lies the dilemma which, arguably, we cannot afford *not* to resolve.

Dilemma Four—**Given the mobility of the population and the globalization of some crime, how should policing be organized? Does it make sense to retain the relatively small-scale local police forces we now have? Or should we be thinking about the creation of national or even a European police force?**

It is one of the ironies of late twentieth-century social policy that 'community' is the title designed to make acceptable so many policy initiatives—community care, community medicine, community policing, and so on—during a period when there is arguably less of a sense of community than at any point in our social history. But that of course is the explanation of the fashion. The promotion of 'community' suggests the restoration of a world that we have lost but hanker for. It follows that we must beware that concepts like 'community policing' will prove little more than rhetorical devices masking an implausible aspiration and a barren operation. Does it any longer make sense to have the local policing infrastructure we have inherited from the nineteenth century?

We need to remind ourselves first of a few constitutional and administrative facts. There are currently forty-three police forces in England and Wales, forty-one of them provincial and related to one or more counties, and two covering London—the Metropolitan Police Force, by far the largest force, and the minute City of London Police Force which covers the approximate square mile of the City. In Scotland there are eight local police forces and Northern Ireland is policed by the Royal Ulster Constabulary. There are other police forces—the British Transport Police, the Royal Parks Police, the UK Atomic Energy Authority Police, and so on—but, unlike most countries in Europe, we have no national police force. The Metropolitan Police provide some national services (the protection of Parliament, the diplomatic corps, and the Royal Family, for example) and with the end of the Cold War MI5 now has a new role in relation to international terrorism and organized crime.[9] But, ever since the beginning of the nineteenth century when the spectre of centralized revolutionary France lay before us, there has been an almost symbolic political abhorrence of the idea of a national police force, as if its creation might spell the onset of a police state.

The proposition that this would be the necessary or even likely outcome is, of course, nonsense. Other stable democracies within Europe—notably the Scandinavian countries—have national police forces. In practice, policing in England and Wales is already highly centralized.[10] The Home Secretary exercises powers to supply common services for all police forces and must use his considerable powers so as to promote general police efficiency. Because central government supplies the bulk of policing expenditure, and because the Government has in recent years tightened its purse strings in this field as in all others, the capacity of the local police authorities, each of which is charged with securing 'the maintenance of an adequate and efficient police force for the area', to determine the overall shape of policing policy, has been progressively curtailed. In practice the local police authorities often made little use of their vestigial powers even when they might have exercised them.[11]

Increased centralization of policing policy has been engineered by means of a number of mechanisms. First, there has been progressive reduction in the number of police forces. Prior to the 1964 Police Act there were 123 forces, later dropping to forty-seven and then to the current total of forty-three. The Police and Magistrates' Courts Act 1994 which amended the constitutional structure for the governance of the police in several important respects, provides the Home Secretary with power to amalgamate forces should he or she consider that step necessary. Secondly, chief constables, who are charged with the direction and control of their force, a provision which has been interpreted by the courts to signify their sole responsibility for 'operational' matters, act in an increasingly corporate manner under the national ægis of the Association of Chief Police Officers (ACPO), an organization which in recent years has developed a series of committees, which formulates policy documents, and is routinely consulted by the Home Office.

Thirdly, the Home Secretary increasingly promulgates policy by means of Home Office circulars issued to all forces, though most usually ACPO is involved from the earliest stages in the drafting of such circulars. Although the circulars are for most part couched in the form of advice, the advice is generally read locally as a requirement which, by one means or another, will be and can be enforced. Fourthly, as far as senior officers aspiring to be chief constables or to take up other national posts are concerned, compliance is ensured by the knowledge that Home Office sponsorship is necessary for their advancement. The Home Office has the power to approve shortlists of candidates interviewed by police authorities and to veto their final selection. Fifthly, there have been developed a number of national or regional police intelligence agencies to deal with a number of issues, appointments to which are decided with the Home Office. Top police officers are 'cosmopolitans' not 'locals'.[12] Sixthly, as far as the police authorities are concerned compliance is ensured through the allocation of the police grant in accordance with 'value for money' rules and 'performance indicators' based on computerized management information promulgated by the enhanced Inspectorate of Constabulary (HMCIC) which annually inspects all forces and may fail to certify a force as efficient, thereby enabling the Home Secretary to withhold all or part of its grant. Seventhly, the work of HMCIC is informed by successive reports from the Audit Commission which has recently published a series of appraisals of aspects of operational police performance. It is not without significance that the Audit Commission has itself stated that: 'The balance has now tilted so far towards the centre that the role of the local authorities in the tripartite structure has been significantly diminished. Account-ability is blurred and financial and management incentives are out of step'.[13] Centralization had gone so far that the theoreti-cally equilateral triangle had become isosceles. By the beginning of the 1990s there had almost developed a national police force *de facto* while there was maintained the *de jure* constitutional fiction of local police forces locally accountable.

The latest development in the constitutional saga of the gover-nance of the police remains controversial and its outcome uncer-tain. This concerns the provisions of the Police and Magistrates Courts Act 1994 which came into force in April 1995. Police authorities are now independent precepting bodies no longer integrated with local government structures. Their membership now includes appointees as well as elected councillors and mag-istrates (generally in a ratio of 5:9:3 respectively), the Home Secretary exercising control over the final shortlist from which a local selection panel appoints the independent members. In addition the Home Secretary is enabled to set national policing objectives and publicize the performance of all forces against national performance indicators. Given that the Act also paves the way for the Home Secretary to issue fixed-term contracts for all officers of the rank of superintendent and above, it has been suggested that these developments might lead to tighter control from the centre with senior officers feeling obliged to comply with central wishes rather than local needs and priorities, and with central wishes couched increasingly in the form of statisti-cal, and probably meaningless, targets to the detriment of more qualitatively imaginative local policing strategies.[14]

Yet it is possible to interpret other provisions in the 1994 Act so as to give limited substance to the Government's claim that the Act represents the devolution of policing policy. Thus, though all forces will henceforth receive a strictly cash limited police grant, chief constables and police authorities will jointly enjoy greater autonomy and thus flexibility in deciding how to use their budgets. They will have greater freedom to decide how many officers to employ and how to mix staff (the balance between officers and civilians), vehicles, buildings, and equipment spending though, ultimately, in the event of an adverse report from HMCIC, the Home Secretary is empowered to fix minimum budgets. Furthermore, every police authority (not the chief constable, though the text is 'drafted' by him or her) is now obliged annually to produce a prospective policing plan which must, *inter alia*, consider any views obtained from the police community consultative committees (PCCGs) universally established under section 106 of the 1984 Police and Criminal Evidence Act, and include performance targets for both the national objectives determined by the Home Secretary *and* whatever objectives the police authority has decided locally to pursue. These new responsibilities may, contrary to the cynical expectations of those critics who see almost every provision in the Act as yet another step in the destruction of local policing and accountability, serve to stimulate greater commitment on the part of police authorities to the process of formulating local policing policies than their predecessors ever demonstrated.[15]

Analysis of the first set of local policing plans indicates that they vary greatly in length, detail, and quality. Only a small minority describe precisely how local consultations contributed to their formulation or what local partnership arrangements with community groups or other agencies will contribute to the achievement of police objectives. A majority, however, stipulate local objectives and set targets for the achievement of both national and local objectives, asserting that they will regularly monitor and report on their achievement. Measurements of public satisfaction with local police services figure prominently among local performance indicators.[16] After this first round, chief constables and police authorities will almost certainly watch closely each others' interpretation of their new responsibilities, and 'good practice' will emerge gradually. How the 1994 Act works out in practice will ultimately depend on how the Home Secretary interprets his responsibilities and whether the Government wishes to stifle or encourage local policing initiatives. If the latter are encouraged then there will be no shortage of ambitious police officers wishing to establish their national reputations by pursuing exciting local experiments.

All of which leads us to the need for and value of local policing responses. We have no doubts on this issue. Local policing responsive to local conditions is vital.

It is true that the British population is now geographically more mobile than ever before. There is a gradual population shift from the North to the South and from the major metropolitan conurbations to the more rural hinterlands. Upgrading the quality of one's dwelling in response to income, or relocating according to employment need or social taste, has become a normal household career step. Three quarters of all households now have the use of a car, nearly a quarter of them two cars. People now commute further and regularly undertake journeys to visit places or people that would have been unthinkable to most people a few decades ago. The idea of community based on *residence* has been eroded in favour communities of *affiliation* or *interest* maintained at a distance, increasingly by electronic means. The size of households has also declined, with one in three now comprising a single person.

These changes in the way we live have had implications for the pattern of crime. 'Natural' surveillance of premises and residences has suffered: we are now less likely to know our neighbours or the identity of persons we see in the street and many households are unoccupied for easily identified and predictable hours of the day or days of the week. The expanding property inventories, including the cars, that we accumulate are easy prey to those inclined to take the new opportunities. Furthermore, offenders, like the law abiding, travel, or their offending tastes—joy riding, for example—mirror the habits of those against whom they offend. An increasing proportion of crime traverses national, let alone county and therefore local constabulary, boundaries. Rounding up the usual local suspects does not provide a solution to some of the dawn raids which are now easily mounted from motorways across the country. At the end of the diverse local car theft chain lies a burgeoning international market for prestigious cars, broken up or disguised, exported, and never recovered. The electronic communications with which most of us play have transformed commercial life and rendered many of the currency and other controls traditionally exercised by sovereign states largely nugatory. This has opened up new vistas for fraud and enabled drug traffickers and organized criminals to wash the proceeds from their enterprises in complex ways almost impenetrable to even specialized law enforcement agencies. Does it really make sense, therefore, to hang on to the Borsetshire Constabulary? Does Borsetshire not, like the Ambridge village bobby (written out of *The Archers* Radio 4 script almost twenty years ago), belong to the conditions of yesteryear? Should we not be reaching for the integrated communicative efficiencies of an English Central Intelligence Agency or Europol?

We shall consider these propositions in Chapter 6. Before we do so, however, we should note that though much crime—including by definition much serious crime—traverses local administrative boundaries, the vast majority does not. Most violence, for example, takes place within the home between people who habitually live together, or is engaged in by young men, sometimes banded together, pursuing amorous or territorial disputes in the neighbourhood clubs and pubs where they regularly take their pleasures. Most burglaries and thefts from stores and cars are not engaged in by professional teams casing joints and using the services of discreet fences far away. They are more typically the occasional opportunistic offences of young people operating within a few miles of where they live. Moreover, it needs to be remembered that the chains that lead to the international professional criminal networks generally have highly localized and very amateurish ragged ends, habitual drug users well known to the local police, for example, selling a bit of this and that in order to raise the funds to feed their habits. Moreover the ecology of crime is for the most part a very localized affair, a patchwork of 'hot spots' and quiet zones symbiotically related to particular residential settings and entertainment foci. These patterns are best understood and policed by officers familiar with the idiosyncrasies of the patches to which ideally they have a long-term attachment and commitment.

There is a need to track the national and international networks within which some crime now thrives. But it remains vital to maintain local policing understandings. Therein lies the dilemma which any future organization of policing, including its accompanying accountability mechanisms, must resolve.

6

OPTIONS FOR CHANGE

When describing trends with regard to crime, policing, and the social context of policing in Britain in Chapters 1 and 2, and the characteristics of, and the dilemmas confronting, British policing in Chapers 3, 4 and 5, we noted that most of what is happening in Britain is in line with developments elsewhere in the industrialized world. It is not surprising, therefore, that policing analysts in other countries are reaching conclusions similar to those to which we are moving. A striking example is provided in a recent book by David Bayley entitled *Police for the Future*.[1] Though his diagnosis and recommendations are geared largely to American conditions, Bayley draws on data collected world-wide, Britain included. We think his analysis is worth summarizing, if only to enable us to delineate where we think British trends, conditions, and, thus, solutions, are and should be distinctive.

Bayley is categorical that the police are in a bind. They cost a lot of money, yet their effectiveness is limited. Their core traditional strategies are of dubious value. They are being put under increased pressure to provide and demonstrate value for money. Their legitimacy is no longer unquestioned. They are facing competition. A real question mark hangs over parts of their mandate. Bayley queries what it is that the police should be asked and expected to do.[2]

Some of Bayley's broad conclusions regarding policing in North America chime well with the situation in Britain. Our police also are in a bind. They are expected to achieve more than they can conceivably deliver. As a service they are being put under increased pressure. Before we address the four major policing dilemmas on which we have chosen to focus, therefore, it may be helpful to see how Bayley answers his own question: what is it the police should be asked and expected to do?

Bayley does not employ the distinction which we have used

between primary, secondary, and tertiary crime prevention, but it is more or less clear that when he talks about crime prevention he refers to most of the measures that might be included under the heading of primary crime prevention, that is, the general environmental conditions which generate the incidence of crime. When he refers to law enforcement he refers to the business of identifying offences and offenders and assembling material for the prosecution of the latter, all of which activity may have secondary crime preventive effects. The key question at issue, as far as Bayley is concerned, is the degree to which in the future the police are to take responsibility for primary crime prevention. He outlines five possible options.

First, there is what he terms 'dishonest law enforcement', which is pretty well what he says is happening at present. 'Dishonest law enforcement' therefore represents more of the same. That is, the police claim to be preventing crime and promise to do it, but actually provide only what he calls 'authoritative intervention and symbolic justice', both necessary and valuable functions but not adequate for primary crime prevention. Thus, public fear of crime is exploited because the value of simple law enforcement is oversold.

The second option, what Bayley terms 'determined crime prevention', occurs when the police take the lead role in analysing the factors associated with the motivation and opportunity to commit crime, recommend what policies should be undertaken by all the agencies whose work has a bearing on those factors, and implement, co-ordinate, and evaluate those policies. It involves the police moving to the centre stage of economic and social policy, a social engineering maximalist role, more interventionist even than that recommended at the end of the 1970s by John Alderson, the former Chief Constable for Devon and Cornwall. 'Determined crime prevention' requires that the police take this central role because, Bayley argues, they have the resources and the information, they are continuously on the spot, they are a power within local communities, and they can deliver in a way that no other agency can. They are best equipped to determine the degree to which force and security should be mixed with ameliorative welfarist intervention, to prevent crime successfully. They are capable of being, as Bayley puts it, the community's resident practical criminologists.

'Honest law enforcement' is Bayley's third option. It involves the police disavowing responsibility for, and the capacity to provide, primary crime prevention thereby cutting the Gordian knot which has been their self-imposed bugbear—namely, promising something they cannot deliver. Henceforth, the police will only do that which they are capable of doing well—authoritative intervention, symbolic justice, traffic regulation, and a few administrative responsibilities—with no pretence that these functions, even well-performed, have much impact on the incidence of crime. 'Honest law enforcement' represents 'old-fashioned policing without the "community" frills', it minimizes the police role, and it should enable politicians to keep a firm lid on the police budget. This is an option that has echoes of the 'minimal policing' model outlined by left realists in Britian in the mid-1980s.[3]

To these three principal options Bayley adds two hybrid options. 'Efficient law enforcement' involves scrapping or radically reorganizing those aspects of law enforcement which contribute nothing to crime prevention and reallocating the resources so as to make aspects of what generally goes by the name of 'community' and 'problem solving' policing more robust—devolving to local police commanders certain budgetry and personnel decisions, liaising and consulting with communities, conducting crime pattern analyses, mobilizing citizens for crime prevention and targeting identified crime-related problems. The restructuring of law enforcement might involve, *inter alia*, civilianizing many police tasks and prioritizing others. Some police tasks—certain administrative functions or aspects of traffic regulation—might even be hived off to other agencies.

An alternative approach Bayley terms 'stratified crime prevention'. It involves limiting responsibility for crime prevention to the activity of front-line uniformed neighbourhood officers, those most closely in touch with communities. Bayley sees this as importing the teamwork tradition of small-town American police forces to the major cities—local patrol officers working closely with other agencies in areas to which they develop a high level of commitment because they are more or less regularly assigned to them.

These, according to Bayley, are the principal choices confronting the police. The choices, he maintains, will have to be made. The question is whether the choices will be made sensibly and openly. With this latter proposition we wholeheartedly agree. Indeed, our view that there is need for a thoroughgoing public debate about policing is the rationale for this book. Policing is too important an aspect of public policy to be left to the police. It is fundamental to our quality of community life. There needs to take place a widespread public debate on how we wish our police to be organized, how we wish them to relate to us, what we want them to do, what methods we think they should employ and how we want them to be accountable to us. How this public debate will best be initiated and fostered is a topic to which we return at the end of this Chapter. We need first, however, to consider whether the overall choices facing us in Britain are quite as Bayley describes them. We think not, and for the following reasons.

First, despite what we have said in previous chapters about the growing emphasis on 'crime-fighting' within much current talk about policing, we do not think that it would be entirely accurate to describe a continuation of the policing *status quo* in Britain as 'dishonest law enforcement'. It is true that the police in Britain, as elsewhere, often ask for additional resources and powers. But in recent years our senior police officers have tended to eschew claims that the number of officers employed, or the powers and resources available to them, determine the incidence of crime to any significant extent . Though police officers on the ground may, in conformity with the 'canteen culture', see themselves as the 'thin blue line' standing between order and anarchy, in recent times most chief constables have tended not to talk publicly about policing in this way. Our senior police officers are in the main well-educated and sophisticated professionals who know very well the limitations of what their forces can deliver. They are familiar with the research literature. Consequently, in spite of the rhetoric to which our politicans are increasingly given, it is accepted orthodxy among those who have considered the evidence—and most of our chief constables scrutinize the evidence closely—that crime levels are largely attributable to the kinds of structural factors we outlined in Chapter 1, and over which the police exercise precious little influence. There may not be as much honesty as there ought to be about the effectiveness of much that the police do, but few serious participants in British policing circles argue that law enforcement is, to quote Bayley's critique, 'an adequate solution to the problem of crime'.[4]

Our starting point, therefore, is different from Bayley's. However much we may regret that British Government policy, as exemplified by the 1996 White Paper, *Protecting the Public*, seems intent on copying some of the excesses of American 'law and order' fashion, we must not lose sight of the fact that in many respects the policing and criminal justice policy scene in the United States remains quite alien. Were our murder rate comparable to that of the US we should have 5,000, not 700, recorded murders each year. If we used prisons as the United States does, we should have a prison population approaching 300,000 rather than 55,000. We have well-advertised problems of police rule-bending, but nothing, fortunately, approaching the tradition of police and local government corruption which is widespread in the United States. There may be a disturbing growth in the use of guns, particularly among the drug-trading fraternity in some of our metropolitan centres, but we are not prey to the collective madness of widespread gun possession and use which disfigures life in the United States. Moreover, our police continue to be against being armed on a routine basis, and our politicians continue to vote against the reintroduction of the death penalty. Though those with liberal sensibilities may feel they are surrounded by politicians and tabloid newspapers with crudely punitive views, compared with the United States there remains in the UK a relatively strong body of opinion that ratcheting up our capacity and resort to force is not really the answer to our crime problems. This is particularly true at senior levels in the police service. Whilst, as will by now be clear, we are very concerned about some of the trends in British policing, we recognize that it is more sophisticated than the description 'dishonest law enforcement' would imply.

This leads us to the second aspect of Bayley's account of possible policing scenarios from which we depart. 'Determined crime prevention' is not, as he describes it, an even remotely plausible role for the police, and this would have been clearer had Bayley made the distinction between primary and secondary crime prevention which we emphasized in Chapter 4. We are not talking here about political traditions, as Bayley suggests, of maximalist or minimalist conceptions of the police role.

Primary crime prevention, conceived as that which addresses the motivation and opportunity to commit crime—and ideally the concomitant consideration of whether behaviour which we wish to discourage is best curtailed by the use of the criminal law or by other measures—involves the whole panoply of socio-economic policy, which is necessarily the directing and co-ordinating role of government itself. Primary crime prevention could not conceivably be the task of the police unless we were by definition envisaging the formation of a police state—a prospect well beyond the vague danger of authoritarianism to which Bayley refers. Bayley himself rules out adoption of his 'determined crime prevention' option on the ground that it does not fit with the liberal-democratic tradition. We rule it out because serious primary crime prevention could not possibly be undertaken by the police even were they to hold the co-ordinating ring when it came to the delivery of all local public services, which they do not.

Our third reservation is that what Bayley refers to as 'honest law enforcement'—the police disavowing a primary crime preventive role and retreating into a laager of authoritative intervention and law enforcement—runs the risk of implying that the police *can* engage in *effective* law enforcement without promoting aspects of the community-style policing which Bayley generally links with crime preventive effort. This is an error and, to be fair to him, Bayley elsewhere in his book provides all the evidence which shows it to be an error. The police, as we showed in Chapter 4, are fundamentally dependent on public trust, co-operation, and assistance regarding their knowledge of the incidence of crime and the identity of offenders if they are to be effective law enforcers. We doubt that Bayley would disagree with this conclusion, but his use of the model 'honest law enforcement' implies that there could be effective law enforcement without elements of what he refers to as 'stratified crime prevention'. We shall return to this point because we think there is a real danger that the government, and some chief constables in Britain, wish to pursue what they may be tempted to describe as 'honest law enforcement' *as if it could be effective* and thus honest. We take the view that such a strategy would be neither honest nor effective. Indeed, such an approach would more correctly be located under the heading 'dishonest law enforcement'.

Fourthly, we need to highlight one significant difference between the United States and Britain which is vital to Bayley's analysis and which should make us think rather less parochially about policing possibilities in Britain. In 1990 the US had 12,228 local police forces, 3,093 sheriffs' departments, forty-eight state police forces, and the Federal Bureau of Investigation—an extraordinarily diversified and decentralized policing system compared to that in Britain.[5] This pattern of policing is interesting because it provides a striking example of how decentralized a policing system *can* be. In Britain we are dominated by the misleading governmental *assumption* that so decentralized a system is almost by definition ineffective, inefficient, and incompatible with an advanced industrial economy. The most recent example of this thinking is provided in the 1993 White Paper on *Police Reform* in which it was suggested that a new round of police force amalgamations would probably make for greater police efficiency.[6] Provision for such amalgamations has been made in the Police and Magistrates' Courts Act 1994. But the extreme *contrast* between small and large police forces in the US naturally influences the thinking of American police analysts in a manner inappropriate to Britain.

In Britain we do not have the organizational extremes characteristic of American police forces. Certainly we have small and large forces—the Metropolitan Police with its 28,000 officers is more than thirty times the size of our smallest forces like the City of London, Dyfed Powys, and Gwent. But this is as nothing compared to the contrast between the New York or Los Angeles Police Departments and the hundreds of local county forces and sheriff's offices, each of which has merely a handful of officers. In the US a central issue for analysts is whether the sorts of community-integrated policing methods pursued by small rural and town forces—in which officers are generalists and are reasonably well-known local figures—can be adopted in the major metropolises by the big city police forces. And secondly, to the extent that it can, what the implications of this will be for command structures, which tend to be different.

In Britain we have no similar hills to climb. Excluding the Metropolitan Police, the difference in scale between our smallest and largest forces is not so large that it has radical differentiating implications for their organization and administration. Further, though members of our largest metropolitan area forces—West Midlands, Strathclyde, Greater Manchester, and particularly the Metropolitan Police—are apt to quip that officers from smaller rural forces operate like 'Noddy in Toyland', knowing nothing about the difficulties of 'real' policing, and thus that their operational experience is largely to be discounted,[7] the truth is that the differences are not so great. There is virtually no force in the country, even the most rural, that does not include its difficult urban pocket. Even the largest metropolitan forces with high crime areas are, for the most part, made up of quiet residential suburban swathes the crime and policing characteristics of which are not very different from many rural areas which commuting and tourism have in recent years made much more difficult to police. Our police forces are *all* perfectly familiar with flexible organizational methods whereby local police administrative areas and officers are able to deliver differentiated policing strategies appropriate to the needs of the area. The pattern which Bayley refers to as 'stratified crime prevention'—the option he favours most and which he derives from the small-town American policing tradition—is, or has been, more or less commonplace in *all* British police forces. The question in Britain is less whether such a system can organizationally be forged, but whether there is a political and police command will to maintain it.

Fifthly, Bayley's analysis concentrates disproportionately on police responsibility for policing. He refers to the competition which *the police* face but thereafter his analysis of the available policy options tends to treat the police as if they operated in a policing vacuum which, as we have repeatedly stressed, they do not. They are part, albeit the most important part, of an increasingly complex and diffuse patchwork quilt of policing activity. The options open to *the police* must incorporate consideration of their role in the overall framework of *policing*.

For all these reasons we believe there may be less need in Britain to clear the ground about fundamental questions regarding the role of the police than Bayley's discussion implies. We are quite content, as was the Independent Committee on the Role and Responsibilities of the Police, to endorse the police service's current Statement of Common Purpose:

The purpose of the police service is to uphold the law fairly and firmly; to prevent crime; to pursue and bring to justice those who break the law;

to keep the Queen's peace; to protect, help and reassure the community; and to be seen to do this with integrity, common sense and sound judgement.

We think this is a perfectly reasonable basis from which to proceed for two reasons, First, because the statement is balanced and acknowledges the multi-faceted role of the police and the multi-functional aspects of nearly all the key activities the police perform. When a police officer is on foot patrol she or he is arguably contributing towards all of the purposes included in the Statement of Common Purpose. The officer's presence should serve to reassure, protect, and deter and the officer is available to persuade, intervene, or act decisively, if necessary by deploying force, if the public interest is best served by so doing. We are not complacent about the need to make the best use of police resources. As we hope to demonstrate, we are not woolly about the police role and we are concerned about value for money. But we are adamant that what is to count as '*best use*' of police resources must acknowledge the importance of *all* the purposes currently endorsed in the Statement of Common Purpose. Though some observers may flinch at the inclusion in the Statement of the word 'firmly', we are content. The vital point is that 'preserving the Queen's peace' enjoys a prominent place: in the Government's 1993 White Paper 'preserving the Queen's peace' was left out of the formulae and 'fighting' crime, or 'waging war against crime' was not just brought in but given first place. That was a dangerous distortion of what the police do and what we believe the British public, when it thinks the issue through, wants the police to do. In response to this it might be contended that the Home Secretary's key national objectives are more rounded, including as they do both a crime prevention objective and the goal: 'to provide high visibility policing to reassure the public'. Nonetheless, it remains the case that leading politicians in both main parties articulate a largely 'crime-fighting' vision of policing. To the extent that they recognize other elements of policing, one is left in little doubt about how the primary task of the police is perceived. We would like to see the Statement of Common Purpose endorsed explicitly by the Home Secretary and his Shadow.

The second reason why we are content to stand by the Statement of Common Purpose is because the questions begged by it, and there are many, will not be solved by formulating a longer and more complex statement about the role and respon-sibiities of *the police*. What is required, and what the government has so far resisted doing, is the definition of the role and respon-sibilities of *other complementary* actors vital to policing and the prevention of crime. We shall address this issue at several points below.

There is one final introductory point that we wish to reiterate before we turn to our four central delemmas:

There are no simple solutions to the crime and policing problems that confront us.

We have made this elementary point before, and we make no excuse for stressing it again. We understand why politicians, when confronted with brief opportunities to make their mark with a wide public, resort to sound-bite slogans, be it 'understanding a little less and condemning a little more', or being 'tough on crime, and tough on the causes of crime', or promising so many thou-sand additional police officers, or making it obligatory for judges to lock up particular categories of offenders for longer. Politicians have to employ rhetorical slogans and symbolic gestures to har-ness the attention and gather the power which will enable serious policies to be constructed for the long term. But these slogans and gestures must not be accepted as substitutes for serious policies. If we proceed incrementally to add a police power here, or slap on an additional sentence there, the public will be ill-served. We believe that the incidence of crime, and the task of preventing it, is too serious a business to be trivialized by a political agenda of police powers or sentencing tariffs. We need rather to address the question of how we think about ourselves as a community and how, as part of that exercise, we police our neighbourhoods and better safeguard our communal safety.

Dilemma One—**How is the almost insatiable demand from the public that it be provided with a visible uniformed police to be faced given that the police increasingly doubt the worthwhile-ness of generalized patrol-work, and governments are unlikely to provide resources so as to make such provision possible?**

The most likely way in which this dilemma will be handled is for the police largely to deny it. For them to claim that they are of course committed to community policing as part of their concept of a police 'service', including the provision of visible local patrols with whatever degree of mobility for officers is considered feasible and appropriate. In some places this stance is likely to be underlined by attractive innovative gestures. In the same way that some police officers can now be seen on roller-blades or mountain bikes in the best-known fun spots in North America so we should expect to see similar apparitions in places like Covent Garden, along the front at Brighton or Blackpool or in the gardens at Stratford-on-Avon. But whatever the occasional street theatre accoutrements, and despite the existence of a specific national objective, the behind-the-scenes reality is likely to be more and more neighbourhood patrol officers being abstracted for other duties that are considered to be more pressing in operational terms. A study conducted for the Home Office in 1989-90 found that only 18 per cent of patrol officers were what might be termed 'community constables' and they were typically abstracted from their beats to peform other duties for 20 per cent of their time.[8] We think that the proportionate availability of officers for the sort of visible neighbourhood patrol that the public will continue to say it wants will almost certainly further decline. The disjunction between community policing rhetoric and reality will continue to grow.

Despite the apparent popularity of 'community policing' and 'problem-oriented policing' currently, it is unlikely that we shall see any significant increase in dedicated patrol by police officers enjoying a high degree of continuous attachment to particular neighbourhoods. In fact, this type of activity, already under pressure, is, if anything, likely to diminish. Relief (reactive) patrols will of course continue and will predominate. Where they are supplemented, this is likely to be by more targeted patrolling of crime hot-spots. Whilst there is much to commend targeted patrol work of this sort, it is unlikely to meet generalized pubic demand for visible patrol. What seems to us clear, therefore, is that supplementary patrols which are already developing alongside the police will almost certainly develop further.

The public wants visible police patrols and its demand for it is unlikely to diminish. As pressures within the police lead to further constraints on general foot patrol, whatever patrol cover the police are able or willing to undertake is likely increasingly to be supplemented in an *ad hoc* manner by local authorities, neighbourhood associations, and commercial consortia. The employment of private security companies will continue to increase, some of it for the purposes of patrolling residential areas as well as institutional and commercial premises. Their paymasters will include local authorities and groups of local residents or local organizations clubbing together to buy a service locally demanded and locally affordable. Some municipal authorities will copy the examples of Sedgefield and Wandsworth. The available evidence indicates that the Sedgefield experiment has been a success. Local people like it and, after some early misgivings, the local police appear to welcome it. The same seems to be true of the Wandsworth Parks Police, and it cannot be long before either that or some other local authority seeks to have 'municipal police' patrolling council estates. Finally, more neighbourhod groups—including those that began life as conventional neighbourhood watch groups—will almost certainly mount volunteer patrols ('street watch'), an activity that will occasionally spill over into controversial incidents or campaigns that will correctly be termed 'vigilantism'.

Of two things we can be almost certain. Whatever form these supplementary patrols take they will generally develop not in the most deprived areas where the risks of victimization are greatest, but in the relatively better-off areas where residents are more articulate and better organized, whose risks of victimization are modest but whose feelings of security are nevertheless more fragile than they think they should be. Secondly, the more police patrols are supplemented by other patrol networks, the greater will be local knowledge of precisely how much, or little, patrol work is being undertaken by the police. Scrutiny of what services the police are supplying will further intensify, as will the demand from the public that its wants as a consumer be satisfied. Consultation over the content of local policing plans may well intensify as a result.

In broad terms, the neighbourhoods least likely to be assisted by these developments are precisely those that need the police most but with whom the police have tended to have the worst relations: the areas with the highest crime rates and in which police officers, now among the best paid public sector workers, have long since ceased to live or have much sympathy with—the discarded public housing estates of the underclass in the rustbelt zones; the residential areas of the long-term unemployed, unskilled, multiply disadvantaged families, relying on residual public services of declining quality; the sorts of areas that during the last fifteen years have become prey to the drugs trade, joy-riding, rampant burglary, and all the other forms of merciless opportunism and transient pleasure that accompany hopeless areal poverty in the midst of complacently uncaring affluence; the sort of neighbourhoods that have experienced occasional riot borne of stop-go policing—feeble withdrawal interspersed with occasional bouts of dramatic force—so eloquently decribed in Beatrix Campbell's *Goliath*.[9] The problem in such locations is not addressed, as Beatrix Campbell has put it, by the 'danger stranger' phenomenon that is the object of neighbourhood watch. The 'dangers' in these high-risk neighbourhoods are well known to most local people. Indeed the 'dangers' (largely masculine) enjoy conspicuous reputations derived from public displays of marauding intimidation. The problem is the absence of understanding, trust, and proactive crime preventive working with not just the police but all the other agencies that provide local services and which might enable the authorities to combine *with* local residents to develop safer communities. The problem in neighbourhoods where crime has been allowed to become rampant is that those individuals who are willing openly to combat the 'dangers' they daily face is that, once revealed, they have to exit the scene. That is the level of threat residents often face. In some cases, of course, even the police with their greater resources and powers, also feel frustrated and impotent.

These deep-seated policing problems in the deprived high-crime areas that are more and more a feature of the increasingly divided Britain we described in Chapter 1, will not be addressed by small residual police community relations departments making forays to formal meetings of the local great and the good—important though such attempts are. Nor will occasional displays of dominant police force, whether it is to clear the streets or arrest an individual or group that has gone way over the top, provide a solution. Areas where community safety is conspicuous by its absence require a dedicated policing presence of persons who know the ground, who are trusted, and can work with other agencies to uplift the neighbourhood. It requires integral policing *with* local people. It requires the police seeking actively to overcome the deep hostility against them which in many areas has been allowed to build up as a result of withdrawal of integral policing and other public support services from neighbourhoods.

We will come below to the issue of who should take primary responsibility for planning community safety. The question here is how to deliver a continuous policing presence, particularly in those areas that need it most.

We think that the police should continue to place as great an emphasis on focused patrolling by 'permanent' beat officers as is possible within the resources that they can command. However, we also believe that experimentation with all the forms of supplementary patrol that we have mentioned should be encouraged, subject to certain limits which we set out in the next section. Despite the misgivings which exist we also think, however, that the time has come to experiment with the introduction of *auxiliary patrol officers* within the police. To this end, we propose that authority be given to mount experiments in selected forces whereby auxiliary patrol officers could be recruited and employed on the basis of personal characteristics, pay scales, and working conditions peculiar to the office of auxiliary patrol officer and which reflect the policing needs of the community. We propose that these auxiliary patrol officers be paid less than other police officers—there clearly would be little point in them were they not. We propose that auxiliary patrol officers have the powers of constables, but that their duties be restricted to patrol work, both mobile and on foot, and that they be trained for, and encouraged to use, a limited range of police actions. Given that the *raison d'être* of such officers is, in part, to increase visibility locally of the police, there would be little to be gained by having such officers dragged away to other duties or spending a significant amount of time processing arrests. An eyes and ears presence, though one that has access to the legitimate use of force, is what we propose.

We think that the introduction of such a rank within the service should provide scope to employ older recruits, both female and male, from a variety of backgrounds, working full or part-time, who would be particularly suited to dedicated local patrol and liaison work, but who would not necessarily be suitable for other types of police work. There is a good deal of room here for more flexible and imaginative career recruitment than has traditionally been displayed by the police service. The office of auxiliary patrol officer would provide a first-rate opportunity to broaden the social base of police personnel and cut into the dominant lower ranks police culture of reactive masculine force.

No reader should expect this proposal to be welcomed by the police representative organizations. To practised eyes this much is apparent from the reports of the 1996 Audit Commission report on Patrol and the interim and final reports of the Independent Committee on the Role and Responsibilities of the Police. Both bodies were drawn to the idea of auxiliary patrol officers, but both drew back from recommending it. The police service, which was very resistant to the idea, played a significant role in this. The consequence was that the Independent Committee, within which the ACPO ranks were heavily represented, made an unspecific recommendation that there there be 'wider experimentation with ways of enabling more public patrolling to be provided by police forces' and the Audit Commission, having reviewed some of the pros and cons of auxiliary patrols, concluded their discussion with a sentence that suggested it was an idea that would probably have to be revisited if other 'improvements fail to increase public satisfaction with patrol levels'.[10]

Let us consider the alleged advantages and disadvantages of auxiliary patrols. The Audit Commission summarized the arguments as in Fig. 42.

Had the scales which the Audit Commission depicted as the background to this statement been drawn so as to reflect the overall relative strength of the competing arguments then, in our judgement, they would not have been shown in balance. It is worth looking at the language employed in the Audit Commission's summary diagram below. First of all, the language implies that the advantages of auxiliary officers are all fairly certain. Thus, they suggest that enhanced visible patrol increases public reassurance; and that auxiliary patrol *would* be subject to the same accountability mechanisms as the rest of the service. To this we would add that we *know* that auxiliaries could cost less than ordinary officers; and, we *know* by definition that they

Advantages	Disadvantages
Enhanced visible presence, so increasing public reassurance.	Appointment of auxiliaries within existing budgets would reduce the number of regular officers; if significant, this could constrain operational flexibility.
Potential to increase overall staffing levels within existing budget.	
Staff are recruited for patrol work only, increasing scope for stable assignments and greater identification with the locality.	Public may lose confidence in the police if auxiliaries are seen as 'second class' PCs.
Keeps auxiliary patrol work within police control and full public accountability.	Auxiliary officers may face situations which they are not trained to deal with; this may impose more rather than less pressure on regular officers.
High-profile patrol work carried out by staff employed and trained just for that role, rather than on sufferance.	

Fig. 42 Advantages and disadvantages of auxiliary patrol officers
Source: Audit Commission (1996) *Streetwise*, London: Audit Commission

would be patrolling and not filling in forms or dashing off responding to calls in other areas. By contrast, as outlined by the Audit Commission, the alleged disadvantages of auxiliary patrols are largely speculative: the public *may* lose confidence *if* auxiliaries are seen as 'second class' constables. The presence of auxiliaries *may* lead to additional pressures being placed on regular officers. Further the argument that the appointment of auxiliaries *within existing budgets* would reduce the number of regular officers is less a substantive argument than a routine managerial consideration that should attend any adjustment in the allocation of personnel. Opportunity costs must always be taken into account and consideration given to whether a net gain is being made in the overall quantity and quality of service delivered. This consideration applied to the additional recruitment to police forces of civilians that has gone on over the past two decades. It will apply to decisions to invest greater personnel resources in intelligence-led proactive, as opposed to reactive, policing. The fact is, as the Audit Commission and the police know very well, the consideration whether auxiliary officers should be introduced is a matter of long-term strategic policy— that is, how best to recruit and use personnel within *steadily increasing* police force budgets.

Whilst those who are against the idea of auxiliary patrol officers claim that the potential shortcomings they have identified effectively undermine the case for such a change, we reject such a charge. Nothing has been said in the debate so far which suggests to us that experimentation would be anything other than valuable. We recognize that the criticisms of auxiliary patrol are all based on legitimate concerns, but we take the view that such criticisms do no more than provide a guide to some of the issues which will have to be taken into consideration when mounting experiments in this area. The possibility exists, of course, that auxiliary patrol will be found wanting in some respects, but we cannot know this unless we examine them in practice.

Not only do we think that some of the criticisms of auxiliary patrol have been overstated, but we consider the Audit Commission reckoning understates the arguments in favour of auxiliary police officers. It may be, for example, that more money could be found for police budgets *if* extra patrol cover were known to be the outcome. Section 24 of the Police and Magistrates' Courts Act 1994, which allows local authorities and others to purchase additional policing, opens up an excellent testing ground for the provision of auxiliaries. If the Wandsworth and Sedgefield municipal examples are any guide, it seems likely that local authorities could be found which would be keen to fund experiments. Such local authorities could, with advantage, consider two developments in the Netherlands, the *Stadswacht* and the *Politiesurveillant*.

The *Stadswacht* means literally the 'city watch' or 'city warden'. There are about 650 of them and they now patrol at least twenty-six Dutch cities. They have no powers beyond those enjoyed by the ordinary Dutch citizen, but they are uniformed and they carry radios. They are available to respond to public inquiries, they provide a reassuring visible presence, they assist in preventing crime, and they control nuisance behaviour. They have a reasonably close reationship with the police, some of them being managed by the police and others being managed by police officers on secondment to the cities. Wardens provide employment for persons who might otherwise be out of work. There are two ways of achieving this. In the first, wardens are appointed for a year during which they attend a training course linked to the job. Many wardens trained in this way subsequently gain employment in the private security industry. In the second, wardens are employed permanently, though their low rate of pay is such that turnover is high. *Stadswacht* provide extra 'eyes and ears' for the police on the streets. They are not auxiliary police patrols as we propose, but supplementary patrols.

The *politiesurveillant*, by contrast, are police patrol auxiliaries along the lines that we propose. In the Netherlands, as in Britain, police patrol work has declined as pressures to deliver other police services have risen, and most of remaining police patrol work is in vehicles. Public demand for more accessible police patrols is undiminished, however. The *politiesurveillant*, or 'police patroller' is a new police rank below that of the ordinary constable but significantly higher that that of the *stadswacht*. Several Dutch cities have introduced the rank. The patrollers are trained full-time for three months and may, after a period of service, seek further training to become regular officers. They wear a full police uniform; the only difference is that theirs has a distinguishing shoulder badge. They have the full powers of constables but they are not allowed to carry firearms and they are managed and supervised in such a fashion as to minimize the likelihood that they will be called upon to use certain powers. They carry radios, handcuffs, and truncheons.

We do not think that the introduction, on an experimental basis, of auxiliary police patrols should be hindered by the inherent conservatism of the police representative associations quite naturally protecting, as all trade unions will, the dearly fought-for benefits now enjoyed by their members. Police services should not be designed to protect the vested interests of existing personnel. They should be designed in such a fashion as will best meet the public interest. That means a balanced police service, part of which should comprise visible integral neighbourhood involvement and patrol by officers who, though we propose they should have the full powers of constables, neither routinely need nor ideally will resort to use of all the powers available to constables. We do not think, for example, that the auxiliary patrol officers should ever be armed. We doubt that they should undertake, at least alone, searches of occupied dwellings or the arrest of known wanted suspects likely to resist arrest.

There is nothing new about all this. The practice of investing personnel with powers that they are not encouraged to use is well understood in the police services and by the criminal fraternity. Special constables have the powers of constables but are often shielded from situations where they might have to resort to their use. Probationer constables are similarly advised. Furthermore, every regular constable patrolling in a sensitive high-risk urban environment is fully aware that there are 'slow-go' areas, 'sensitive' neighbourhoods where the management roof will fall in on her or him if he or she is foolish enough to 'have a go' in a situation where back-up—greater numbers, more experience, or access to greater force—is manifestly required. Given this, there is no reason to believe that deploying auxiliary patrol officers will add significantly to the burden on regular officers. That does not appear to be happening in the Netherlands, Wandsworth, or Sedgefield. On the contrary auxiliary patrols appear to complement existing police services and, we suggest, could involve more mature officers, female and male, from more diverse backgrounds (socially and ethnically), who might better build bridges with disaffected neighbourhoods than the very junior, young, regular male officers who, under current arrangements, are most likely to be deployed on patrol duties. Indeed research on the role of the communty constable suggests that officers who realize they cannot themselves resort to force, and cannot readily call for back-up force from relief patrols without endangering their hard-earned trust in the community, are forced to look for alternative means of defusing the difficult situations with which they are often confronted.[11] This is often the better way forward and serves to dispel rather than exacerbate tensions. It would be advantageous if performance indicators other than the number of arrests made were devised for auxiliary patrol officers.

Finally, it will be claimed by some that the cheapness of auxiliaries is a myth. We do not seek cheap but cost effective solutions to the dilemma we have identified. But auxiliaries would be relatively cheaper. The Audit Commission has estimated that auxiliary patrol officers might cost approximately £25,000 compared to £32,000 *per annum* per regular officer. We think that the difference in annual unit cost might be even greater than this. But, just as importantly, we think that auxiliaries might be employed on a more flexible basis than is the practice with regular officers.

In conclusion, it will be argued by some that the possible advantages for which we have argued are no less speculative than the disadvantages posited by the Audit Commission. In which case let there be experimentation so that we can fully evaluate this idea. We can, after all, follow the Audit Commission's example in relation to auxiliaries and construct a table which considers the advantages and disadvantages of using *regular* police officers for patrol work. How, we would ask our readers, are the arguments balanced when we consider the existing arrangements?

We will not overstate the case for community beat officers. We argued in Chapter 2 that unless community beat patrol officers' activities are related to meeting the concerns of local communities, there is a real risk that any increase in their number will go unnoticed and therefore fail to achieve the objects of either public reassurance or the enhanced flow of information from the public to the police. We suggest that the introduction of auxiliary patrol officers provides an opportunity for realizing the potential of dedicated community patrol officers that current arrangements often fail to realize. The evidence is that most young constables currently allocated to community patrol work do not wish to continue in it,[12] an unsurprising outcome given that few dedicated patrol officers believe their forces value patrol work as important.[13] Moreover, it appears that, as presently organized, much patrol work achieves little. For example, since 35 per cent of patrol officers fail during the course of a shift to initiate any sort of contact with a member of the public (do not say 'hello' or offer any sort of greeting to anyone), it comes as no surprise that 65 per cent of them also report having failed to gather any sort of

Advantages	Disadvantages
PCs are highly trained and have a broad range of competencies.	PCs are relatively expensive and are frequently abstracted for other duties
PCs enjoy the trust of, and have legitimacy with, most members of the public	PCs attach low status to community patrol work.
PCs bring a full range of powers with them in any situation they encounter and can call on a considerable range of back-up resources from other regular officers	PCs allocated to community patrol work tend to be the most junior and least experienced officers.
PC patrol officers are part of the mainstream regular force	PCs allocated to community patrol work therefore reflect the characteristics of the mainstream police culture: they are overwhelmingly male, young, white and looking for 'action'.

Fig. 43 Advantages and disadvantages of using regular police officers for community beat work

intelligence during the course of a tour of duty.[14] The low level of activity generally reported by patrol officers scarcely squares with the claim that the police are overwhelmed by the demands made on them. Neither does it suggest that the role of patrol officers is well defined and their activities closely monitored and appraised so that they *are visible*. The introduction of auxiliary patrol officers will need to be accompanied by the development of performance indicators geared specifically to their role.

There are dangers, as we have outlined, in becoming too pre-occupied with *police* solutions to contemporary dilemmas in *policing*. Accordingly, although we have outlined a fairly forceful case for experimenting with the police patrol function. We suggest also that one of the means of responding to the first dilemma is to increase municipal involvement in policing. Later in this section we will outline our views of the proper role of local authorities in community safety. Suffice it to say for the moment that we consider that local authorities should take a significantly more active role in community safety than is currently the case. One of the ways in which local authorities can demonstrate their commitment to community safety is, of course, to provide appropriate resources for the police locally. They can also enter into a variety of partnerships with the local police. In addition, we believe that they might give consideration to providing a municipal patrol service as a supplement to local policing. Akin perhaps to the Sedgefield example, this would be an 'eyes and ears' supplement. Being provided by the local authority, it would automatically be a service which could be held accountable by elected representatives and, moreover, it would be a service for whose standards the local authority could also be publicly held to account.

Investing in this very direct way in community safety—that is providing a service that people overwhelmingly say they want— seems to us not only a proper, but a highly constructive use of public money. Moreover, because in this case the service would be provided by the 'local state', rather than bought by groups of residents banding together, some of the problems of access and 'need' that we outlined above might be overcome. Thus, it would be perfectly possible for a local authority to identify those areas in which it believed some form of uniformed presence might be most valuable, and then target this municipal resource toward those areas. In addition to planning and playing a central role in the provision of the variety of community safety initiatives focused on vulnerable neighbourhoods, local authorities might also be encouraged to play their part in ensuring that a visible patrol presence was maintained where it was most needed.

Dilemma Two—**How is the growth of self-help and private policing provision to be responded to: should the burgeoning sectors be encouraged and brought into the fold, or should they be resisted on the grounds that they represent sectional interests whose activity will undermine the integrity of the state?**

Whether or not our first dilemma is addressed by introducing a new police rank—the dedicated auxiliary police patrol officer—there is no doubt in our minds that supplementary patrols and other forms of private security provision will continue to burgeon. We think this growth may in part be stemmed if the police are able to maintain a visible public presence, which is why we have advocated the auxiliary patrol officer. Such officers would form part of the police and would therefore be fully publicly accountable and could be used wherever and in whatever manner the police authorities, in conjunction with their chief constables, considered would best serve the public interest. In our judgement equitable policing within the framework of the rule of law would thus be most satisfactorily safeguarded. But even if this is done, supplementary patrol activity will take place, and because the services that some local authorities, agencies, and neighbourhoods will continue to want and be able to pay for—like the protection of private property and space to which the public have access, for example—services that cannot, and arguably should not, be provided out of the public purse, then our second dilemma remains a challenging one which we think must now be addressed.

Because private security firms occupy a position of trust for those who employ them to protect their persons and property, because the evidence suggests that individuals and groups defer to people who wear uniforms designed to conjure the authority of the police, and because those who provide security services are in a position to abuse that deference and trust, we do not think it is any longer tenable to allow the private security industry to continue unregulated. There is evidence of abuse. There are undoubted cowboys on the loose and there is nothing currently to prevent disreputable and criminally-minded operators from offering any security service they wish. Indeed, even a Government ideologically committed to reducing the amount of regulation has latterly come round to the view that some form of control of the private security industry is now necessary. In August 1996, the Home Office announced that a statutory body to vet people wanting to work in private security was to be established, and that new criminal offences of employing an unlicensed guard and working as an unlicensed guard would be introduced.[15] Given that these plans are both vague and not accompanied by any timetable for implementation, we set out our views on the regulation of the industry below.

There is currently no statutory licensing or regulative system of any kind for the private security industry in Britain. This contrasts with almost all other European countries. Britain stands virtually alone in not having admission requirements for firms offering security services and, together with Germany, not setting performance requirements for private security operatives. Austria, Belgium, Denmark, Finland, France, Germany, Greece, Italy, the Netherlands. Norway, Portugal, Spain, Sweden and Switzerland all have some form of legislative control over their private security industries.[16]

The system of control, such as it is, in Britain is one of self-regulation by the various trade associations covering the industry, the two biggest of which are the *British Security Industry Association* (BSIA) and the *International Professional Security Association* (IPSA). These bodies, together with a host of other smaller trade organizations, comprise the network of self-registration and regulation for private security in the United Kingdom. Clearly, there need to be important reasons of public interest to introduce statutory regulation in a sector of commerce and employment which has hitherto been free of it. We agree that the labour market should be allowed to function with the minimum of regulation compatible with the public interest. The reasons we have come to the conclusion that it is necessary now to introduce a degree of regulation over the private security industry can be grouped under three broad headings: standards of conduct; the reliability of staff; and standards of product and service. The degree to which any of these are relevant varies depending upon which section of the industry is being considered. The police staff associations have for many years contended that it is all too easy for people with inappropriate criminal histories to gain employment in the security industry. A 1988 ACPO report highlighted a number of alleged deficiencies within the private security industry, the largest of which was 'employer/employee having a criminal record'.[17] The same allegation was put before the recent review of the private security industry by the Home Affairs Select Committee. ACPO claimed the relatively widespread presence in the industry of employees with criminal records.[18]

There are currently two major impediments to the effective vetting of private security staff. First, companies cannot submit names for checking on the Police National Computer: without the applicant's permission they are therefore unable to check their employees' possible criminal records. Secondly, the provisions of the Rehabilitation of Offenders Act 1974 restrict the checks that companies can make on employees. The Act allows for convictions for offences which have resulted in sentences of up to two and a half years in prison to be 'ignored' if the offender stays out of trouble for a specified time after the first conviction. Some of the private security trade associations argue that, though it is important to protect the rights of ex-offenders with respect to most forms of potential employment, an exemption should be made for jobs in the private security industry because of the specific circumstances involved. Granting a recidivist burglar or robber access to the details of locks, alarms, and other security arrangements might be considered the equivalent of granting a repeat child abuser responsibility for the welfare of a group of young children. Following its consideration of the current situation in 1995 the Home Affairs Select Committee concluded that: 'vetting procedures for the industry as they currently stand are, in our opinion, inadequate'.[19]

It is not clear whether the Government's new proposals will go wider than introducing licenses for the guarding sector of the industry. Providing a poor standard of service is a criticism that has most often been levelled at the intruder alarm sector, despite the application for some years of British Standards.[20] 97 per cent of intruder alarm activations are false alarms.[21] This has represented a substantial and wasteful burden for the police and led in 1990 to the introduction by ACPO of a national burglar alarm policy. The policy involved the withdrawal by the police of response for a set period to devices that frequently generated false alarms. The initiative appears not to have been very successful. The number of false activations of intruder alarms reported in the 1990 National Intruder Alarm Statistics published by the ACPO Intruder Alarms Sub-Committee showed only a 3 per cent decline on the previous year: the proportion of false alarms to which the police respond is still very high.

In Chapter 2 we showed how important the private security industry is becoming in the 'policing' of Britain. The public is increasingly engaged in activities in areas where policing is undertaken by private organizations. More and more households, neighbourhoods, and institutions (both public and private) are becoming reliant on commercially provided surveillance technology and patrols for their sense of security. As demands on the police have expanded, so the police have become dependent on skills available in, and services provided by, the private sector. This is largely to be welcomed, and positive co-operation between the public and private sectors needs to be encouraged. There are many benefits to be gained from constructive partnership. But it is vital that this partnership be based on integrity. The public, let alone the police, must have confidence that the very highest standards are being upheld in any agency with which the police are engaged in partnership. For these reasons we conclude that the time has come to introduce a system of official or statutory regulation of the private security industry.

Our view enjoys widespread support, and we do not mean only from leading providers within the industry, firms that would undoubtedly derive competitive advantage from the operation of a regulative system the effect of which would probably be to raise costs and drive out smaller, less well-established operators. In 1995 the Home Affairs Select Committee (HAC) recommended that an agency be created empowered to license both individuals and companies in the manned guarding sector.[22] In 1996 the Independent Committee on the Role and Responsibilities of the Police concurred.[23] The question is: what exactly needs to be regulated and how?

Before providing our answer to that question there is a vital preliminary issue to be dealt with. What powers should be available to private security personnel? Should they, as in many countries, be empowered to bear arms? Should they have greater powers of arrest, search, and detention than those available to the ordinary citizen?

We can see no case for granting private security personnel powers not available to the ordinary citizen and, as far as we have been able to discover, there is no demand from either within or without the industry that such powers should be granted, except in very particular circumstances. One such circumstance is provided by the contracted-out management of prisons. The Criminal Justice Act provides that the prisoner custody officers employed by the security companies now managing five prisons are empowered to search prisoners and their visitors and to use such force as is necessary to prevent prisoners from escaping. But this sort of exception apart we can see no reason why citizens' powers are inadequate for dealing with the type of situations with which private security personnel are likely to be confronted when guarding or on patrol. Indeed, quite the contrary. We consider that the fact that security personnel have no powers beyond those available to the ordinary citizen itself provides a desirable check on their activities and clearly demarcates, both in law and in the eyes of the public at large, what is otherwise becoming an increasingly fuzzy boundary between the police and private 'policing' enterprises. The reality of private security is that their personnel are *not* like ordinary citizens. They may not have additional powers, but they have specific responsibilities, they are *organized*, they are generally recruited because of their *physical* suitability, they are dressed in a manner to emphasize their capacity to intimidate, they may be trained in self-defence or have experience in how to 'handle themselves' in situations thought to justify reasonable force, they are more likely to employ force, and so on. All these predisposing conditions suggest, given the widespread concerns about the *de facto* power wielded by private security personnel whose integrity is uncertain, whose public accountability is non-existent, and whose allegiance is by definition to whomsoever pays the piper, that there ia a very strong case for ensuring that in law they exercise no more right to employ force than the rest of us. We conclude that no change in citizens' powers of arrest is justified.

Which parts of the private security industry should be regulated? The key area, we would argue, is where private security staff are involved in the policing of space which is public—streets, housing estates, and so on—or which the public considers to be *public*, even though it is actually *private*, that is places like shopping malls, football grounds, hospitals, and so on. We think any new form of regulation should certainly cover the work of private security guards, including contract and in-house guards. The Home Affairs Select Committee excluded in-house staff from its recommendations for regulation. However, though the evidence indicates that there are fewer complaints about in-house security services, the fact that there is significant mobility between the contract and the in-house sectors leads us to believe that any new system of licensing should cover both. Moreover, given their role in relation to either private property or private space to which the public have access, both nightclub door staff and installers of electronic surveillance and security equipment ought, in our judgment, also to come within a new system of regulation.

This leaves the question of how the licensing should be done. We agree with both the House of Commons Home Affairs Select Committee and the Independent Committee on the Role and Responsibilities of the Police that an independent licensing authority should be established accountable to the relevant minister, the Home Secretary, who in turn would be accountable for its operation to Parliament. This body would be responsible for managing and implementing a system of accreditation for those companies working in the areas of private security identified above. Licensing would be of the firm rather than the individual employee. However, the issuing of a licence would be dependent on compliance with a set of standards which would include vetting of staff, the provision of adequate training, the holding of appropriate insurance, and the investigation of complaints against staff. The licensing system, and in particular the standards set, would need to be flexible, taking account of the differing functions and responsibilities in various parts of the industry. A system of independent and rigorous inspection would also need to be instituted, as would the establishment of an independent complaints mechanism—though the latter could be an arm of the licensing authority itself.

In our judgement the establishment of a regulatory mechanism on these lines would provide the basis for public confidence in private security provisions and allow the police to forge a partnership with accredited firms in situations where the public interest, as agreed by chief constables together with their police authorities, considered it appropriate. This partnership should not involve the sharing of privileged information, however. It would not be proper for police forces to share with private security personnel confidential information to which access should not be given to any other citizen.

Dilemma three—Given all the evidence that the incidence of crime is only to a very limited extent related to anything that the police do, where should the locus of responsibility for crime prevention and community safety lie: should it remain with the police who currently have the task and wish to keep it, or should

it be given to others whose involvement would be appropriate but who show no great enthusiasm for taking it on?

At the beginning of this Chapter we argued against Bayley's proposition that the police are uniquely well placed to take the lead in primary crime preventive activity. We did so because Bayley implicitly assumes a police monopoly over policing activity, which is less and less the case. Further, as we showed in Chapter 3, the division of labour within the police is complex and their culture difficult to change. The consequence is that any arrangement giving the police responsibility for a version of crime prevention going beyond analysis of crime patterns, limited problem-solving exercises in liaison with other agencies where crime 'hot spots' arise, and the targeting of known offenders, is likely to be marginalized in terms of the allocation of police resources and police organizational commitment. Thus, though law enforcement is, of course, a powerful tool in crime prevention, it is not, nor arguably will it ever be, central in what we, following other analysts, have termed primary crime prevention.[24]

Most people, most of the time, do not abide by most laws out of fear that they will be caught and punished: they do so because they subscribe to the values embedded in the law. There are, of course, some laws conformity with which many of us calculate at the margin. We may risk parking our cars in places where, or at times at which, parking is not allowed if there is no parking warden in the vicinity. We may exceed speed limits by up to 10 or 15 per cent in the belief that this is tolerable. But most of us do not refrain from stealing from our fellow citizens or damaging public property because we think a police officer may spot us. We respect the property of others, and in turn expect our own property rights to be respected. We value public facilities and derive benefit from them. The legitimacy of the law is not something primarily inculcated by the police: it is part of a value system into which we are progressively socialized by all the institutions with which we have contact and of which we are a part—family, school, church, neighbourhood club or association, workplace, and civic network—and in which, ideally, by the time we reach adolescence and adulthood we have a stake. Or not.

Crime is a product of the degree to which we constitute in reality what we say we are in theory, a community of common interest based on principles of democracy, fairness, and justice. In this process every citizen has a part to play. But the framework within which we play our separate parts is primarily the responsibility of government, not the police. The police are not responsible for the public infrastructure which supports or contradicts the values to which as a community we say we subscribe, nor can they be made to be.

Yet there has to be some local agency responsible for the day-to-day trouble-shooting and long-term planning which, even in the best regulated society, are necessary to maximize what we have chosen to call community safety. And it seems to us self-evident that, though Bayley is right to emphasize that the police have a key role in identifying where and how safety is lacking, because the police are not responsible for providing the range of public services that have a bearing on community safety—roads, street lighting and road safety, housing and refuse collection, education and youth and community facilities, recreational facilities, health services, employment and regional development, and so on, *as well as policing*—it makes no sense to impose the primary responsibility for primary crime prevention on the police. The police are responsible for only one service among many and, as we have seen, they are not even wholly responsible for the policing services on which we more and more rely.

The problem of course is that there is no longer a branch of the local state in Britain which *is* responsible for the delivery of most, let alone all, of the services that anyone planning primary crime prevention would naturally wish to bring under a planning umbrella. For the Conservative administration from 1979 onward the local authorities came progressively to represent the antithesis of everything they set out to achieve and counter. Local authorities were associated with profligate public expenditure spent on allegedly inefficient monopolistic public services controlled by Labour councillors opposed to all reform. During the last twenty years local government has been progressively dismantled—this seems a more accurate description than 'restructured'[25]—responsibility for different services being parcelled out to a plethora of public bodies, many of them no longer democratically elected, or contracted out to commercial and other providers. Moreover, the administrative boundaries within which the different major services are organized coincide less and less. Commitment to market principles in the delivery of most of the major public services has allowed practically all semblance of civic identity and inter-agency co-ordination to be swept away, each provider being allowed to design its own administrative structures according to its own assessment of efficiency with little or no regard to the corporate whole.

Thus Training and Enterprise Councils have assumed responsibility for further education and training alongside local authority education departments, and further education institutions have become corporate bodies detached from their former parent local authorities. Individual schools have been allowed to opt out of local authority management, thereby rendering overall local planning for education services difficult, if not impossible. Urban Development Corporations and Housing Action Trusts have assumed a measure of responsibility for development in addition to the local planning authorities. Most transport and waste-disposal services have been privatized. Hospital trusts have been set up outside local authority control. In the wake of the abolition of the metropolitan authorities, joint boards have been established to oversee policing and fire services and to provide oversight of transport and refuse disposal. And, most important of all, is the ongoing process of local government reorganization which, in addition to the creation of further joint boards, will see the formation of a variety of forms of unitary local authority alongside a diminished number of two-tier systems of local government.

Not even the criminal justice system any longer carries the pretence of being an administratively co-ordinated system at a local level. The Crown Prosecution Service, the Prison Service, the Probation Service, and the courts have all recently been reorganized so that none of their local administrative units converge or are consistent with the boundaries of the forty-one provincial police forces. No wonder that in 1992 it was thought necessary to create a national Criminal Justice Consultative Council and parallel local fora in which representatives of all these agencies meet together and attempt some semblance of joint problem-solving and co-ordinated anticipation of what the knock-on consequences of their separate policy initiatives might be for the rest of the so-called 'system'.[26]

The local state is now a pale shadow of what it once was and the scope for overall planning has, by central government design, been substantially reduced. It is possibly no coincidence, therefore, that public feelings of community safety have reached what is almost certainly an all-time low ebb this century. The very phrase 'civic dignity' sounds almost painfully old-fashioned—a voice from the condemned past of relative local authority supremacy. Yet even though the process of local government dismantlement has continued since the Morgan Committee reported in 1991—including the diminished role of local authorities in the governance and finance of the police service—we can see no sensible alternative to the core conclusions to which the Morgan Committee came. Namely, that community safety be confirmed as the legitimate concern of local government. Morgan recommended that:

local authorities, working in conjunction with the police, should have a clear statutory responsibility for the development and stimulation of community safety and crime prevention programmes, and for progressing at a local level of multi-agency approach to community safety.[27]

We agree with this proposition, but it needs adapting to the situation now prevailing in the wake of the Police and Magistrates' Courts Act 1994.

We, like the proverbial Irishman asked by a traveller for directions to his destination, might find it easier to describe the route if we were not starting from here. We have no rose-tinted spectacles about the history of local government in Britain or the administration of some of our major public services. But we think there is a powerful case for having integrated public services and strong local or regional government through which people are able to shape public services to suit local circumstances and develop innovative local identities. In the same way that it is typically argued that legal 'ownership' of property tends to promote pride in and responsibility for that property, so we believe that civic pride in people's immediate environment and quality of life is best promoted by their being able to exercise a high degree of control over planning for that environment and arranging the facilities within it—local residents 'owning' and taking responsibility for their immediate environment. We attach importance to the promotion of civic dignity. This can only effectively be achieved, however, if local people are able, in an integrated manner, to bring the major strands of policy together and to determine the allocation of resources. We do not think this is currently sufficiently the case. Britain is now a more centrally directed state than most countries in Europe. There is no effective counterweight to Westminster. Moreover the apparent devolution of power that has taken place to a variety of local agencies and groups is so dispersed and fragmentary that the relationships between services at a local level, relationships increasingly structured on market principles, sometimes border on anarchy.

By the same token we think that the relative ineffectiveness of police authorities prior to the Police and Magistrates' Courts Act—and we do not quarrel with that diagnosis—was to a large extent the product of their membership (we have never been persuaded of the case for having unelected lay magistrates as members), the all too frequent predominance of petty party political squabbling, the fact that the police authorities were in no real sense *responsible* for policing policy in a context of declining responsibility for the finance and delivery of continuous public services, and because of what was often an overly-broad interpretation of the doctrine of constabulary independence. It is scarcely surprising, therefore, that police authority members occasionally acted *irresponsibly* or largely failed to exercise their vestigial powers. We think that in an ideal world police authorities would be democratically elected, though quite probably assisted by co-opted members, and that councillors had substantial responsibility for the delivery of other public services.

So, ideally, we would not start from here. Yet we *must.* And we must build on the positive aspects of recent policy developments, primarily the provisions for the governance of the police in the Police and Magistrates' Courts Act 1994.

The Act requires each police authority outside London to publish before the beginning of each financial year 'a plan setting out the proposed arrangements for the policing of the authority's area during the year'. The plan must contain the authority's priorities for the year and the financial resources expected to be available and their proposed allocation. It must also include any local objectives that the police authority wishes to set, in addition to the key objectives set nationally by the Home Secretary. Further, the Home Office guidance issued in 1994 on the preparation of plans suggests that they should include a description of the consultation undertaken locally in order to prepare the plan and—a specific prompt—an outline of what partnership initiatives are to be pursued by the force or the authority with local groups or agencies.[17]

We think there should be a statutory obligation placed on unitary local authorities (which will form the majority of local authorities) to prepare a draft Community Safety Plan (CSP) and that the manner of its preparation should be dovetailed with the police authorities' statutory obligation to prepare a Policing Plan (PP). We have recommendations for how this will best be done. but at the centre of what we propose lie the Police Community Consultative Groups (PCCGs) which in most areas have been in existence since the early 1980s and which, though now well-established, have generally failed to realize their practical problem-solving potential. What we propose could breathe new life into what was one of Lord Scarman's most important propositions and what, following section 106 of the Police and Criminal Evidence Act 1984, is now a statutory requirement—namely that local communities be consulted about the policing of their areas. We think this should be done because we agree with Lord Scarman's contention that a police force that fails to consult will fail to be effective, a contention which we have demonstrated logically flows from all the evidence as to *how* the police are able to police. We also think that one can helpfully think of an accountable police force as being a police force that pursues the methods and priorities of which the public broadly approves.

We do not pretend that this is an easy objective to achieve, not least because there are many publics and what those publics want from the police may conflict.[18] Moreover, the public often wants inconsistent things—visible local patrol, rapid response to emergencies, *and* intense proactive investigation of serious repeat offenders. But in our judgment this is the only doctrine of policing by consent worthy of the name, and it is one that we should consciously and continuously strive to realize.

We recommend, therefore, that the PCCGs established under PACE should be adapted so that the areas they cover coincide with the boundaries of local authorities rather than the police administrative areas which is currently generally their foundation. There is no difficulty surrounding this proposition. In most parts of the country the police authorities decided in the first half of the 1980s when PCCGs generally got off the ground that they should be established by police division or sub-division. but this was not invariably the case. In London where, controversially, there is no elected local police authority, the Home Office provided that PCCGs be established for each of the London boroughs. This was a way of tying borough councils—most of whom resented the absence of local democratic accountability—into the consultative process. Further, in a few of the provincial police forces, PCCGs were tied to local authority boundaries because the police organizational map was itself based on those boundaries.

On balance the evidence suggests that placing PCCGs on a local authority foundation has been advantageous. Most observers are agreed that the London borough PCCGs have been among the most vigorous groups in the country.[19] The borough councils rather than the police have provided the administrative support for groups, from the beginning meetings have been held on civic rather than police premises, a more inclusive basis for membership of PCCGs was adopted and greater success has generally been achieved in involving the public, with all the benefits that may then accrue for public education and joint problem solving. For much the same reasons the introduction of 'lay visitor to police station' schemes has generally also been a greater success in London than in the provinces.[20] It is noteworthy that some provincial police authorities—Northamptonshire, for example—have already taken steps to re-orient some of their section 106 arrangements towards local government by establishing Community Safety Groups, with a core of democratically elected members, based on district councils. A similar move has been made in Brighton, Sussex.[21]

Whatever the areal basis of PCCGs there is a slight problem of representation if police and local authority boundaries differ. If a PCCG straddles two or more police administrative units then the consultative group has necessarily to deal with more than one police commander, who may be pursuing slightly different policies. If a PCCG straddles two or more local government areas then by definition each authority must be represented at all levels on the PCCG, both elected councillors and officers running services. On balance it is easier to represent more than one police administrative unit than several local authorities, because at least the different police administrative units are drawn from the same constabulary and are therefore subject to the same corporate direction.

We suggest, therefore, that a new Home Office circular on the interpretation of section 106 be issued, and that this recommend a revised framework for consultation. There is no need for further legislation on this matter. Section 106 merely requires that:

arrangements shall be made in each police area for obtaining the views of the people in that area about matters concerning the policing of the area and for obtaining their co-operation with the police in preventing crime in the area.

There is no blueprint on how consultation is to be achieved in the 1984 Act. Interpretation of the statutory requirement that there be consultation has been determined entirely by means of Home Office administrative *advice* issued in a series of circulars. It follows that were the Home Office to issue new advice on the lines that we suggest, then we envisage that the police authorities and chief constables would readily accede, as they have done in the past.

We propose, therefore, that in drawing up their draft Community Safety Plans—a requirement for which there *will* need to be new legislation—the local authorities should be required and empowered to bring together all the relevant local authority departments, agencies, and other bodies within its borders to draw up the plan. We are not proposing that there should be transferred to the local authorities new executive powers to implement measures or that they should be required to implement particular measures. We are simply proposing that the local authorities be given a statutory responsibility to take the lead in bringing together all the relevant parties in order that a draft Community Safety Plan be prepared. As part of this, statutory responsibility for organizing police–community consultation would have to pass from police authorities to local authorities. Local authorities should also have to monitor execution of the final plan by those responsible for implementation. The latter will include the police authority and the police, who should be able to influence the content of local authority Community Safety Plans in the light of decisions adopted in the Policing Plan. We recognize that, at least while such arrangements bed down, there is the potential for some conflict between police authorities and local authorities over priorities and objectives. We do not consider this to be a problem. Indeed, the existence of such conflict would probably indicate that the relevant parties were taking their revised roles in policing and community safety seriously and conscientiously, a development wholly to be welcomed.

The planning process, we suggest, should take the following form. Each local authority would have as many PCCGs as is judged necessary to represent local neighbourhoods with distinctive crime and policing characteristics. Each PCCG should generally include, as at present, a member of the police authority (outside London), the relevant local police commander(s), local councillors and representatives of local institutions, the various statutory agencies and community groups, and so on. Membership should be determined by the local authority so as to ensure that local views are represented to the maximum extent. We believe that experience of PCCGs hitherto favours an open and inclusive structure with at least occasional meetings being held at which the widest possible public attendance is encouraged. In order that PCCGs be effective, particularly when preparing their submissions to the local authority for the CSP, and the police authority for the PP, the police should make available to them local crime and incident pattern analyses and provide information about the normal allocation of police resources for their area. When the draft CSP and PP have been prepared, PCCGs should be invited to comment on them, particularly those parts that relate to their areas.

Our central objective is to ensure that the PP which each police authority is now required to prepare should be made as effective as possible by being informed by the CSPs of its constituent local authorities. It follows that the timetable for local authority CSP and police authority PP planning cycles should be co-ordinated, thereby enabling PCCGs to consider policing and other issues together. That way the likelihood of genuine problem-solving partnerships of the sort that the government says it wishes to encourage will be maximized.

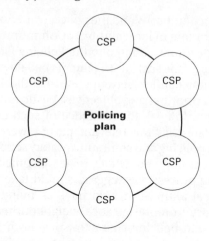

Fig. 44 The relationship between the policing plan and community safety plans

The arrangements which we propose would ensure that the local authority would have a clear channel of communication to the police authority via its PCCGs. The police authority would, through the PCCG, have a natural channel to the local authority when preparing its Policing Plan. Moreover, the local authority would have a mechanism through which to start thinking about community safety needs and plans. Thus, we believe, the potential of the PCCGs might be better realized, not least because a local authority that was dissatisfied with the policing of its area would have a vested interest in using the PCCG mechanism to demonstrate the fact. By the same token, if local CSP discussions were not primarily about policing—and it is worth stressing that many of the topics discussed currently by PCCGs are *not* about policing—but were more about the deficiencies in other community facilities and services—the paucity of youth facilities, inadequate street lighting, poor road design, and excessive traffic speeds, the tardiness in effecting repairs to council properties, the lack of refuse services, and so on—then that would emerge from PCCG deliberations and the police and the police authority should, through their representation on the PCCGs, be able to press home the point to the representatives from the local authorities.

Three important administrative points remain to be addressed. First, what of those parts of the country where there will not be unitary local authorities but where two-tier local authority arrangements will continue? This is difficult, but we think that statutory responsibility for preparing a Community Safety Plan should fall on the district councils with reference to district council areas, i.e. the lower tier. Though two-tier arrangements will mean that the authorities concerned will have even less control over the relevant public services than elsewhere, and will necessarily have to ensure that the heads of services run by county councils are consulted when Plans are being drawn up, we think that the district councils are generally of a more manageable size when it comes to ascertaining the safety needs and opinions of local residents. People are generally quite parochial in their community safety concerns. They know about the conditions in their street, block of flats, neighbourhood, or town centre. They are generally not keen to discuss, and do not know about, what is happening in the next town or village or a neighbourhood some twenty or thirty miles away. We think the arrangements we propose will work best if the deliberating and planning unit is as local as possible.

Even so, and this is the second administrative issue, given the variable size of the local authorities on which PCCGs will be based, it may be necessary, as is already the case in some parts of the country, for some PCCGs to establish sector or neighbourhood sub-groups, particularly in areas experiencing particular local community safety problems. We stressed in Chapter 1 that crime patterns and other community safety issues are often extremely localized. Public order problems, prostitution, drug trading, and even burglary or street robbery are often concentrated in particular ecological zones.[22] These 'hot-spots' need to be the subject of focused consideration by those residents and decision-makers most closely concerned. Moreover the way local problems are handled needs to be sensitive to the traditions and experiences of different social groups, whose attitudes to the police may be less than warm.

Thirdly, and most importantly, there is the vexed question of London and the Metropolitan and City of London Police forces neither of which reports to a police authority with majority elected representation. The Metropolitan Police reports directly to the Home Secretary, who is now 'advised' by an unelected Metropolitan Police Committee, and the City of London Police reports to the Common Council of the City of London. the Metropolitan Police is by far the largest police force in England and Wales, and in addition to its geographically natural national functions—the protection of Parliament, the diplomatic corps, and the Royal Family—it has over the years accrued a broader national role in which the Metropolitan Police provides specialist services such as those in relation to terrorism, and in connection with immigration, passports, and extradition. The City of London Police is the smallest of the forty-three area police forces in England and Wales and owes its constitutional arrangements for governance to the historic role of the City and the guilds. We can see no good reason for the London forces not having local police authorities with majority elected representation as elsewhere in England and Wales.

This is not the place to argue that case: it has been eloquently argued elsewhere, and the Opposition political parties have at various times committed themselves to remedying this deficiency in the accountability arrangements for London. Not only do we think police authorities with majority elected representation should be introduced, but we think that analogous mechanisms to those that we propose for the rest of England should be introduced for the purposes of promoting community safety in London. Namely, each of the London boroughs should by statute be required to prepare an annual CSP. As and when the London police forces acquire local police authorities with majority elected representation, then those authorities should also have responsibility for preparing annual Policing Plans.

In conclusion, therefore, we think that the structure and process of preparing CSPs and PPs should be that set out in Figures 45 and 46.

Nothing we have proposed should be interpreted as meaning that we think there should be a rigid blueprint for the process of consultation with the public about policing. On the contrary, flexibility is vital. Arrangements should be geared to local circumstances and needs. Thus the existence of PCCGs, or Community Safety Groups, based on district council boundaries would in no way preclude the continued operation of forces or city-wide consultative groups designed to address the problems,

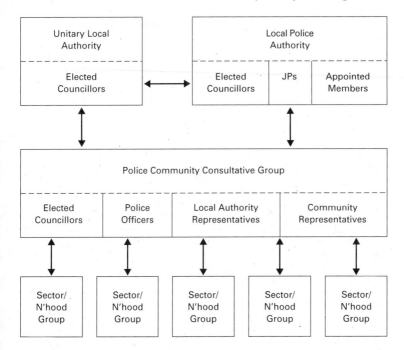

Fig. 45 Consultation and community safety

Source: Report of the Independent Committee of Inquiry into the Role and
Responsibilities of the Police

such as racial harassment, of particular sections of the population.

Dilemma four—Given the mobility of the population and the
globalization of some crime does it make sense to retain the relatively small-scale local police forces we now have? Or should
we be thinking again about the creation of a national or even a
European police force?

In Chapter 1 we noted that many of the demographic and socio-
economic changes which provide the context for the crime
trends which preoccupy the police and public reflect global
changes. The majority of the population is mobile—whether that
mobility relates to employment and housing moves, the taking
of holidays, or the daily pattern of commuting to work or the

The consultation process

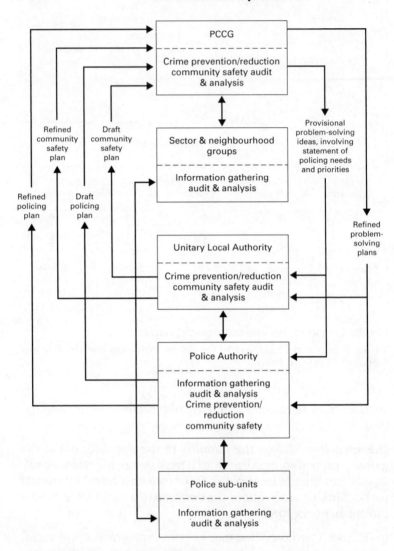

Fig. 46 The consultation process

Source: Report of the Independent Committee of Inquiry into the Role and Responsibilities of the Police

buying of groceries—to a degree scarcely imaginable twenty or thirty years ago. Our wants—whether it be the drinks we consume, the clothes we wear, or the consumer durables we earnestly desire—are shaped by mass advertising put out by multi-national corporations through mass media whose reach is into practically every household, rich or poor, from Wigan to Woking, Winnipeg to Warsaw. We are tied increasingly into a global economy which has opened up unprecedented opportunities for the transfer of funds, exchange, trade, and marketing and rendered much talk about national sovereignty little more than fraudulent posturing. The huge expansion of global networks and interchange has increased the scope for profit while it has simultaneously reduced the capacity to control.

Crime is part of this pattern. Crime and crime control have always constituted a sort of symbiotic game of leap-frog—property holders developing new defences for their assets, criminals devising new techniques for penetrating those defences and relieving owners of their assets, and the police devising techniques for identifying the pillagers and their methods. The game is becoming ever more complex and global and, almost inevitably, the diplomatic advance of international legal agreement and reaction is lumberingly slow, trailing in the wake of the entrepreneurial crime networks capable of exploiting technological opportunities which, hitherto, the lawyers, the police, and the courts have little known about let alone understood.

This is the contemporary reality. It follows that however much we may cherish our domestic policing traditions and arrangements a sensible approach to policing and crime control involves close analysis of the nature of the crime we wish to control, following which we must devise policing structures and processes appropriate to the task and consistent with principles of justice and public accountability, not *vice versa*. There is nothing sacrosanct about having a given number of police forces or a police force for a particular area. There is no principle of justice or accountability which dictates that there should be local chief constables accountable to local police authorities as opposed to a national police force accountable through the Home Secretary directly to Parliament. Within other jurisdictions in Europe there exists a great range of police structures—comprehensive national forces with more or less devolution of decision-making to local administrative units, local police forces not unlike our own, parallel national and local forces, or more than one national force, pursuing a division of labour. The fundamental question is: what will provide for the most effective policing, given our political culture and traditions?

There can be no clear-cut answer to such a question. We do not have a *tabula rasa*. Given, as we have argued, that the effectiveness of police work depends crucially on public co-operation and trust, it follows that the policing arrangements likely to work best are those with which the public are broadly familiar and which inspire confidence. Devising police force structures is not like setting up a business to produce plastic yo-yos. Policing is *with* the people, and thus conservative caution, whatever we have said above, must inevitably be built into the policy-making equation. It would almost certainly be foolhardy to seek other than incremental change. We suggest that the following considerations should guide our approach to this difficult question.

First, there is growing evidence that relatively highly organized criminal networks whose activities cut across local, regional, and national boundaries are becoming more common. Entirely localized policing structures are ill-equipped to counter these criminal networks. We need effective international, national, and regional police organizations to deal with the threat. The physical mobility of the general population also means that groups who might present a public order threat—whether they be football fans and the gangs that attach themselves to groups of fans, striking workers, social protesters or youth cult adherents—may gather in large numbers in any part of the country at short notice. The police must be able to mobilize a response to such gatherings, and this response may need to draw on resources not permanently available locally.

Secondly, the vast majority of the crime and nuisance about which the public is concerned and with which the police deal is very local. A study in Newcastle-under-Lyme found that almost one half of burglaries were committed within 0.8km of the burglar's home,[23] and researchers in Sheffield found that approximately three-quarters of 'breaking' offences occurred within two miles of the offender's home.[24] The bulk of what the public is primarily concerned about comprises disputes and offences within households or between neighbours, the activities of young people clustering at some street meeting point or inebriated late-night customers spilling from a particular pub or club, assaults in the town centre between young men coming in from the fringe estates, break-ins, and shop-thefts carried out by local burglars and thiefs. This is the bread-and-butter stuff which takes up most police resources and time.

Of course a little of this local activity feeds into national, or even international, networks. The kids who get used to taking cars for joy-riding or getting home may eventually feed into the lucrative international stolen car trade whose journey's end is in the Middle East or Eastern Europe. The heroin circulating among a relatively small coterie of persons in almost every town in the land originates from the Golden Triangle or South America. But the global networks are profitable only because there are grass roots, grass roots whose habits are generally very familiar to local police officers whose experience has taken them regularly to the magistrates' court. Most of the material on which the police work is highly parochial and there is a premium to be placed on developing policing arrangements which maximize local continuity, intelligence, and networks of trust. The paradox of globalization is that its socio-economic impact—in the form of the 'rustbelts' and 'sunrise' zones of which we spoke in Chapter 1—makes focused localized policing, as well as international co-operation, even more important.

Thirdly, the larger that police units become, the greater the geographical areas they cover, the greater the likelihood that local continuity of police personnel attachments will diminish. There are currently forty-three police forces in England and Wales. The vast majority of police officers serve in only one force for the whole of their careers. The exceptions are the fast-track, more senior officers. Indeed the police promotion rules *require* that promotion through the ACPO ranks—chief constables, their deputies, and assistants—shall involve service in more than one constabulary. But this pattern is the exception. Most retiring officers, be they constables, sergeants, inspectors, or superintendents, have served their twenty to thirty years in the same force, albeit probably on several patches within the county or counties that their force covers. Their stock of local knowledge is typically considerable, though not as intimate as that which their predecessors would have had forty years ago when there were over 100 forces and most officers saw service in only a single county or city. Were we to amalgamate our existing forty-three forces and develop, say, ten to fifteen regional police forces, then it is almost inevitable that officers of every rank would move greater distances than they do now, would typically live at a greater distance from their current posting, and be less familiar with and to the locality policed. It ought to be possible to prevent this happening, but experience of larger organizations suggests that greater career mobility is invariably the outcome.

Of course some career mobility is desirable. We think the rules requiring that candidates for chief constable posts should have moved are wise. A fresh pair of eyes as little clouded by local alliances or enmities is usually an asset. Moreover the small-town corruption so characteristic of policing arrangements in the United States and which blighted some small police forces in Britain half a century ago is something probably more easily avoided by having larger units less easily influenced by local power brokers. Precisely what is the optimum size for a police force in terms of these and other factors—not least economies of scale—is a difficult issue to determine.

Fourthly, whatever form police units take—be they local, regional, or national—we have no doubt that they should be directly accountable to a body the majority of whose members are democratically elected and capable of determining the broad direction of policy. We think this is both a principle and a requirement for long-term public confidence. We will not engage here in a detailed discussion of what that accountability should comprise, or the extent to which the nature of policing requires a degree of operational autonomy greater than that generally considered appropriate for other public services. There is a huge literature on that topic,[25] the product of the disputes and intensive debates about policing which characterized the early 1980s. It will suffice if we indicate that we do *not* think there is anything particularly distinctive about the office of constable compared to, say, the professional responsibilities of doctors, social workers, or teachers. Each quite properly requires a degree of operational autonomy within which professional judgement may be exercised untrammelled by political or other influence. We see no conflict between the exercise of a degree of operational autonomy and a requirement that the overall direction of

policy be determined by the people through their democratically elected representatives, be it in Parliament, or through local
councils, or both.

We have expressed some reservations about the make-up of
police authorities, both before and after the Police and
Magistrates' Courts Act 1994, in the sections above. On the other
hand we see a number of potentially positive developments arising from the new Act and we particularly welcome the requirement under the Act that the production of an annual Policing
Plan should be the responsibility of each police authority.
Though this requirement applies to all provincial police forces it
does not, as yet, apply to regional or national police bodies. The
remaining questions therefore are, should police bodies other
than provincial forces be subject to the requirement to publish
an annual policing plan and should some of these policing plans
be laid before Parliament for debate?

In Chapter 2 we outlined, in brief, some of the developing
regional, national, and international policing structures that
have grown up in recent years. Many of these structures have
grown a little like Topsy and have not so far been matched by
robust systems of public accountability. There is at best a flimsy
statutory basis for most of the international and supranational
arrangements, for example.[26] At the other end of the spectrum
there is no statutory basis for the existence of the Regional Crime
Squads—other than the provision of section 13 of the Police Act
1964, which enable voluntary collaborative agreements to be
established between forces. Since the RCSs cover larger areas
than are provided for by the normal lines of police accountability to the police authorities they exist in a sort of accountability
limbo.

We have no doubt about the need for regional and national
structures and for a formal basis for international policing liaison, intelligence exchange, and proactive action. The developing
international criminal networks are, as we have argued, no
respecters of national boundaries, and it is quite clear that a collection of relatively small local police forces provides an inadequate organizational basis to counter such activity. However, we
think there is almost certainly now a case for grasping a nettle
about which there is general political and police reluctance to
talk—namely the need for a national police force with a remit to

tackle organized national and international crime. We think that there ought to be what the Government claims the National Crime Squad will not be—namely, a national police force.

The reluctance among political and senior police circles to back the creation of a national force is not surprising. The forty-three chief constables are likely to see such a body as a threat to their own power and autonomy. Both they and the Home Secretary are likely to be able to exercise greater control over the resources and the policies of regional and national squads that exist in the murky interstices of the tripartite arrangements for the governance of the local police forces. This largely hidden territory provides for the minimum public interference, questioning, and scrutiny, which is precisely why the arrangement needs to be reformed.

We have no doubt that the existing lack of clarity regarding the mechanisms for holding regional and national policing bodies to account has been profoundly damaging for public confidence. During the 1984–5 Miners' Strike, for example, the operation of the National Reporting Centre—the Centre periodically instituted to organize 'mutual aid' between police forces to cope with major movements of citizens that arguably might give rise to threats to public order—became the cause of widespread dispute and suspicion. It matters little whether, in reality, the National Reporting Centre was directed by ACPO or the Home Office. The point was that whoever was directing the Centre, they *were not effectively accountable to a democratically elected forum for whatever direction was being given.* This angered police authority members as much as it did Members of Parliament. There was altogether too close an identity for comfort between the operational policing decisions being taken under the ægis of the National Reporting Centre and the proclaimed interests of the government in winning the battle against the miners. The perceived political impartiality of the police was jeopardized as a consequence. No such suspicions have yet been aroused by the activities of the regional and national squads that have since been established. But the same accountability breach attends them.

We think it is time to take up the proposition last systematically considered by the 1962 Royal Commission on the Police. Should we have a properly constituted national police force accountable to the Home Secretary and Parliament? The Royal Commission thought there was a substantial case for creating a national police force—they thought it would in many respects be more logical organizationally and might be more efficient for crime fighting and handling road traffic. Furthermore the Commission saw no objection to such an arrangement, constitutionally or politically.[27] But they implicitly took the view—mistakenly in our opinion—that the choice had to be *between* local and national policing arrangements. In the end their majority view (one of their number dissenting) was that local arrangements would better achieve the other objects which they recommended.

In our judgement there is no need to choose. We can have the best of all worlds—a national policing structure accountable to Parliament—which would mean that its Policing Plan could properly be debated in Parliament in a manner that the priorities and methods of the existing national and regional squads and agencies are not. *And* we can retain local forces on much the sort of pattern we have at present.

What objections will be raised to this proposal? There will of course be cultural objections. Within the British political tradition the very title—a National Police Force—smacks of repugnant Napoleonic visions; it conjures up the spectre of a centralized politically-driven force threatening the civil liberties of the British citizen. In the opinion of one senior police officer the whole idea of a national police force is mistakenly associated with political tyranny.[28] But close scrutiny of the policing arrangements which we have for long suffered indicates that the reverse is potentially more true. During recent decades there are three developments on which every serious commentator on policing has been agreed and the contours of which we have ranged over in earlier chapters: there has been creeping centralization of the direction of policing policy while what is largely the constitutional fiction of local autonomy has been maintained; policing policy has become more and more party-politicized, thereby making policing structures which are effectively unaccountable more hazardous; and the major changes in the direction of policing policy have not been properly debated in either Westminster or the local police authorities.

What we propose will help remedy this unsatisfactory

situation. The national police force will be accountable to Parliament. The local police forces will be accountable to both the Home Secretary and to their police authorities. Given that all police forces now have to agree their policies in the form of an annual plan, the creation of a properly constituted national force should mean that *all* the key aspects of policing policy will have to be publicly debated in fora where the majority of members are democratically elected.

Furthermore, the formation of a national police force will, paradoxically, better safeguard the local policing tradition which the British people favour. The constant political threat of local police force amalgamation, most recently raised by the provisions for amalgamation in the Police and Magistrates' Courts Act 1994, recurs because of the alleged inefficiency of small local forces to counter serious crime that spans county boundaries. If the latter threat is principally the business of a properly constituted national force, then it follows that local police forces can be left in more secure long-term peace to get on with the bread-and-butter business with which all local police forces predominantly deal. Indeed, were we to create a national police force we might even consider the prospect of de-amalgamation, breaking up some of the larger metropolitan forces which many commentators think unwieldy, and which, in some corners of the country, have always been resented as alien forces. Coventry, for example, has never been happy to be part of the West Midlands Police. The Metropolitan Police has long since been regarded as too large, as evidenced by its constant reorganization. There is a serious case to be put for *more localized policing*. We think this is most likely to be achieved, ironically, as part of a process in which a national police force is created.

It will of course be said that there will inevitably be antagonisms between the national force and local forces and that this will lead to competition, mandate disputes, and inefficiency. We take this objection seriously, though, given the benefits which allegedly accrue from competition, this will be an odd objection if it is voiced by Conservative government spokespersons.

All divisions of labour involve some disbenefits, and in this regard policing organizations have been no exception. Communication between the CID and uniformed branches have often not been of the best, and there has always been a good deal of suspicion among provincial forces about the alleged untrustworthiness and arrogance of the Metropolitan Police—a feature of the Operation Countryman investigation to which we referred in Chapter 2. Similar tensions have always surrounded relationships between mainstream policing bodies and the 'elite'—as they are generally seen to be—regional and national squads. It follows that the 'lack of co-operation' and 'territorial' objections likely to be levelled at the idea of a national police force apply equally to the government proposal that there be a National Crime Squad. In our judgement these disputes are less likely to arise if the mandate of the national force is set down clearly in a statute and if its Policing Plan has to be laid annually before Parliament. The core of its mandate should revolve around the collection of intelligence regarding national and international organized crime networks, combating serious organized crime and the performance of certain national policing functions currently the responsibility of the Metropolitan Police—protection of the Royal Family, Parliament, foreign embassies, and the diplomatic corps. This transfer of responsibilities from the Metropolitan Police would pave the way for thinking radically about the possible break-up of the Metropolitan Police into more manageable, possibly separate, sectoral police forces concentrating their attention unequivocally on the local services that Londoners want and need.

7

NEXT STEPS

The four dilemmas on which we concentrated our attention in Chapters 5 and 6 by no means exhaust the difficult decisions confronting policing policy makers. But we selected these four—providing the visible patrols the public want, the relationship between state and non-state police, the responsibility for crime prevention planning, and the organization of police forces—because we think their resolution provides the key which will better unlock subsidiary dilemmas. Take, for example, the question on which the Audit Commission concentrated its attention in its 1993 report, *Helping with Enquiries: Tackling Crime Effectively*. The Commission recommended a shift from reactive to proactive policing. It proposed that crime intelligence be given a more pivotal place in the allocation of policing resources and that police concentrate rather less on offences and rather more on prolific offenders. These shifts would better enable crime to be *managed*. The Audit Commission's proposals are undoubtedly evoking a response, and some police forces, or at least their senior officers, are now enthusiastic advocates of a model of 'intelligence-led policing' which by all accounts is involving substantial changes in the manner in which police personnel are used.[1]

The Audit Commission's proposals—given fulsome support in the Government's most recent White Paper[2]—do of course reflect the Government's view, set out in the 1993 White Paper on *Police Reform*, that crime fighting is and should be the police's key role. It should be no surprise, therefore, that the 'intelligence-led policing model' raises questions about the degree to which other policing functions and activities can be satisfied and carried out. How important is it to victims, for example, that their calls are responded to even if police attendance at the scene of their crime is not likely to lead to the identification of the offender? What happens to dedicated local police patrols which, however much they may reassure the public, are not considered, in the short term at least, to contribute much to the clear-up of crime or the nailing of persistent offenders? How marginal and specialized does the task of liaising with local community groups become? What happens to primary crime prevention?

We take what we think is a more balanced view of the police role. We have endorsed the service's current Statement of Common Purpose and we are sceptical of claims that the police can, alone, 'tackle crime effectively'. All the evidence shows that they cannot. We think it vital, therefore, that the police be tied organizationally into civic life so that whatever it is that they want to do, they have actively to carry the public with them. We do not doubt the value of 'intelligence-led policing'. On the contrary. We also think there is a powerful case for concentrating a good many police resources on identifying and bringing to book persistent offenders. However, we do not think this is a policing panacea. And the key question is: how many policing resources are to be devoted to this as opposed to other, in our opinion, *equally important* police objectives?

The *leitmotif* running through all our proposals, therefore, is *policing by consent, partnership,* and *shaping the policing organization to fit the problem,* not vice versa. We want the police to develop a partnership with non-police patrol options which we hope will develop and to experiment by creating their own patrol rank— the auxiliary patrol officer—in order to deliver a service that the public undoubtedly wants. We want Policing Plans to be dovetailed with local authority Community Safety Plans so that crime prevention becomes a shared responsibility and the basis for all that the police do. And we want the real challenge of organized national and international crime to be faced up to by means of a national police force accountable to Parliament. Our argument is that, once these mechanisms are in place, then the dilemmas inherent in deciding the balance that needs to be struck between reactive and proactive policing is more likely to be informed by public debate, understanding, and consent. As we said at the beginning of this text policing is far too important to be left to the police and we should not lightly throw away a British police tradition which, for all its faults, still commands the strong support of most of the British people. In our judgement failure to tackle the four dilemmas which we have identified will do just that—prejudice a fine policing tradition which lies at the heart of the British way of life.

How then should we proceed? In recent years there have been repeated calls, particularly from the Liberal Democratic Party, for a Royal Commission on the role, responsibilities, and organization of the police. We understand this call—particularly in the period running up to the Police and Magistrates Courts Act 1994 when it appeared that the government was prepared to push through far-reaching changes to our policing system which had been the subject of little or no consultation and consideration— but we do not support it, for the simple reason that we think the options facing us are well known and understood, albeit probably only by those specialists who make it their business to consider policing policy. Moreover we have a wealth of research evidence—possibly a greater wealth than any other country in Europe—about what the British people want from their police, what the police spend their time doing, what works and how policing policy decisions are made. What we need is not the research studies that a Royal Commision might put in hand, or the wise deliberations of the great and the good. What we require is, rather, politicians prepared to take the problem of crime seriously—which means less sloganizing and posturing behind tough but misleading rhetoric—by mounting local experiments so that we can see how the people and the police take to some of the practical propositions that we have suggested.

Some of the developments that we have suggested—placing a statutory responsibility on local authorities to prepare Comunity Safety Plans, the creation of a National Police Force, and proposals for the regulation of private security (broadly defined; not just guarding)—should be the subject of a White Paper setting out the proposed detail and, subsequently, will require legislation. But other proposals—the development of the auxiliary patrol rank and partnerships with non-police patrol groups—need to be the subject of well considered, well publicized and well evaluated *experiments* which could be organized by the Home Office and which different forces might *bid* to conduct. There might be appointed a Home Office Advisory Committee—comprising police and local authority representatives and some independent persons with research, business, and other expertise—

whose task it would be to oversee this process of experimentation. The Advisory Committee could approve the nature of the experiments to be conducted, supervise the tendering/bidding process, organize the evaluations (which might themselves be contracted out), and publicize the results by, among other methods, holding regional seminars and other discussions. The Advisory Body should then make recommendations as to how these ideas might be developed nationally and institutionally.

Above all these experiments and evaluations should include a process of public consultation and participation. This process would *itself* help to achieve three things. It would ensure that public opinion becomes an essential criterion to be considered for success. It would ferment a public debate about the desirablity of the arrangements. And it would help forge the partnership between police and community which is essential to all effective policing and crime preventive effort. So should we proceed.

NOTES

INTRODUCTION

1 The cartoon was described by Professor Robert Reiner in his Inaugural Lecture 'Fin de Siecle Blues: Policing a Postmodern Society' at the London School of Economics in 1992.

2 *Hansard* House of Commons debates, 12 July 1977, col. 231.

3 Quoted in Rawlings, P. (1991), 'Creeping privatisation? The police, the Conservative government and policing in the late 1980s' in Reiner, R. and Cross, M. (eds.), *Beyond Law and Order: Criminal justice policy and politics into the 1990s.* London: Macmillan.

4 Baker, K. (1993), *The Turbulent Years: My life in politics*, London: Faber and Faber, 450.

5 Mayhew, P., Elliott, D., and Dowds, E.A. (1989), *The 1988 British Crime Survey*, Home Office Research Study No.111 London: HMSO

6 See, for example, *Police Review*, 20 May 1985.

7 Reiner, R. (1992), *The Politics of the Police*, Hemel Hempstead: Harvester Wheatsheaf; Sheerman, B. (1991), 'What Labour wants', *Policing* vol. 7 no. 3.

8 Home Office (1993), *Police Reform: A Police Service for the Twenty-First Century*, Cm 2281, London: HMSO.

9 *Ibid.*, para. 2.2.

10 Sheehy Report (1993), *Report of the Inquiry into Police Responsibilities and Rewards*, Cm 2280, I, II, London: HMSO.

11 'Police threaten 'open conflict''. *Financial Times*, 1 July 1993.

12 'Police leader fears coercive national force', *The Guardian*, 5 February 1994.

13 Home Office (1994,) *Review of Police Core and Ancillary Tasks: Interim Report*, London: Home Office.

14 *Ibid.*

15 Audit Commission (1996), *Streetwise: Effective Police Patrol*, London: Audit Commission.

16 Audit Commission (1993), *Helping With Inquiries: Tackling Crime Effectively*, London: Audit Commission.

17 Audit Commission (1993), Summary 2.

CHAPTER ONE

1 Commission on Social Justice (1994), *Social Justice: Strategies for National Renewal*, London: Vintage.
2 See Green A. (1994), *The Geography of Poverty*, Warwick: Institute of Emloyment Research.
3 Joseph Rowntree Foundation (1995), *Income and Wealth: Report of the JRF Inquiry Group, Summary*, York: Joseph Rowntree Foundation.
4 Willmott, P. (1994), *Urban Trends 2*, London: PSI.
5 Bottoms, A. E and Wiles, P. (1994), *Crime and Insecurity in the City*, Paper presented at the International Course organized by the International Society of Criminology, Leuven, Belgium, May 1994.
6 House of Commons Home Affairs Select Committee (1995), *Organised Crime*, Session 1994–95, London: HMSO.
7 Lord Scarman (1982), *The Scarman Report: The Brixton Disorders, 10–12 April 1981*, Harmondsworth: Penguin, 120.
8 Hough, M. (1995), *Anxiety about crime: findings from the 1994 British Crime Survey*, Home Office Research Study No.147, London: Home Office, 43.

CHAPTER TWO

1 Chibnall, S. (1977), *Law and Order News*, London: Tavistock, 71, quoted in Reiner (1992) n. 3 below.
2 For a general account of these developments see Cox, B., Shirley, J., and Short, M. (1977), *The Fall of Scotland Yard*, Harmondsworth: Penguin.
3 For an account of this period see Reiner R. (1992), *The Politics of the Police, op. cit.*, Ch. Two.
4 All the figures quoted are drawn from *Social Trends*, vols 11–19, London: HMSO.
5 Home Office (1983), *Manpower, Effectiveness and Efficiency in the Police Service*, Circular 114/1983, London: Home Office; Home Office (1988), *Applications for increases in police force establishments*, Circular 106/1988, London: Home Office.
6 Morgan, R., and Maggs, C. (1985), *Setting the PACE: Police community consultation arrangements in England and Wales*, Bath Social Policy Papers No. 4, University of Bath.
7 Jones, T., Newburn, T., and Smith, D.J. (1994), *Democracy and Policing*, London: PSI.

8 Lustgarten L. (1986), *The Governance of Police*, London: Sweet and Maxwell, 87.

9 Reiner, n. 3 above, 223.

10 Lord Scarman (1982), n. 7, ch. 1.

11 *Ibid.*, para. 3.110.

12 *Ibid.*, para. 5.3.

13 *Ibid.*, para. 4.57.

14 Cmnd. 8092 (1981), *Report of the Royal Commission on Criminal Procedure*, London: HMSO.

15 For general reviews see Ashworth A. (1994), *The Criminal Process: An Evaluative Study*, Oxford: Oxford University Press, Chs. 4 and 5; and Sanders A. and Young R. (1994), *Criminal Justice*, London: Butterworths, Chs. 2–4.

16 See Morgan R. (1995), *Making Consultation Work: A Handbook for those involved in police community consulation arrangements*, London: The Police Foundation.

17 See Morgan R. (1992), 'Talking about policing' in Downes D. (ed.), *Unravelling Criminal Justice*, Basingstoke: Macmillan.

18 Maguire, M., and Corbett, C. (1991), *A Study of the Police Complaints System*, London: HMSO.

19 Skogan, W. (1994), *Contacts between police and public: findings from the 1992 British Crime Survey*, Home Office Research Study No. 134, London: HMSO.

20 Cm 2263 (The Runciman Report) (1993), *Report of the Royal Commission on Criminal Justice*, London: HMSO.

21 Home Office (1992), *Police Reform: A Police Service for the Twenty First Century*, Cm 2281, London: HMSO.

22 See, for example, Reiner, R. (1993a), Police Accountability: Principles, patterns and practices, in, Reiner, R., and Spencer, S. (ed.), *Accountable Policing: Effectiveness, Empowerment and Equity*, London: Institute for Public Policy Research.

23 Sheehy Report (1993), *Inquiry into Police Responsibilities and Rewards*, Cm 2280.I,II, London: HMSO.

24 Home Office (1994), *Review of Police Core and Ancillary Tasks: Interim Report*, London: Home Office, para. 6.

25 Cm 2281 (1993), Preface.

26 Home Office (1995), *Review of Police Core and Ancillary Tasks: Final Report*, London: Home Office.

27 Conservative Party (1979), *The Conservative Manifesto 1979*, London: Conservative Central Office, 19.

28 Conservative Party (1983), *The Challenge of Our Times*, London: Conservative Party.

29 Conservative Party (1987), *Our First Eight Years: The Next Moves Forward*, London: Conservative Central Office, 55.

30 Cornish Report (1965), *Report of the Committee on the Prevention and Detection of Crime*, London: Home Office.

31 Alderson, J. (1979), *Policing Freedom*, London: Macdonald and Evans; see also his evidence to the Scarman Inquiry in Alderson J. (1984), *Law and Disorder*, London: Hamish Hamilton, App. A.

32 Home Office (1978), *Juveniles: Cooperation between the police and other agencies*, Circular 211/1978, London: Home Office.

33 Home Office and others (1984), *Crime Prevention*, Circular 8/1984, London: Home Office.

34 See Tilley, N. (1982), *Safer Cities and Community Safety Srategies*, Police Research Group, Paper 38, London: Home Office.

35 Home Office (1996), *Protecting the Public: The government's strategy on crime in England and Wales*, Cm 3190, London: Home Office, para. 2.4.

36 Pease, K. (1994), 'Crime Prevention' in Maguire M., Morgan R., and Reiner R., *The Oxford Handbook of Criminology*, Oxford: Oxford University Press, 683.

37 See, for example, Weatheritt M. (1986), *Innovations in Policing*, London: Croom Helm.

38 See Smith L. J. F. (1984), *Neighbourhood Watch: A note on implemenation*, London: Crime Prevention Unit, Home Ofice.

39 Dowds, L., and Mayhew, P. (1994), *Participation in Neighbourhood Watch: Finding from the 1992 British Crime Survey*, Home Office Research Findings No. 11, London: Home Office.

40 *Protecting the Public*, n. 35 above, para. 2.26.

41 See Bennett T. (1990), *Evaluating Neighbourhood Watch*, Aldershot: Gower.

42 *Protecting the Public*, n. 35 above, para. 2.29.

43 Audit Commission (1993), *Helping with Enquiries: Tackling Crime Effectively*, London: Audit Commission.

44 *Ibid.*, para. 78.

45 Audit Comission (1996), *Tackling Crime Effectively Volume 2*, London: Audit Commission.

46 Home Office (1996), *op. cit.*, para. 335.

47 House of Commons Home Affairs Committee (1995), *Organised Crime*, Session 1994–95, London: HMSO.

48 *Ibid.*, para. 3.34.

49 *Ibid.*, para. 3.36.

50 Shearing, C., and Stenning, P. (1983), 'Private security: implications for social control', *Social Problems*, vol. 30, no. 5, 493–506.

51 Jones, T., and Newburn, T. (1995), 'How big is the private security sector?' *Policing and Society*, 5, 221–32.

52 I'Anson, J., and Wiles, P. (1995), *The Sedgefield Community Force: the results of a survey of the public's response to the introduction of the Force*, Sheffield: Centre for Criminological and Legal Research, University of Sheffield. .

53 Wiles, P. (1996), *The Quality of Service of the Sedgefield Community Force: The results of a customer satisfaction survey on the work of the Force*, Sheffield: Centre for Criminological and Legal Research, University of Sheffield.

54 Comparable figures for the police are contained in Bucke, T. (1996), *Policing and the public: Findings from the 1994 British Crime Survey*, Home Office Research Findings No. 28, London: Home Office.

55 See Jones, T., and Newburn, T. (forthcoming), *Private Security and Public Policing*, Oxford: Clarendon Press, chs. five and six.

CHAPTER THREE

1 Home Office (1993), *Police Reform: A Police Service for the Twenty-First Century*, Cm 2281, London: HMSO .

2 The cover description on Anthony Martienssen's 1953 book *Crime and the Police*, (London: Penguin) opens with the sentence: 'The police forces of Britain have the reputation of being the best in the world'; see also Weinberger B. (1995), *The Best Police in the World?*, Aldershot: Scolar.

3 Quoted in Critchley T.A. (1967), *A History of Police in England and Wales 900–1966*, London: Constable, 201.

4 Quoted in Emsley, C. (1983), *Policing and its Context 1750–1870*, London: Macmillan.

5 Manning, P. (1977), *Police Work*, Cambridge Mass.: MIT Press, 56.

6 Research on neighbourhood policing in London in the 1980s found that although approximately nine tenths of supervisors felt that great emphasis should not be placed on making large numbers of arrests, less than one fifth of constables held a similar view. Being seen to be engaged in making arrests, issuing summonses, and stopping and searching suspects was, from their perspective, a necessity for anyone interested in being transferred to the more favoured CID work or, more generally, in promotion. See Irving, B., Bird, C., Hibberd, M., and Willmore, J. (1989), *Neighbourhood Policing: The natural history of a policing experiment*, London: The Police Foundation.

7 Reiner, R. (1991), *Chief Constables*, Oxford: Oxford University Press.

8 Hagan, J. (1977), *The Disreputable Pleasures: Crime and Deviance in Canada*, quoted in Jones *et al.*, 1986, 123.

9 Hough, M. (1985), 'Organisation and resource management in the uniformed police', in, Heal, K., Tarling, R., and Burrows, J. (eds.), *Policing Today*, London: HMSO.

10 Comrie, M. D., and Kings, E. J. (1974), 'Urban Workloads', *Police Research Bulletin* 23, 32–38.

11 Ekblom, P., and Heal, K. (1982), *The Police Response to Calls from the Public*, Research and Planning Unit Paper No. 9, London: Home Office.

12 Skogan, W. (1990), *The Police and Public in England and Wales: A British Crime Survey Report*, Home Office Research Study No. 117, London: HMSO.

13 Jones, T., MacLean, B., and Young, J. (1986), *The Islington Crime Survey*, Aldershot: Gower.

14 Skogan, W. (1990),n. 12 above, 12.

15 Punch, M., and Naylor, T. (1973), 'The police: a social service', *New Society*, 24, 358–61.

16 Smith, D.J. (1983), *Police and People in London III: A survey of police officers*, London: Policy Studies Institute.

17 Bittner, E. (1974), 'Florence Nightingale in pursuit of Willie Sutton: A theory of the police', in Jacob H. (ed.), *The Potential for Reform of Criminal Justice*, Beverley Hills: Sage.

18 Audit Commission (1996), *Streetwise: Effective police patrol*, London: Audit Commission.

19 Bayley, D. (1994), *Police for the Future*, New York: Oxford University Press. .

20 Smith (1983), n. 16 above.

21 Bayley (1994), note 19 above, 20.

22 Home Office (1993), n. 1 above.

23 Diez, L. (1994), *The Use of Call Grading: How calls to the police are graded and resourced*, Police Research Series Paper 13, London: Home Office Police Research Group.

24 Waddington, P. A. J. (1994), *Calling the Police*, Aldershot: Gower; see also Diez, L. (1994), n. 23.

25 Graef, R. (1990), *Talking Blues: The police in their own words*, London: Fontana.

26 Audit Commission (1993), *Helping with Enquiries: Tackling Crime Effectively*, London: Audit Commission, Exhibit 10.

27 Maguire M., and Norris C. (1992), *The Conduct and Supervision of Criminal Investigations*, Royal Commission on Criminal Justice Research Study No 5, London: HMSO.

28 Ogilvie-Smith, A., Downey, A., and Ransom, E. (1994), *Traffic Policing: Activity and Organisation*, Police Research Series Paper No. 12, Home Office, Home Office Police Research Group.

29 'Privatisation of motorway policing under review', *Independent*, 10 March 1994.

30 Ogilvie-Smith *et al.* (1994), n. 28 above.

31 Mayhew, P. Mirrlees-Black, C., and Aye Maung, N. (1994), *Trends in Crime: Finding from the 1994 British Crime Survey*, Home Office Research Findings No. 14, London: Home Office.

32 Southgate, P., and Crisp, D. (1992), *Public Satisfaction with Police Services*, Research and Planning Unit Paper No. 73, London: Home Office.

33 Sherman, L. (1983), 'After the riots: police and minorities in the US, 1970–1980', in N. Glazer and K. Young, (eds.), *Ethnic Pluralism and Public Policy*, London: Heinemann.

34 Reiner, R. (1989), 'Race and criminal justice', *New Community*, 16:1, 5–22.

35 Reiner, R. (1991), *Chief Constables*, Oxford: Oxford University Press.

36 Aye Maung, N. (1995), *Young people, victimisation and the police: British Crime Survey findings on experiences and attitudes of 12–15 year olds*, Home Office Research Study No. 140, London: HMSO.

37 Jones, T., Maclean, B., and Young, J. (1986), *The Islington Crime Survey*, Aldershot: Gower.

38 Skogan, W. (1990), n. 12 above, 24.

39 Ekblom, P., and Heal, K. (1982), *The Police Response to Calls From the Public*, Research and Planning Unit Paper 9, London: Home Office.

40 Bucke, T. (1995), *Policing and the Public: Findings from the 1994 British Crime Survey*, Home Office Research Research Findings No.28, London: Home Office.

41 *Ibid.*

42 There is some evidence that this can be done. See Jolowicz, C., and Read, T. (1994), *Managing demand on the police: An evaluation of a crime line*, Police Research Series Paper 8, London: Home Office Police Research Group.

43 Storch, R. (1975), 'The plague of blue locusts: police reform and popular resistance in Northern England 1840–57', *International Review of Social History*, 20, 61–90.

44 Skogan, W. (1996), 'Public opinion and the police', in Saulsbury, W., Mott, J., and Newburn, T. (eds.), *Themes in Contemporary Policing*, London: Police Foundation/Policy Studies Institute.

45 Joint Consultative Committee (1990), *Operational Policing Review*, Surbiton: Surrey.

46 Skogan, W. (1996), n. 44 above.

47 Consumers' Association (1996), *Policy Report: Police and the Public*, London: Consumers' Association.
48 Jones, T., and Newburn, T. (1996), 'Policing Disaffected Communities', in *Annual Report of the Standing Advisory Commission on Human Rights*, London: HMSO.
49 Fielding, N. (1995), *Community Policing*, Oxford: Clarendon Press.

CHAPTER FOUR

1   See Downes, D., and Morgan R. (1994), 'Hostages to Fortune'? The Politics of Law and Order in Post-War Britain' in Maguire, M., Morgan, R., and Reiner, R. (eds.), *The Oxford Handbook of Criminology*, Oxford: Oxford University Press.
2   Davis, M. (1992), *City of Quartz: Excavating the future of Los Angeles*, London: Vintage.
3   Currie, E. (1996), 'Is America Winning the 'War' on Crime—and Should Britain Follow Our Example?', NACRO 30th Anniversary Lecture, London, 18 June.
4   *Ibid*. For a critical survey of all these issues, see the paper by Currie and the report of the National Criminal Justice Commission (1996), *The Real War on Crime*, New York: National Criminal Justice Commission.
5   To take one example, there were as many Criminal Justice Acts between 1982 and 1993 as there were between 1948 and 1977.
6   'Home Office's £40m private security bill', *The Guardian*, 3 October 1994.
7   Galbraith J. K. (1958), *The Affluent Society*, London: Hamish Hamilton; Galbraith J. K. (1967), *The New Industrial State*, London: Hamish Hamilton.
8   Hagell, A., and Newburn, T. (1994), *Persistent Young Offenders*, London: Policy Studies Institute.
9   Graham, J., and Bowling, B. (1995), *Young People and Crime*, Home Office Research Study No.145, London: Home Office.
10 Lord Scarman (1982), *Report of an Inquiry into the Brixton Disorder, 10–12 April 1981*, Harmondsworth: Penguin, para. 5.62.
11 Waddington, P. A. J. (1993), *Calling the Police*, Aldershot: Avebury.
12 *Ibid*.
13 Mawby, R. (1979), *Policing the City*, Farnborough: Gower; Hough, M. (1996), 'The police patrol function: What research can tell us', in Saulsbury, W., *et al*. (eds.), *Themes in Contemporary Policing*, London: Policy Foundation/Policy Studies Institute.
14 Burrows, J., and Tarling, R. (1982), *Clearing Up Crime*, Home Office

Research Study No. 73, London: HMSO; Brown, D. (1991), *Investigating Burglary: The effect of PACE*, Home Office Research Study No. 123, London: HMSO.

15 Bottomley, A. K., and Coleman, C. (1981), *Understanding Crime Rates*, Farnborough: Gower; Maguire, M., and Norris, C. (1992), *The Conduct and Supervision of Criminal Investigations*, Royal Commission on Criminal Justice Research Study No. 5, London: HMSO.

16 See Reiner, R. (1992), *The Politics of the Police*, Hemel Hempstead: Harvester Wheatsheaf, 152. .

17 Cox, B., Shirley, J., and Short, M. (1977), *The Fall of Scotland Yard*, London: Penguin; Greer, S. (1994), *Supergrasses: Anti-Terrorist Law Enforcement in Northern Ireland*, Oxford: Oxford University Press.

18 Audit Commission (1993), *Helping with Enquiries: Tackling Crime Effectively*, London: Audit Commission, 84–6.

19 For a fuller discussion of these issues see Dunninghan, C., and Norris, C. (1995), 'The detective, the snout, and the Audit Commission: the real costs in using informants', Paper presented at the British Criminology Conference, Loughborough, July.

20 Mayhew, P., Mirrlees-Black, C., and Aye Maung, N. (1994), *Trends in Crime: Findings from the 1994 British Crime Survey*, Home Office Research Findings No 14, London: Home Office, 4.

21 Hanmer, J., and Saunders, S. (1984), *Well-Founded Fear: A community study of violence to women*, London: Hutchinson.

22 Johnston, L. (1996), 'What is vigilantism?', *British Journal of Criminology*, 36, 2, 220–36.

23 Mayhew, P., Aye Maung, N., and Mirrlees-Black, C. (1993), *The 1992 British Crime Survey*, Home Office Research Study No. 132, London: HMSO, 26.

24 Carr-Hill, N. A., and Stern, N. H. (1979), *Crime, the Police and Criminal Statistics*, London: Academic Press.

25 Clarke, R., and Hough, M. (1984), *Crime and Police Effectiveness*, Home Office Research Study No.79, London: HMSO; Heal, K., Tarling, R., and Burrows, J. (eds.), (1985), *Policing Today*, London: HMSO.

26 Kelling, G., Pate, T., Dieckman, D., and Brown, C. (1974), *The Kansas City Preventive Patrol Experiment*, Washington DC: Police Foundation.

27 Audit Commission (1996), *Streetwise: Effective Police Patrol*, London: Audit Commission, Exhibit 5.

28 Clarke and Hough (1984), n. 25 above.

29 Bieck, W. (1977), *Response Time Analysis*, Kansas City Police Department, Kansas City; Spelman, W., and Brown, D. (1981),

Calling the Police: Citizen reporting of serious crime, Washington DC: Police Executive Research Forum; Ekblom, P., and Heal, K. (1982), *The Police Response to Calls from the Public*, Research and Planning Unit Paper No. 9, London: Home Office.

30 Police Foundation (1981), *The Newark Foot Patrol Experiment*, Washington DC: Police Foundation; Trojanowicz, R. C. (1986), 'Evaluating a Neighbourhood Foot Patrol Programme', in Rosenbaum, D. (ed.), *Community Crime Prevention: Does it work?* London: Sage.

31 See Maguire and Norris (1992), n. 15 above.

32 Burrows and Tarling (1982), n. 14 above.

33 The Government's plans for mandatory minumum prison sentences for repeat offenders is a further part of this strategy. See Home Office (1996), *Protecting the Public: The Government's Strategy on Crime in England and Wales*, Cm 3190, London: Home Office, chs. 10–12.

34 See Maguire, M., and John, T. (1995), *Intelligence, Surveillance and Informants: Integrated Aproaches*, Crime Detection and Pevention Series Paper 64, London: Home Office Police Research Group, 55.

35 Skolnick J. (1966), *Justice Without Trial: Law Enforcement in a Democratic Society*, New York: Wiley.

36 For discussion see Maguire and Norris (1992), n. 15 above, ch. 3.

37 Rubenstein, H., Murray, C. Motoyama, T., Rouse, W. V., and Titus, R. (1980), *The Link Between Crime and the Built Environment: The current state of knowledge*, Washington DC: National Institute of Justice.

38 Knutsson, J., and Kuhlhorn, E. (1992), 'Macro-measures against crime: the example of check forgeries', in Clarke, R. (ed.), *Situational Crime Prevention: Successful Case Studies*, New York: Harrow and Heston.

39 Ekblom, P. (1986), *The Prevention of Shop Theft: An approach through crime analysis*, Home Office Crime Prevention Paper No. 5, London: Home Office.

40 Webb, B., and Laycock, G. (1992), *Reducing Crime on the London Underground: An evaluation of three pilot projects*, Crime Prevention Unit Paper 30, London: Home Office.

41 Brown, B. (1995), *CCTV in Town Centres: Three case studies*, Crime Detection and Prevention Series Paper 68, London: Home Office; Scottish Office Central Research Unit (1995), *Does CCTV Prevent Crime? An Evaluation of the use of CCTV Surveillance Cameras in Airdrie Town Centre*, Crime and Criminal Justice Research Findings No. 8, Edinburgh: Scottish Office.

42 Weatheritt, M. (1986), *Innovations in Policing*, London: Croom Helm.

CHAPTER FIVE

1 Johnston, L. (1996), 'What is Vigilantism?', *British Journal of Criminology*, 36, 2, 220–36.
2 Southgate, P., and Ekblom, P. (1984), *Contacts Between Police and Public: Findings from the British Crime Survey*, Home Office Research Study No. 77, London: HMSO.
3 Reiner, R. (1992), *The Politics of the Police*, Hemel Hempstead: Harvester Wheatsheaf, 73.
4 Evans, T. (ed.), (1991), *An Arresting Idea: The Management of Police Services in Modern Britain*, London: Adam Smith Institute.
5 Jones, T., and Newburn, T. (forthcoming), *Private Security and Public Policing*, Oxford: Clarendon Press.
6 A Commission in British Columbia, Canada, in 1994 noted that it was no longer feasible 'to expect the police to respond to all reports of offences or community problems' and that 'some types of law enforcement work can, and should be, done by non-police personnel such as civilians, private security firms or auxiliary officers'. Quoted in Shearing, C. (1996), 'Public and Private Policing', in Saulsbury, W. *et al.* (eds.), *Themes in Contemporary Policing*, London: Police Foundation/Policy Studies Institute, 89.
7 By contrast, *secondary* crime prevention in this classification refers to changing people, particularly those at high risk of embarking on a criminal career. Lastly, *tertiary* prevention is concerned with truncating criminal careers, generally through the treatment or punishment of known offenders: Brantingham, P. L., and Faust, F. L. (1976), 'A Conceptual Model of Crime Prevention', *Crime and Delinquency*, 22, 130–46.
8 Harvey, L., Grimshaw, P., and Pease, K. (1989), 'Crime Prevention Delivery: The Work of Crime Prevention Officers', in Morgan and Smith (eds.), *Coming to Terms with Policing*, London: Routledge; Johnston, V., Shapland, J., and Wiles, P. (1993), *Developing Police Crime Prevention: Management and Organisational Change*, Police Research Group Crime Prevention Unit Series Paper No. 41, London: Home Office.
9 Security Service Act 1996.
10 Reiner, R. (1993a), 'Police Accountability: Principles, Patterns and Practices', in Reiner, R., and Spencer, S. (eds.), *Accountable Policing: Effectivenes, Empowerment and Equity*, London: Institute for Public Policy Research.
11 Spencer, S. (1985), *Called to Account: The Case for Police Accountability in England and Wales*, London: NCCL; Jones, T.,

Newburn, T., and Smith, D. J. (1994), *Democracy and Policing*, London: Policy Studies Institute.

12 Reiner, R. (1991), *Chief Constables*, Oxford: Oxford University Press.

13 Audit Commission (1990), *Footing the Bill*, London: HMSO.

14 Loveday, B. (1992), 'The Local Accountability of Police in England and Wales—Future Prospects', Birmingham: Institute of Public Policy Research, University of Central England.

15 Jones, T., and Newburn, T. (1995), 'Local Government and Policing: Arresting the Decline of Local Influence', *Local Government Studies*, vol. 21, 3, 448–60.

16 Weatheritt, M. (1995), *Policing Plans: The Role of Police Authority Members*, London: Association of County Councils.

CHAPTER SIX

1 Bayley D. (1994), *Police for the Future*, New York: Oxford University Press.

2 *Ibid.*, ch. 5.

3 See, for example, ch. 9 in Kinsey, R., Lea, J., and Young, J. (1986), *Losing the Fight Against Crime*, Oxford: Blackwell.

4 Bayley (1994), n. 1 above, 124.

5 *Ibid.*, 90.

6 Home Office (1993), *Police Reform: A Police Service for the Twenty-First Century*, Cm 2281, London: HMSO, paras. 10.5 –10.10.

7 In the late 1970s this was the gibe frequently made about John Alderson's 'community policing' vision because of his position as commander of the Devon and Cornall Constabulary.

8 Bennett, T., and Lupton, R. (1992), 'A survey of the allocation and use of community constables in England and Wales' *British Journal of Criminology*, 32, 2, 167–82.

9 In which she describes the 1991 riots in Ely (Cardiff), Blackbird Leys (Oxford), and Meadowell (Newcastle). See Campbell, B. (1993), *Goliath: Britain's Dangerous Places*, London: Methuen.

10 Independent Inquiry (1996), *The Role and Responsibilities of the Police*, London: Police Foundation and Policy Studies Institute, para. 4.24; Audit Commission (1996), *Streetwise: Effective Police Patrol*, London: Audit Commission, para. 96.

11 Fielding, N. (1995), *Community Policing*, Oxford: Clarendon Press.

12 Bennett and Lupton (1992), n. 8 above.

13 Audit Commission, (1996), n. 10 above, para. 59.

14 *Ibid.*, Exhibit 26.

15 'Security guards will be licensed to curb cowboys', *Daily Telegraph*, 15 August 1996.

16 de Waard, J. (1993), 'The private security sector in fifteen European countries: Size, rules and legislation', *Security Journal*, 4, 58–63.

17 ACPO (1988), *A Review of the Private Security Industry*, London: ACPO.

18 ACPO (1994), *Evidence to the House of Commons Home Affairs Select Committee on the Private Security Industry*, London: ACPO.

19 House of Commons Home Affairs Select Committee (1995), *The Private Security Industry*, First Report, Session 1994–5, London: HMSO, para. 48.

20 George, B., and Watson, T. (1992), Regulation of the Private Security Industry, *Public Money and Management*, 12, 1, 55–7.

21 Waddington, P. A. J. (1993), *Calling the Police*, Aldershot: Avebury.

22 House of Commons Home Affairs Committee, (1995), n. 19 above.

23 Independent Inquiry (1996), n. 10 above, para. 5.17.

24 Brantingham, P. J., and Faust, F. L. (1976), 'A conceptual model of crime prevention', *Crime and Delinquency*, 22, 130–46.

25 See Stewart, J and Stoker, G. (1995), 'Local government restructuring 1979–94: an evaluation' in Stewart, J., and Stoker, G. (eds.), *Local Government in the 1990s*, Basingstoke: Macmillan.

26 This followed the recommendation of the Woolf Report (1991), *Prison Disturbances April 1990, Report of an Eenquiry by the Rt. Hon. Lord Justice Woolf (Parts I and II) and His Honour Judge Stephen Tumim (Part II)*, Cm 1456, London: HMSO, paras. 10.157–10.188.

27 Standing Conference on Crime Prevention (1991), *Safer Communities: The local delivery of crime prevention through the partnership appraoch*, London: Home Office.

28 For an outline of what the first set of authorities' plans looked like see Weatheritt, M. (1995), n. 16 (Chapter 5) above.

29 See Morgan, R. (1987), 'The local determinants of policing policy', in Willmott, P. (ed.), *Policing and the Community*, London: Policy Studies Institute.

30 See Morgan R. (1992), 'Talking About Policing' in Downes D. (ed.), *Unravelling Criminal Justice*, Basingstoke: MacMillan.

31 Kemp C., and Morgan R. (1990), *Lay Visitors to Police Stations: Report to the Home Office*, Bristol: Bristol Centre for Criminal Justice.

32 See Demuth, C. (1989), *Community Safety in Brighton: Report of a survey and consultation*, Brighton: Brighton Council Police and Public Safety Unit.

33 For a full discussion of such issues see Bottoms, A. E. (1994), 'Environmental criminology', in Maguire, M., Morgan, R., and Reiner, R. (eds.), *The Oxford Handbook of Criminology*, Oxford: Oxford University Press.

34 Evans, D. J., and Oulds, G. (1984), 'Geographical aspects of the inci-
    dence of residential burglary in Newcastle-under-Lyme, UK', in
    Tijdschrift voor Economische en Sociale Geografie, 75, 5.
35 Baldwin, J., and Bottoms, A. E. (1976), *The Urban Criminal*, London:
    Tavistock.
36 See, for example, Lustgarten, L. (1986), *The Governance of Police*,
    London: Sweet and Maxwell; Day, P., and Klein, R. (1987),
    Acccountablities, London: Routledge; Reiner R. (1992), *The Politics
    of the Police*, 2nd edn., London: Harvester Wheatsheaf, ch. 6.
37 See den Boer, M., and Walker, N. (1993), 'European Policing After
    1992', *Journal of Common Market Studies*, 31, 1, 3–28.
38 Home Office (1962), *Report of the Royal Commission on Police*,
    Cmnd. 1728, London: Home Office.
39 Oliver, I. (1987), *Police, Government and Accountability*,
    Basingstoke: Macmillan, 223.

CHAPTER SEVEN

1 Amey, P., Hale, C., and Uglow, S. (1996), *Development and
   Evaluation of a Crime Management Model*, Police Research Series
   Paper 18, London: Police Research Group.
2 Home Office (1996), *Protecting the Public: The government's strategy
   on crime in England and Wales*, Cm 3190, London: Home Office,
   para. 3.21.

INDEX